C000263362

LIFE, DEATH AND HIP HOP

HAU LĀTŪKEFU
AND
CHRISTOPHER RILEY

PENGUIN BOOKS

UK | USA | Canada | Ireland | Australia
India | New Zealand | South Africa | China

Penguin Books is part of the Penguin Random House group of companies
whose addresses can be found at global.penguinrandomhouse.com

First published by Penguin Books in 2022

Copyright © Hau Lātūkefu and Christopher Riley, 2022

The moral right of the authors has been asserted.

All rights reserved. No part of this publication may be reproduced, published, performed
in public or communicated to the public in any form or by any means without prior written
permission from Penguin Random House Australia Pty Ltd or its authorised licensees.

*This book is a memoir. It reflects the author's present recollections of experiences over time.
In some instances, events have been compressed and dialogue has been recreated.
Some names and distinguishing details have been changed throughout.*

Cover photograph by Rush
Cover design by Seth One. Logo vectorisation and photo retouching by MGO.
Internal design and typesetting in 12/17.5 pt Minion Pro by Midland Typesetters, Australia

Printed and bound in Australia by Griffin Press, an accredited
ISO AS/NZS 14001 Environmental Management Systems printer

 A catalogue record for this
book is available from the
National Library of Australia

ISBN 978 1 76104 630 8

penguin.com.au

We at Penguin Random House Australia acknowledge that Aboriginal and Torres Strait Islander
peoples are the Traditional Custodians and the first storytellers of the lands on which we live
and work. We honour Aboriginal and Torres Strait Islander peoples' continuous connection
to Country, waters, skies and communities. We celebrate Aboriginal and Torres Strait Islander
stories, traditions and living cultures; and we pay our respects to Elders past and present.

To Maila and Aki. You are the past, present and future.

It's an absolute must I acknowledge and pay my respects to the custodians of the land I put this pen to paper on – the Gadigal people of the Eora nation. I also must acknowledge the custodians of the lands I grew up on – the Ngambri and Ngunnawal people of the Ngunnawal nation. I extend that love and respect to all Aboriginal and Torres Strait Islanders. I recognise that sovereignty has never been ceded. It always was, and always will be, Aboriginal land.

CONTENTS

PART 1
LEARN
1976–1993

The Parliament Houses, War Memorial, the High Court,
The National Library, scenery to die for, easy living,
Good schools and low crime,
 a few corrupt cops but we try to pay it no mind,
Telstra Towers, the Floriade flowers, the legal brothels,
Tidbinbilla Tracking Station, the Summer Nats shamozzle
The National Gallery, the mint making your money,
The Canberra Raiders and Vikings, plus the ACT Brumbies,
And that's Canberra. I'm just setting the scene,
 the city that gave birth to a team destined for dreams
Larger than life, isolation made me fiend harder for mics . . .

– 'All City', Koolism, 2002

VISITING CELLY

It's been a while since I've done this. I went to see my mate Mahem in jail when they were housing him in Parramatta, but that must have been at least twenty years ago. Man, I felt physically sick when I set foot inside that place. Mahem was just like me – around the same age, same background – but he was doing it tough. We may have seemed similar on the outside but Mahem lived an entire life before I ever even met him. Which, I guess, explains why his path took him to Parramatta and mine to the ARIAs. I had a real sense that it could've just as easily been me on the other side of that visiting table. To be honest, the guard who checked my ID that day clearly thought as much. After looking at everyone's credentials on the visitors' list, he let them through, but he kept mine to double-check that I didn't have any priors. He couldn't quite get his head around a Brown fella with no criminal record.

This time feels different. In the waiting room, I see a mother and father preparing to visit their son. It looks like they've been here before; sitting in silence, they stare straight ahead, waiting to be called in. There are no tears, just a look of weary resignation, a numbness that protects them from the harshness of this place – this place where time slows down and dreams come to die. I think of my eight-year-old son, Aki. The thought of being separated from him brings on such a rush of fear that I quickly take a deep breath to stifle the emotion. Not now, I tell myself.

Along with a few of his friends, I'm here to visit Celly, a young brother with roots in the Pacific Islands and South America, who started a rising rap group from Western Sydney by the name ONEFOUR. I've been helping the rest of the crew – J Emz, YP, Spenny and Lekks – for the past few months, but I've never met Celly. I'm interested to hear what he thinks about the work we've been doing in his absence. I helped the boys produce a track called 'Spot the Difference' a few weeks back, and the numbers are going crazy. We're talking millions of views in just a few weeks. That might be normal in the States, or even the UK, but in Australia? Never.

It's difficult to predict where these boys can take this, considering their legal troubles. It's not just Celly – both YP and Lekks are fighting cases that could see them gone for a few years, too. I mean, I'm probably risking a heart attack even considering signing them to my label, but who else is going to help an all-Pasifika rap group with a criminal record? Particularly with the Sydney papers doing a good job of ensuring a cloud of controversy follows their every move. Labelling them gang members, the media claim the boys' violent lyrics are accurate depictions of crimes, rather than just a group of young men from Mount Druitt describing the environment in which they grew up. But I'm not about to give up on them that easily.

When we get to the visiting room, Celly tells us he's been writing some lyrics while inside.

'Go on, let us hear it,' the boys ask, egging him on. Celly obliges and raps a quick sixteen-bar acapella, which prompts a few stares from *around the visiting room. As someone who's spent most of his adult life as a professional rapper, a lot of people have asked to spit bars for me over the years, and nine times out of ten it's bad. Like,* really *bad. This isn't. Similar to Lekks, Celly is a real rapper's rapper – as a student of the game he understands flow and rhyme patterns more than most experienced pros. Listening to him, he reminds me somewhat of me.*

The rest of the visit finishes as quickly as it started. Celly wants to discuss life on the outside, so we barely get to any ONEFOUR stuff. That's cool; I'm not going to rush things. We shake hands and agree to keep talking. One of the guards collects Celly and walks him back to his cell while we are escorted to the exit. Once outside, I take a deep breath of fresh air, as if to remind myself I'm free.

On the way home I think about just how many Black and Brown men were inside that visiting room. The world has grown used to seeing us in this light, to hearing only one side of our stories. But those times are changing. For too long, the world has looked at Dwayne Johnson as the only Pacific Islander doing cool shit. Don't get me wrong, I love The Rock as much as the next guy, but it's about time our talents started getting the attention they deserve. We can be movie stars, we can be rappers, and we can be politicians and scientists. We can be anything. Whether it's lads like ONEFOUR, or even a rapper turned radio host like myself, we have the mic now. It's our turn.

But let's get one thing clear: my story is not Celly's and it's not Mahem's. It doesn't involve crime and violence (okay, maybe a little) and it doesn't end in jail (fingers crossed). It's a story about a kid from the 2620 who dared to dream. But my story doesn't start with me. Just like Celly and Mahem, and every other child of immigrants, mine begins in the motherland . . .

SUPPORTER OF THE KING

Queen Sālote Tupou III was the first Tongan to become a global celebrity. A game-changer for our country, she won the hearts and minds of people overseas, giving my parents' generation the courage to leave behind the tiny island they called home in search of new opportunities. All because she refused an umbrella.

It was 2 June 1953, and royals from all over the world were in England for the coronation of Queen Elizabeth II. The procession began at Buckingham Palace before horse-drawn carriages rode to Westminster Abbey for the ceremony. On the way back to the Palace, it started raining. The royals, dressed to the nines in their best wedding 'fits, closed the hoods on their carriages to protect themselves from the pouring rain. All but one.

Near the back of the procession, Queen Sālote's carriage remained open. Unbothered, she smiled and waved happily to the adoring crowds as the rain bucketed down on her.

The reason she did this was simple: Tongans are humble people. Our customs dictate that you shouldn't elevate yourself to the same position as the person you are honouring. And Queen Sālote was there to pay her respects to Queen Elizabeth, so while the British monarch was free to protect herself from the elements, Queen Sālote humbly declined.

And the crowd loved it, showering her with cheers and applause almost as heavy as the rain itself. The next day, *The Telegraph* wrote that she 'won an extraordinary quantity of affection from the British people', while *The Times* described her as 'the outstanding overseas figure of the celebrations'.

It was the one and only time Queen Sālote went to Europe, but the image of her riding proudly through the rain has remained, to this day, a symbol of Tongan humility. After Queen Sālote blazed a trail and won affection for Tongans overseas, people like Mum and Dad felt they could do the same.

While Mum and Dad were inspired by Queen Sālote Tupou III, they were the ones who inspired me. Growing up as I did, surrounded by the comforts of life in Australia, it was important for them to remind me and my big sister, Sabne, of our Tongan background. For Dad, this was especially important. His eldest brother, Sione, used to share stories every Christmas about how they were raised, an upbringing that saw their father work the land every day in the plantations near their home, while their mother fished and cared for the family. With a dozen or so mouths to feed, life was far from easy.

Dad doesn't say much himself, but when he does, you listen. On the rare occasions he'd continue Sione's tradition of recounting stories of their life in Tonga, he'd point out that his dad, my grandfather, didn't work the fields like they do here in Australia, with machines and technology. It was all done by hand; backbreaking work in the sweltering heat. But with Dad, he'd more often than not remind us of what they had, not what they lacked. And what they had was each other. His older brothers, after moving to Australia, would send money home so that he, as the youngest, didn't have to worry. If you mention their name to Dad even now, he'll tear up thinking of the sacrifices they made for him.

But when it comes to Mum and Dad, my favourite story of all is how they met. Dad went to school in the bush, so they had a runner who'd head to town every few days to pick up supplies from the shops, mail their letters and so on. One day, Dad gave a note to the runner to pass to Mum, whose school was near the centre of town. He'd seen her around and wanted to ask her out. But when Mum got the note, she had no idea who this 'Lesoni Lātūkefu' was. When the runner pointed him out a few days later, she wasn't impressed. Thinking he wasn't handsome enough, Mum ignored the letter and Dad was 'left on read'. Brutal, I know.

Fast-forward a few years and both of them were in Australia. They found themselves at the same wedding for a mutual friend, and when Mum arrived, Dad was in the entrance singing some traditional Tongan hymns on his guitar. *Now* she was a fan. They ended up singing a song together, and by the time they finished, they were holding hands. A few months later, they were engaged.

When Mum tells the story, you'll see Dad offer a cheeky wink that says, *I knew she'd come back.* It always cracks me up but the reason I never get tired of hearing it is because it says so much about them, and therefore about me. Dad with his quiet confidence in pursuing Mum, and Mum with her headstrong opinions and refusal to be swayed (unless you bring out a guitar, that is). I reckon I'm equal parts of both, but I've definitely got my dad's emotional side. Just the mention of family will set him off crying. I'm the same. Thinking about our family spread across Australia, Tonga and New Zealand brings to the surface all these memories of sacrifice and perseverance but also joy and laughter. Growing up, our house was always a place of laughter.

That's what this book is all about: sacrifice and perseverance; joy and laughter. Because any good story – and life – involves a bit of both.

Tongan hymns may have brought Mum and Dad together, but their upbringing couldn't have been more different. Mum went to Tonga College, which was, and still is, the most prestigious school in the country, accepting only the top thirty-five students each year. Her dad, my grandfather, was a maths and Tongan language teacher there, so she spent her whole upbringing at Tonga College, learning from the best of the best. Dad, meanwhile, was brought up in the bush and attended a missionary school, where it was all about learning cultural traditions and practical skills rather than what most would consider a 'conventional' education.

The eldest of twelve siblings, when Mum decided she wanted to move to Australia, it was on her to figure out a way. She ended up applying for a Rotary Club scholarship to study nursing, and after a delay in getting her visa sorted, she marched herself into the office of the Ministry of Education in Tonga and demanded to know what was causing the hold-up.

'These things take time,' they told her. But Mum wasn't about to take that shit for an answer.

'Give me the address of the president of the Rotary Club and I'll do it myself.' (She was all of seventeen.) They handed it over, probably just wanting to get rid of her. Either way, it worked. After receiving her letter, the president flew to Tonga to meet her personally, and she was on a plane to Australia a few weeks later. My mum is a do-it-yourself kind of woman. If you're in her way, she'll give you the big 'don't argue' and keep going. *Respectfully*.

Dad, on the other hand, had a habit of skipping school. As the youngest of nine siblings, he'd hit up one of his older brothers at the start of each term for school fees. He'd take those few dollars and, rather than enrolling, spend it on a boat fare to one of the neighbouring islands. Dad would stay there all term long, returning only when the footy season started.

One year, he had to go back to the mainland sooner than expected. He'd received a letter from his brothers, who by this point were already in Australia.

'Pack your bags, Lesoni,' they told him, 'your plane leaves in two days.' And that was that. He joined his brothers in Canberra later that week, and he's been there ever since. That's Dad: quiet, humble and completely devoted to his family (and his footy).

Just like him, I'm the baby of the family and have had a wide network of uncles and cousins as well as my sister, Sabne, who would literally do anything for me. You could call me spoiled – in fact, my sister does, a lot. To this day, I'm saved in her phone as 'brat'. But there's that other side, Mum's staunchness, that shines through when it's needed. Like I said, in any good story you need a bit of both.

The Lātūkefus were the first Tongans to set foot in Canberra. They arrived in the early '70s, a few years after the PM Harold Holt abolished the 'White Australia' policy. (For anyone in need of a quick history lesson, that was a government policy in place since 1901 that aimed to forbid any non-Europeans from immigrating to Australia. Come on, don't tell me that surprises you?) Think about that for a second: just a few years before, their arrival would have been illegal. None of their countrymen had ever made the same journey, and they had no way of knowing what to expect. But they did it anyway.

My dad's older brothers set themselves up in a big old house just outside Queanbeyan, near the NSW–ACT border. It was a true Aussie bush home: creaky, a bit creepy, with a dark, dingy outside bathroom. From the plantations of Tonga to rural Australia, my uncles made that house their home for years before they started to have their own families. When I think of my uncles I see them all together under that one roof, working, playing footy, drinking and getting acquainted with the local white girls on the weekend. Not a bad life.

My uncles were gun players, so I reckon that helped their transition into the local culture. Australia's a country that harbours a distrust of my dark-skinned brothers and sisters, but a lot can be forgiven if you know what to do with a footy ball in your hand. Racism and rugby are two of Australia's favourite things, and very occasionally one can cancel the other out.

After my mum and dad got married, his eldest brother, Sione, decided they wouldn't stay in the bush house with everyone else. Instead, he bought them their own place altogether. Can you believe that? He put down a deposit and said, 'Here you go, bro, this is yours.' When I say my family would do anything for each other, I mean it. But, if I'm honest, there's probably another reason behind Sione's decision. In the Lātūkefu house, just like in the family in general, Sione's word was law. My dad and his other brothers respected him, the eldest, as the head of the family. Mum on the other hand, well, she holds her tongue for no one. Sione knew he'd met his match.

Queen Sālote Tupou III went on to serve nearly forty-eight years, the longest of any Tongan monarch. She died in New Zealand in 1965, and one of the last things she did was invite Uncle Sione to come and stay with her.

You see, Uncle Sione, like Queen Sālote, was a trailblazer. He was the country's very first historian and was commissioned by Queen Sālote to write a book on Tonga's political development. It basically puts to rest any theories that the missions were solely responsible for the creation of its constitution. (White people love taking credit for shit they didn't do.)

At times, the book reads more like a thriller, offering first-hand accounts of key moments in Tongan history, like when Captain Cook arrived in 1773. Apparently, old mate loved it, describing the people as friendly and welcoming, and even though he saw some evidence of weapons, he said the locals walked around unarmed. You can just imagine it: Cook putting his bayonet down for a brief second, grabbing himself a coconut and dipping his toes in the water. Good times. But what he didn't know was that these friendly locals were plotting to kill him. The only reason they didn't was because the chiefs couldn't agree whether to attack at day or night.

I didn't know whether to laugh or cry when I read this. As unbelievable as it may sound now, it says a lot about the ways in which Tongans are underestimated. We're joyous people who like to love and laugh and smile. However, do not mistake our kindness for weakness.

Cook was able to leave unharmed, and thirteen years later he 'discovered' Australia. The rest, as they say, is history. Or, let's be real, *his-story*.

After nearly ten years of hard work, Sione was about ready to finish the book when I was born. And as Sione was head of the family, Mum and Dad asked him to name me. He came up with Lāngomi-e-Hau, which translates to Supporter of the King, and Hau on its own means 'King'.

It took a few years for me to really understand what Uncle Sione was getting at. Tongan society looks a lot like a feudal system with a clear hierarchical structure. Each village has a noble, and beneath them there's what's called a *Tauhifonua* ('guardian of the land'), who acts as their ceremonial stand-in when the noble is not present.

The *Tauhifonua* is appointed either by the noble or, depending on the bloodline of the individual, directly from the King himself. For generations, that responsibility has been with Dad's family, so in some ways, Sione was placing me alongside the legacy of my ancestors, making sure I knew from the moment I was born that I was a King. Whenever I say my name, I'm reminded of who I am and those who have come before me. The sacrifices, the perseverance, the joy, the laughter.

But the line doesn't stop with me, because as Uncle Sione knew, real Kings support the next line of Kings and Queens. They empower those around them so that they can do it even bigger, ensuring the legacy continues to grow.

So, no pressure then.

FOOTBALL, FEASTS AND FAMILY

I'm sitting on the floor in the living room watching cartoons when my cousins arrive. My uncles greet my parents with big, firm hugs before Tevita picks me up and puts me on his shoulders. Like all my uncles, Tevita is a powerful man with big, leathery hands, but his touch is gentle. He takes me outside and sets me on his lap as he joins his brothers by the barbecue.

My dad hands out a round of beers – massive gold cans as big as my head with droplets of condensation trickling down the sides and the letters 'KB' printed on the front.

'Cheers!'

I watch as they clink the cans together before taking long, grateful sips. Someone mentions this morning's footy match and my uncles start laughing; I don't follow what they're saying, but I don't have to. Their deep, joyous laughter is the soundtrack to my childhood.

Tevita passes me to Dad, who holds me in one hand while tending to the barbecue with the other. Today, we've gone all out: a whole pig on the spit. Dad started the fire before everyone arrived, so the smell of sizzling meat fills the air and the pig's skin is starting to turn a light brown. The pig's feet, I've come to learn, taste the best and they fall off first. Following my gaze, Dad pulls off one of the trotters with his barbecue tongs and passes me a bite with a wink. I gobble it down, savouring the crispy goodness.

This is my dad at his happiest: surrounded by his big brothers, beer in hand and a plate of food on the way. *What more could you want?* He is content. We all are. All we have is each other, and that's just fine with us. We don't need anyone else.

These are my first real memories. Big family barbecues every weekend with my cousins, aunts and uncles, cocooned in our small but growing Tongan community. Like most people, these early memories appear to me today through the rosy lens of nostalgia. The reality was, we were on our own, and while I was too young to know this at the time, that forced us to adapt. Our house in Queanbeyan was surrounded by the same bushland as everyone else in the neighbourhood, and the beers my dad and uncles loved so much were the same beers every other Aussie bloke enjoyed. But being the only Tongans for miles in a country that just a few years before made our presence illegal, we couldn't rely on anyone else for help.

Uncle Sione knew this better than anyone. He was the playmaker, making sure the family was self-sufficient so we didn't have to rely on our neighbours. The first thing he did was ensure everyone had a place to live, then the next order of business was jobs. Sione lined my dad and his other brothers up with a range of careers so that everyone could help each other out. My dad was a house painter, so if anyone needed help on their house, he was the go-to guy. To this day, the smell of paint reminds me of him.

Then there was Uncle Tevita, who lived just round the corner. Sione got him a job as an architect and, like my other uncles, Tevita would always be lending his services to the community either for free or for cheap. He was the only one married to a white woman, so he wasn't at the drink-ups as often as the others. His wife, my aunt Helen, loved us and we loved her, but I don't think she had the same need to be surrounded by family every weekend as we did. But living so close, he'd pop in more or less every day anyway. Uncle would walk up to chat with my folks and always ask me to 'fix him a cuppa', a term I'd never heard before. (I think he got that from Aunty Helen.)

Next up, Uncle Maile. He ran a bookshop and worked in Aboriginal Affairs, so he had a steady stream of income, and because he didn't have kids 'til later, he would spoil me and Sabne rotten. One time I got it in my head that I wanted a motorbike. Despite being barely ten years old, Maile said, 'Sure,' and he actually drove me to go buy one. Mum caught wind of this and quickly put a stop to the plan, but it's always stuck in my mind as proof that Maile would have done anything for me.

Uncle Talia'uli was a mechanic, so his front yard would be full of cars every weekend because every Tongan in Canberra would go to him for repairs. He was the best footy player in the family and was even named in the Tongan team of the century. When he moved to Australia, he soon got the call-up to rep the green and gold, but it was for a tour of South Africa during apartheid, so you know how that went. Over the next ten years or so, whenever I played rugby, whether for school or club, I'd be asked, 'Are you Talia'uli's nephew?'

Finally, Uncle Ano, who was my mum's brother and an accountant, so if you had trouble balancing the books, he was your man. He was also a minister and had the responsibility of saying grace at family gatherings. Then there was the Langi family nearby, made up of Singa, his wife Colleen, and kids Shani and Simon. Singa was from Dad's village back in Tonga, so the Langis were like family too. Plus, there were all my aunties and uncles in Tonga but we'll get to them in a bit.

***

At some point in the afternoon, the music would come on. It was always traditional Tongan music played on cassette tapes – lots of guitars, drums and a harmony of voices. After a few more drinks, my uncles would get up and start dancing, then we'd all follow. It was a bit of fun, but it was also more than that: it was a way for my family to keep in touch with Tonga. Music and dance are in our souls; it's our history written into song. Whether we were in Queanbeyan or Tonga, it was our anchor.

After a few hours of drinking and cooking, it was time to eat. It would usually be a mix of classic Aussie barbecue food – lamb chops, burgers, snags – and traditional Tongan fare. Occasionally we'd have an *'umu*, which is like an underground oven popular in Tonga. My dad and uncles would dig a hole then start a fire inside it, putting large stones on top of the flames. Then we'd put meat and veggies on the stones – in Queanbeyan we'd cover them in tin foil; in Tonga we'd use taro leaves – before covering the hole with a potato sack. A few hours later, we'd have perfectly cooked and tender meat. It was a long process but always worth it.

Chicken giblets were another favourite. They're basically the insides of a chicken, like the liver, heart and neck, all thrown together. I didn't know what they were; I just knew they tasted delicious. We'd throw them on the barbie then drench them in soy sauce and salt. There was another dish we'd often have called *sipi*. Common in Tonga, these are flaps of mutton.

I didn't realise 'til later that these aren't exactly common dishes in Australia. It wasn't until I started eating Chinese food – ya know, *traditional* Chinese food, like chicken feet and all the rest – to understand what was going on. Countries like Australia might be able to afford just using the meaty parts of an animal, but in places like Tonga and China, we use every part on offer. This would involve cheap cuts of meat with high fat content. It's things like this that contribute to obesity and high blood pressure in the Islands. In fact, the importing of *sipi* in Tonga was made illegal in 2020 because of its link to obesity. But we didn't know – or care – about any of this at the time. It would be a few happy years before we'd start to pay the price.

ROCK STEADY

Entering primary school, my parents were worried about me – for a number of reasons. First off, I was born with a club foot, so Dad was concerned I wouldn't be able to play footy. In a family where footy is more like a religion than a sport, that caused a few issues. Thankfully, the doctor was able to fix it in surgery, so by age six I was running around just like my cousins. The first time I kicked a ball, Mum and Dad cheered so much from the sidelines you would have thought I'd won Olympic gold.

Mum had a different set of concerns. Not only did I come into this world with a club foot, I came in punching too. I was a happy kid, but if you crossed me there was a small chubby right hand swinging like a fat gold chain. When I was brought along to a parents evening at Sabne's school, I ended up punching on with one of the other kids, Matt Beckenham. Man, Mum was mortified! But Matt and I went on to become good mates, so no hard feelings.

A few terms into primary school, Mum was worried again. This time it had nothing to do with my fighting or footy; it was about the company I kept. For some reason all my friends were from single-parent households, and Mum was concerned a pattern was forming

19

and that these kids might be a bad influence on me. She came into school one day and spoke to my teacher.

'Should I be worried?' she asked. Thankfully Miss put her fears to rest.

'Mrs Lātūkefu, it's a good thing,' she explained. 'Hau looks out for the other kids.'

I don't think I was doing it consciously, but if there was one thing I knew, even then, it was that family was everything. So if you somehow didn't have a big, loving family like mine, in my eyes you could do with a little help. I'd like to think I tried to fill in any gaps they had. I had one friend Patrick, who'd come over to our house so often that Uncle Maile asked him why: 'Don't you have a home to go to? Won't your mum be looking for you?'

Completely serious, Patrick looked at my uncle and told him, 'No, Mum's not worried. She knows I'm with Hau and that he'll look after me.'

Growing up Tongan Australian made me feel special. Raised on a diet of Vegemite and Passiona, I was as Aussie as anyone else in primary school. But I also had VIP access to a whole other world. Mum and Dad took me to Tonga when I was four years old, but I was mainly passed from one adoring family member to another, not yet familiar with my surroundings. It existed in my mind as an almost magical place, where family greeted our arrival like we were royalty, and I swam at the beach with my cousins until my skin turned a deep dark brown.

In many ways it was like a dream. When I told Patrick and my other school mates of my experiences in Tonga, they would become more romantic, the colours more vibrant, the memories more vivid. It was something they could never truly understand, and that was okay – it was just for me. But the thing about dreams is they can turn to nightmares in a second.

That's what happened in Year 3. I was having breakfast before school one morning when Mum explained to me that Tonga had just experienced a cyclone.

'What's that?' I asked between mouthfuls of cornflakes.

'It's almost like a tornado,' Mum explained. 'In some places, the winds are so strong, they're destroying . . .'

I stopped eating and started panicking. *What does she mean, 'destroying'*? Mum carried on talking but I only heard bits and pieces. *Houses blown apart. Buildings wrecked. People killed.* I didn't have the words to process it and couldn't understand why Mum and Dad weren't as worried about it as I was. *What will happen to my cousins and grandparents?*

By the time I arrived at school, I was on the verge of tears. We started the day with news time, and Miss asking each student to share some stories from our weekend. Someone spoke about a new pet they had just been given, another about scoring the winning try in a footy match. When it got to me, I couldn't hold it in any longer.

'Tonga's destroyed!' I said, bursting into tears. 'It's all gone.'

Confused, Miss asked what I meant.

'It's destroyed!' I repeated. What part didn't she understand?

After some consoling, Miss explained everything. Tonga was going to be okay – they had just had an accident. A cyclone, she told me, was almost like a big storm. They will have to rebuild some things, but Tonga was definitely still on the map. Relieved, I stopped crying. The picture in my mind regained its shape, and I was whole again.

Friday night was movie night in our house. We'd go to Today's Video, Tonight, a movie rental store on the main street in Queanbeyan,

> 21st September, 1987
> Antonyms and synonyms
> Antonyms mean the opposite and Synonyms
> meen the same.
> 1. a. uneducated b. incorrect c. imperfect ✓
>   d. iregular ✓ e. irevelant ✓ f. unessesary ✓
>   g. impossible ✓ h. independent ✓
> 2.
>   a. stretch   ✓ b. sight ✓
>   c. friend   ✓, 4. d. flower ✓ e. tears ✓ 13/13
>   21st September 1987
> *I think that it would be like leaning
> off the edge of disaster. There would be
> no pictures, take-aways, video tapes etc.
> We would be very, very poor. We won't be
> able to get some much grocery. But
> luckily my parents do work and we go
> to the movies etc.'
> *If Mr. my parents didnt work.
>   It's good to realise how
>   lucky you are sometimes,
>   isn't it? L

and Sabne and I would pick one while our parents would do the same. Before watching the movie, Dad would bring my and Sabne's mattresses into the living room so we could have a sleepover. There're few things as exciting for a kid than being able to wake up on a Saturday morning and watch cartoons *immediately*. No asking permission, no chores – just a few hours of uninterrupted TV time.

And it was even better when Sabne had a netball game first thing which meant I was in charge of the remote. *Finally!*

My parents' room was down the end of the hallway, and if no one was looking I'd sneak in and steal gum out of my dad's pants pocket. Either Juicy Fruit or PK, I'd sneak a couple pieces, being careful not to take too many so as to alert my dad, then rush back to the couch. With the remote in my hand and gum in my mouth, I was in my element.

When it came to TV, my first love was professional wrestling and my favourite was Haku aka King Tonga. Apparently, Mum used to know him from the homeland back in the day. When I first saw Haku, he was part of a tag-team duo called The Islanders, alongside a Samoan named Tama. Samoa, in particular, has a rich history when it comes to wrestling, but most of the Polynesian wrestlers didn't overtly rep their background. Haku, on the other hand, was all about Tonga, straight out the gate, and I lapped up every minute of it. Plus, he was one certified bad man. Watching Haku, you couldn't tell me wrestling was fake. With arms bigger than my thighs, he threw opponents around the ring like dirty washing into the laundry basket. Haku had a few moves he would pull out regularly: the karate side kick, the across-the-chest chop and, of course, the headbutt, using his big coconut.

Most weekends, when my cousins and I weren't playing footy, we were wrestling, which meant me doing my best impression of King Tonga. In all, I've got literally dozens of cousins – too many to name – but in Australia they were divided into two age groups. The older bunch, led by Uncle Sione's son 'Alopi, included Sabne, along with my cousins Sione and Maikeli. Then it was me, Hounga, Mai, T'ui and 'Uli, who was the baby of the group. Being the oldest in our little posse, I was the ringleader, directing everyone into position.

'OK, Hounga and Mai, you be The Hart Foundation. Tu'i and me, we'll be The Islanders,' I announced one morning.

'Who am I?' asked 'Uli.

'For now, you just watch.'*

Dismissing 'Uli's protests, the match started with me against Mai. I stomped my feet and slapped my hands one by one across my chest just as I'd seen King Tonga do to psych out his opponents. We circled each other like two predators sizing each other up. Waiting for an opening, I dove low and grabbed Mai's legs, tackling him to the ground. Immediately I got him into a figure-four leg lock; I was going for the kill.

Mai groaned out in pain before managing to tag Hounga in. I stood back up and looked down at Hounga, who was two years younger than me and a foot shorter. Easy prey. Ignoring Tu'i's calls to tag him in, I grabbed Hounga by the scruff of his pyjama top.

'And Haku has him . . .' I called out, now simultaneously wrestling and commentating. 'Oh my God – he's preparing the Tongan death grip!'

I began simulating a choke hold on Hounga, who obliged and began feigning being strangled. But I wasn't done; I had him right where I wanted him. As Hounga began to fall to his knees, I dropped down into a squat to build momentum and picked my little cousin up off the ground . . .

'Haku with the choke slam!'

As I threw Hounga against the couch with all the King Tonga energy I could muster, his trailing foot caught the edge of a plate that still bore the evidence of our morning's toast. As Hounga hit the couch, the plate went flying across the living room, finding its

---

* This aged well! Who could have guessed that 'Uli would go on to become a successful actor and score a role as the younger version of one of the greatest wrestlers ever, Dwayne 'The Rock' Johnson, in the NBC sit-com *Young Rock*. All that practice clearly paid off! Proud of you, bro.

resting place as a pile of shards spread out across the floor. A look of mortal fear took over Hounga's face as Mum came running in to find out what the noise was about.

I gave the others a look that said, *Don't say a word.*

'Sorry, Mum, we were playing and Hounga must have accidentally knocked a plate over,' I said. 'Don't worry, I'll clean it up.'

After wrestling came the music videos. There was a show called *Sounds* that would start at 9 am and one called *Countdown*, hosted by Molly Meldrum. They'd interview musicians and play a bunch of songs, and all the while I'd sit there, eyes glued to the screen, bobbing my head to whatever pop or rock came on. This was the New Wave era – groups like Culture Club and Duran Duran – and I was a *fan*. The outfits, the attitude, the hair – I was into it all.

But another thing caught my attention – and kept it. A group called Rock Steady Crew came on *Countdown*. They were from a place called New York City, and they were a crew of dancers: *B-boys*. I'd never seen anything like it. They wore matching blue tracksuits that looked more like parachutes, and when they danced their bodies moved in ways I didn't even understand. Moves that had names like the 'turtle' and the 'jackhammer'. My young brain was in overload. I immediately got up and tried to follow what they were doing.

The knee spin looked the easiest for me to master, so I started there. I knelt down onto my right knee and, studying the way Rock Steady did it, used my left leg to spin me around. I ended up on the floor on my first try, and again on my second. Undeterred, I got up and did it again and again until I'd managed to achieve one full rotation.

My next lesson came courtesy of Debbie Harry. Yeah, you heard me – Debbie Harry, one half of the rock group Blondie. Harry had this beautiful voice, but on her song 'Rapture' she did something else, something I'd never heard before. Instead of singing, she . . . *talked*? Over the music, she spoke in a rhythmic tone that sucked me right in.

You had to wait for the second verse to hear it, but whenever the song came on *Sounds* or *Countdown*, I watched right until the end. Harry, strutting her stuff through an alleyway with graffiti in the background and a guy dancing in a white suit and matching top hat. I didn't know what I was watching, but I knew I needed to hear more.

Then there was Herbie Hancock's song 'Rockit'. The video used to creep me out with its headless mannequins moving as if they were alive. This time there was no rhyming, but throughout the song the beat would stop and go back and forth, as if someone were pressing pause then messing with the song somehow. The mannequins and other robots started dancing to the beat, their movements tied to the rhythm of the back and forth.

I didn't know it at the time, but Blondie and Herbie Hancock had just introduced me to three of the core elements of hip hop: rapping, scratching and graffiti.

One Friday night, Sabne and I rented a film called *Beat Street*. It was one of the few occasions where Sabne and I could agree on what to watch, and just like the Rock Steady Crew it was based in New York, a city that was quickly becoming my Narnia. At the centre of the film is Kenny Kirkland aka Double K, who's trying to become a DJ. Then there's his buddy Ramon, who's a graffiti artist, and Kenny's little brother Lee, who's got moves as smooth as butter and is on his way to becoming a breakdancer.

Man, I cried my arse off when Ramon died. But, to be honest, I wasn't there for the plot. Because *Beat Street* is full of Black and

Brown kids doing cool shit. They're making music, dancing, doing graffiti . . . Whatever they wanted to do, they did it. Yes, they weren't like us, ethnicity-wise – they weren't Islanders – but at the same time, they *were* us. Minorities see themselves in each other, and I saw myself in Lee and Double K and Ramon. In Australia, we didn't have stories like this. I had King Tonga, and I had my uncles and my older cousins, but when I turned on the television I didn't see myself reflected back. Looking at *Beat Street* and the Rock Steady Crew, I thought, *I can do that.*

LU'ISA, AKA MUM

When Hau was young, we needed a new car. We'd always had these small little cars, and Hau's dad decided to get a bigger one because he said I'd look good driving it. On the day they were supposed to pick it up, Hau was excited to go with his dad to the dealership. But instead of going home, Hau's dad drove the car to the Tongan high commissioner's house in Canberra and left it there. The high commissioner at the time was a noble from Hau's dad's village in Tonga, and he would drive around Canberra with his family in this little car. Hau's dad couldn't have them driving a smaller car than us, so he let them borrow it until they got a new one. They had it for about six months before they gave it back.

It was hard to make Hau understand why his dad had done that. But it's just the way his father was brought up. I would never have done that – that's not my background – but Hau's dad is very traditional, and in Tonga it's all about loyalty and respect. And the thing about Hau – he always had our respect.

He wasn't a kid who wanted something all the time. He always saved for it. He even had a go at me for having a credit card once. He was only a kid and he asked, 'Why do you have to have one of them, Mum? Why can't you just save up and then get it when you've got enough?'

Because that's what he did. We never got our Christmas present 'til they had the sales. Every year he'd get on a bus and go to Sydney for the post-Christmas sales, so every year we got our Christmas presents late. We just got used to it.

Even at school, the teachers trusted him. Sabne used to get into trouble, but there were only a few times I had to go into school to speak to Hau's teachers. Once they were doing a nativity play, and Hau was one of the wise men. He wanted to wear a gold crown, so I said I'd make him one. Then he went to school the next day and when he came back, he said, 'Oh, don't do it, Mum. The teacher said we all have to wear the same crown.' I said, 'No, that's not fair. We're gonna make yours gold.' So, I went and saw the teacher and said, 'I'm sorry, but Hau would like the gold crown. I've already made it so I think you should let him wear it.'

She could see I wasn't about to be gotten rid of!

·12·15 t.eN. PRESENTS:

DAd: summER shoRts oR tie   shoRts : $10
                                      tie :   RocK

Mum: eaRings oR : $10
     scaRf :   RacK

Sabne:

Me, y-s the x-Kwizit one, the Know Hau: mixER: $60
                                     designed hat: $13

things I plan to get: 2 turn tables
               1 MIXER
             moRe· RecoRds
            2·R1 mic(s) and
    definately mo· noney dis D·V·K·E·H·N·n

HOW DARE YOU!

I'm nine years old and Mum has just sent me inside the convenience store to grab a soft drink while she waits in the car. Clutching the dollar she just handed me, I'm on my way to the back where the drinks are kept when I see the range of chocolate bars stacked neatly on the shelves next to the magazines. I stop for a second. Without thinking, I pick up a Chokito bar – my favourite – and slip it in my pocket. *Smooth.* I turn to leave, and as I do I see my reflection in a pair of sunglasses. But I'm not alone. Lurking behind me, at the end of the aisle, is a security guard. He's big, he's white, and he's pointing me out to the shopkeeper. *Crusted.* I can feel the Chokito bar burning a hole in my pocket, a sign of my impending guilt. But I keep my composure. Continuing down the aisle away from the security guard, I manage to slip the chocolate bar onto a shelf along the way. Forgetting all about the drink, I make it to the entrance of the store when the security guard stops me.

'Excuse me, empty your pockets please, young man,' he tells me.

Putting on my best confused face, I shrug and pull out my now-empty pockets. Then I leave the guard looking disappointed and race to get in the car with Mum.

'What did that man just say to you?' she asks as I sit down.

'Oh, nothing.' I shrug. 'He thought I stole something.' Before I could say anything else, Mum jumps out the car and catches the guard before he returns inside the store.

'What did you just say to my son?' she demands, her face red with rage. The man tries to explain that he caught me red-handed, but Mum's having none of it.

'How *dare* you accuse my son of stealing?' she says, drowning out his protests. 'HOW *DARE* YOU!'

At this point, the security guard realises Mum isn't backing down. He apologises before she gets back in the car and starts the engine. I watch the man from the side mirror – hands on hips, confused, he slowly recedes from view as we drive off.

We never spoke about this incident. Mum never asked if I actually did take something, and I never told her. I felt guilty about it for some time – after all, I *was* stealing. But I learned two things that day: one, if you're gonna steal, don't get caught; and two, Mum is gonna be there for me no matter what. Even if I'm in the wrong, she wasn't letting *anybody* tell me what to do.

I was in my last year of primary school when things like this started happening regularly, whether I was stealing or not. One of the convenience stores near our house was the worst. I started to feel the lady behind the counter treating me differently. She'd scowl whenever she saw me and would be super short whenever I bought something. I never stole anything from that store, so I never understood it. Every time I went in, I'd leave asking myself, *Why doesn't she like me?*

And it wasn't just her. I'd get followed around most shops I went into; the security guard – or whoever it was – would pretend to look at items a few feet from where I was standing. *How convenient.* It confused me more than anything. I wanted to shout over a megaphone, *Guys, I learned my lesson, Okay? I'm NOT stealing!*

It wasn't 'til later that I heard the term 'racial profiling' and connected the dots. Then it all made sense and my confusion turned into an uncomfortable sadness, one that I tried to ignore. I didn't talk about it with my parents or my sister – I didn't really know how – but looking back on the Chokito bar incident, I reckon that was my mum's way of warning me. I know that now, and I'm grateful to her, but as any Black or Brown person will understand, just *knowing* that you're in the right doesn't go all that far. Having those eyes burn into you with judgement; those looks that say, *I know your type*; those old white ladies who clutch their bags or cross the road when they see you coming. It all has an impact, whether you admit it or not. It weighs on you like you're dragging some invisible object everywhere you go.

As I got older I learned tactics to deal with other people's perceptions of me. Whenever I enter a room, I'm overly friendly to make sure everyone knows they can relax and feel comfortable. *Big Bad Brown Hau is not gonna hurt anyone.* If I buy something from a store, I'll wait outside for a few minutes to put the shop owner at ease. *No, I did not steal something; I'm here acting casual because I've done nothing wrong and have nothing to hide.*

At nine years old, I didn't have these tactics in my armoury. I would experience things and store them away in a folder labelled 'Things I Don't Understand'. But whether I understood them or not, they left their mark.

THE MOTHERLAND

I loved visiting Tonga; it had the excitement of a holiday and the familiarity of home all rolled into one. We spent the summer holidays there every other year or so from when I was about four years old, leaving a week after school was finished and returning just before term started again. We never bothered with sunscreen back then and there was no mosquito repellent, so I'd come back several shades browner and covered in bites. I'd pick at them, so more often than not the bites would turn into what they call *pala*, which are boils – big, gross, pus-filled sores – all over my arms and legs. But that was a small price to pay.

Before Tonga there was Aotearoa, more commonly known as New Zealand. In those days, you couldn't catch a direct flight from Australia to Tonga, so we would fly via NZ (or Fiji) and visit Mum's family along the way. They lived in Mount Roskill in Auckland, and it would always bug me out how many Islanders were there. Because the country is so close to the Pacific Islands, New Zealand is the first stop-off point for anyone wanting to immigrate, so there's way more Pacific Islanders there than in Australia. I couldn't believe it – at the airport, in the shops, even on TV – Brown people were everywhere.

After spending time with my Maʻilei family in NZ – Uncle Tonga, Aunty Tisiola and my cousins Andrew, Liz and Alexandria – weʼd jump back on the plane to Tonga. Two and a half hours to New Zealand then another two and a half to Tonga. There was no in-flight entertainment, so Iʼd pass the time doodling in my notepad, counting down the minutes until I could see the first sign of Tonga on the horizon: coconut trees. They are *everywhere*, and as soon as I saw those trees, it was on!

Mum and Dad would spend the flight engrossed in conversation – no doubt super excited to see the family again – so I was free to take advantage of the refreshments. Without needing their permission, I got jacked up on orange juice and waited eagerly to land. One year I took it too far and threw up everywhere, covering the seat in front of me in chunks of orange mess. But I wasnʼt about to let a bit of spew stop me. I wiped it off and got back to my notepad.

ʻPlease put your seatbelts on, we will begin our descent in five minutes,ʼ came a voice over the intercom. ʻ*Mālō ʻAupito.*ʼ Thank you.

I looked through my window and there they were: lines and lines of coconut trees, as far as you could see. I grabbed Sabneʼs arm next to me. We were home.

As soon as the plane doors opened, we were hit by two things: the heat and the smell. Because we always went during summer, it would be at least 30 degrees. And because things like waste management werenʼt really present in Tonga, most households would burn their garbage. Combine that with the dry heat and the native trees and youʼve got this sweet, almost musky smell. Itʼs hard to describe, but itʼs very distinct. If you know, you know. Just like the sight of coconut trees, the smell filled me with excitement and reminded me I was in Tonga. Sometimes even now I get a small whiff of that scent in Australia and it transports me straight there.

There would always be legions of family waiting for us when we arrived. No matter how often we went, it was always a big deal. Cousins, aunts, uncles, family friends – there seemed to be more waiting for us each time we visited. It was especially important for Mum's side. She left when she was seventeen and, being the oldest child in the family, her return was always an event. Before I was born, she'd visited Tonga for Christmas with a few friends from her nursing degree, and there was a news crew waiting for her. She was even on the radio; it was like having a celebrity visit – which, I guess, in many ways she was. The path Mum took – getting herself to Australia off her own back, starting a new life while supporting family back home – isn't one many get to travel.

Of course, there was another reason that our visits caused such a stir. Being 'foreigners', family would expect money from us. We were comfortable, but we were never wealthy. For Tongans living in Tonga, that's difficult to understand. *You live in a Western country, you're rich.* Simple as that.

We'd make our way off the tarmac, by now already dripping in sweat, before going through security. These sorts of things on the island could take ages, but thankfully we knew the right people. Mum's brother held a senior position in the post office, and in Tonga that carries a lot of clout. With him by our side, we'd get waved right through.

Once we cleared customs we'd jump in the back of one of my uncle's trucks and the trip would really start. This was the moment I most looked forward to: no seatbelt, the wind in my face, the smell of Tonga in the air. We were off, and my heart was full.

My sister has a special status in our family. As the eldest daughter of the eldest child (my mum), Sabne's what's called *fahu* in Tonga.

It basically means you're the matriarch of the generation and receive a different kind of respect from the family. The *fahu* gets special treatment at family functions; for example, if there's a twenty-first, some of the gifts would be given to them rather than the birthday person. It wasn't until we were in Tonga that I really understood the full extent of what her status as *fahu* meant. One day, Sabne was playing with the daughter of our grandmother's maid, running around in the garden, like kids do. In the midst of playing, Sabne tripped and fell. She wasn't hurt – it was just a minor trip – but my grandmother saw and completely lost her shit. She gave the maid's daughter such a beating that day. Apparently, the girl should have been more careful in taking care of Sabne. Meanwhile, we just watched on in shock, not sure what to do or say.

We started each holiday with Mum's side of the family, where she and Sabne were doted on like royalty. Not only was Sab *fahu*, but Mum, as the eldest child, had all sorts of responsibilities to fulfil. It took its toll on Mum, and even from a young age I could feel the pressure weighing on her. There was always something going on: different parts of the community were requesting her presence at events; people were coming to visit and pay their respects. Whatever it was, Mum could never really relax.

As the youngest, Dad could just chill and enjoy himself, so our time with the Lātūkefus was always a lot simpler. They lived on the west side of the island, which was roughly a half-hour drive, and still worked on the plantations there. Dad's side would literally give you the food off their plate without a second thought. All Tongans are like that, but Dad's family take selflessness to a whole other level. It's funny – they, like a lot of Tongans, live hand to mouth, but we never thought of it as poverty. You have that little money in a place like Australia and you're in dire trouble – you're on your own. But in Tonga, because it's such a small island and nearly everyone knows each other, there's a real sense of family and community. People look after one another.

That said, things were definitely different when Dad was a kid. I'll never forget the moment I made an offhand comment about being hungry. There was no food in the fridge, and like a spoiled brat, I said those fateful words: 'I'm starving!'

My dad took one look at me, disappointment on his face, and told me calmly but sternly, 'Son, you don't know what starving is.' *Sheesh.* That shut me up.

I knew he was speaking from experience, but it's hard to actually wrap your head around things that have affected your parents and not you. It's like it's all happened in a different time, a different world even, almost like to characters in a book or film. I could *hear* what Dad was saying, but at the same time it was hard to *feel* it. Then my cousin Maikeli, who grew up in Australia with me, went back to Tonga for an exchange year, attending the same school my dad went to. When he came home he must have been half the weight he was when he left. It was a boarding school, and all meals from Monday to Saturday would be *manioke* – which is Tongan for cassava, the starchy root vegetable. On Sundays the students would go home for a proper meal with family, then on Monday it was back to *manioke* for three meals a day. My cousin told me that one of the boys got hold of a small portion of rotten meat. They were so hungry that they snuck out into the bush and ate it, even though they knew they were going to get sick. And here I was 'starving'. *Damn.*

When we were visiting Dad's side, we'd stay with 'Uaisele, or as we more affectionately called him, Uncle Sele, who still lived in the village where he and Dad grew up, called Kolovai. As soon as we arrived, we were met by a pack of four or five dogs. I don't want to call them feral but . . . well, they were. I guess you could call them feral dogs that had a permanent residency at Uncle Sele's. Alongside them would be pigs, and even a few horses – that was normal, to get around on horse and cart. I used to love being thrown onto the back of the horse then riding around to help my uncles run errands or work in the fields. You don't get *that* in Queanbeyan.

Uncle Sele was as strong as an ox, probably from all the farm work he did. He was a huge guy with an even bigger smile, and you always knew when Sele was around because you would hear his husky, bellowing laugh from a mile away. He loved taking photos with us kids, holding us up in the air with one hand, a cigarette hanging loosely from his lips. His house had a big mango tree in the front yard that would act as the meeting point for me and my cousins. We'd play, hang out, or when it was too hot just nap in the shade provided by its overhanging leaves. It was almost like a member of the family; it has been there for us ever since I can remember.

There was electricity but no fridge at Uncle Sele's, so all the food was kept in the cupboards. Not being able to open the fridge door for a quick snack whenever I wanted took a little getting used to. Even worse was the showers. There was no hot water, which was fine during the day because it was so hot, but at night it would mean I'd shower in approximately three seconds. Chuck some water under my armpits and *voilà*! No wonder my mosquito bites always ended up getting infected.

When low tide arrived, we'd walk out for what seemed like ages past the shoreline, the water still by our ankles. There, we'd check the fish nets to see if we'd caught anything. Sometimes there'd be starfish and bits of coral that we'd have to pick out and throw back in so we didn't ruin the nets, and other times there'd be fish for us to take home and barbecue. Once, I saw Dad take a small fish from the net, skin the scales off with a knife and then pop it straight in his mouth – whole. Now that's sushi! Eating raw fish in Tonga is pretty common, actually. We have a dish called 'ota 'ika, which is raw fish marinated in citrus fruit and coconut milk. I guess Dad was too hungry to wait for the marinade. I tried most things when I was in Tonga, but eating raw fish straight out the ocean? Not my steelo at that age.

When we were in Tonga, cultural traditions were always more strictly enforced than back home. There are all sorts of things in Tongan culture that you can and can't do: you can't touch your father's hair; you can't enter your sister's room; you can't eat off your father's plate. We were aware of these things, but back in Australia they were never a big thing in our household. Our parents realised that it wasn't going to be the same for us. Growing up in Queanbeyan, our ties to this strict cultural background would always be slightly looser than if we had grown up in Tonga. So they educated us without enforcing the rules all that much.

Some Tongan families in Australia really struggled with that generational disconnect. The parents expected their kids to fully adhere to cultural traditions, just like they did, but in Tonga, you can rely on the sanctity of these customs to prevail. Because *everyone* adheres to them, there's far less risk of a kid rebelling. They don't know any other way. While in Australia, life was different. Kids wouldn't pay as much attention to these things, and depending on how strict your parents were, that could cause issues. Thankfully, our family were good communicators, so it wasn't such a problem for us.

But Mum and Sabne clashed all the time anyway. Sabne was way more of a rebel than me. She'd sneak out to hang with her friends, talk back, even break curfew. It's funny because Mum is where Sabne gets her rebellious streak from. Mum is a real traditionalist, but she also resents any time she's expected to play a role. Often in Tonga she would have to defer to my dad, and she hated having to be submissive. At the same time, she'd expect Sabne to be the 'good Tongan girl'. Sis was having none of it.

There was one tradition that even Sabne and I couldn't get out of: Sundays. It's a day of worship and rest, and in Tonga they take that very seriously. It was the *worst*: no music, no games, no laughter. It felt a lot like that movie *Footloose*, where the local pastor bans rock'n'roll and dancing. Man, it was so boring. My cousins and I would sneak into one of the bedrooms and play cards in silence, mouthing words to each other for fear of being caught. If one of us let out a giggle, it was always Uncle Samisoni who would remind us *who* we were and *where* we were. Uncle Soni, as we called him, lived just round the corner from Uncle Sele and, being an ex-cop, he was the strictest in the family.

The day would start with church, then we'd have a big family meal followed by an afternoon of silence and rest before often going to church again. Church *twice* in one day; it was brutal. Whether it was in Australia or Tonga, all church services would be conducted in Tongan, so we barely understood a word. Mum and Dad chose not to teach us the language as they worried it would put us at a disadvantage at school, so we would try – and fail – to follow along using the few words we picked up during our trips. More often than not, I'd daydream until the hymns.

The singing in Tongan churches is beautiful – nothing like the stuffy hymns you hear in white churches, which only feature melodies. In Tongan services, depending on your age or gender, everyone knows their place within the harmony. Even with no musical instruments, it goes *off* during hymn time. As I got older and started making music of my own, I realised how much my development was based on my time in church. Okay, church *and* Jodeci.

After five weeks, it was time to go home. I'd always have mixed feelings; I didn't want to leave my uncles or my cousins, but at the same time I was used to the comfort of our house in Queanbeyan. The cold water, the mosquitoes, the silent Sundays – there would always come a time when I was ready for life back in Australia. Mum was the same. She missed her hot baths and her red wine. Not Dad. If he was happy at our family barbecues in Queanbeyan, man, he was in his element when he was in Tonga. If it wasn't for his kids, and now grandkids, I have no doubt Dad would move back to Tonga in a heartbeat.

But he did what a lot of Tongans do; he left for a better life. That doesn't mean he, or any of us, ever fell out of love with Tonga. It's just the way life goes. Although, as we were about to find out, even for those who did leave in search of better opportunities, it didn't work out for everyone.

DAWN RAID

It's still dark when they come: two white men in black suits banging on our front door, piercing the morning's birdsong and sending the house into a sleep-deprived panic.

'Who's that?' I hear Mum ask from her bedroom.

Dad answers the door while I stand in the hallway. Still wearing my pyjamas, I wipe the sleep from my eyes.

'We have reason to believe you are harbouring overstayers,' one of the men tells Dad.

Overstayers? Harbouring?

My dad lets the men in and they say something about searching the house. Confused, I step back, creating space between myself and these two strange men and their black suits. *Are they policemen? Are we in trouble?*

I watch as the men approach the laundry door. The one asking the questions goes to open it, but the door gets stuck. He turns to Dad, annoyed.

'Why is this locked?' he demands. 'Who's behind there?'

'It's not locked,' Dad explains. 'You just have to . . .' Dad yanks the laundry door open, revealing the contents of our laundry basket.

Disappointed, the men look at each other and, without saying a word, continue their search.

It doesn't take them long to find what they're looking for. My aunties. Aunt Valeti, Aunt Lu'isa and Aunt Tuitui, mum's cousins, have been staying at our house for the past few months after visiting from Tonga. They're still asleep in the back room when the men come in.

At this point, Mum and Dad close the door, and I can only hear muffled voices from the room where my aunties are. *Have they done something wrong? Are we in trouble?*

After a few minutes, the door opens and my aunties walk out holding their suitcases, the strange men staying close by their side, as if they're worried my aunties might run away. Mum says something to me that I don't hear as the men take my aunties outside and put them in the back of a van.

Confused, I follow them and watch as the men drive away with my aunties. As they disappear down the hill, I hear the sound of birdsong again, before my dad takes my arm and leads me inside.

'Come on, Hau. Let's get you ready for school.'

I loved it when family came to stay. At any point in time, family from Tonga – Mum's cousins, her brother, even members of the Tongan marching band – would be staying over. They'd usually crash on the couch or, sometimes, take my room, which would mean I'd bunk with Sabne. Okay, I didn't like that part as much, but having family close by was always a good thing.

I especially liked Aunty Valeti. She worked as a maid at one of the hotels in town and would always bring treats home to me and Sabne on payday. I started looking forward to the first of the month, knowing when I got home from school that Aunty Valeti would be waiting for me with candy, the sort Mum would *never* let me have.

There was no more candy after the men in suits came. Mum explained to me after school that day that my aunties weren't allowed to work while they were in Australia; they had to go back to Tonga. I didn't understand. I wasn't angry, or even sad, just confused. *Why can't they work? How are they supposed to buy things?*

Mum said my aunties were being kept in a 'detention centre' in Canberra, whatever that was. A week later, they were gone.

I soon learned we weren't the only family this happened to. Turns out, these visits even had a name: Dawn Raids. When I heard that term, it all made sense. The authorities were catching people who had over-stayed their visas, arriving before dawn so they (*we*) wouldn't have time to react. And clearly, the plan was working.

The policy started in New Zealand. The country went through an economic boom in the '50s, and as a result, the government encour-aged people from the Pacific Islands to emigrate to New Zealand in order to support the growing workforce. Lots of people from Tonga, Samoa and Fiji obliged, and set off for Aotearoa. It was a win-win for everyone: New Zealand had more hands to work on the ship-yards and in the factories, and those arriving were able to support their family with their new jobs. Until New Zealand decided they no longer needed the extra hands.

When it got to the '70s, the boom was over and then-Prime Minister Kirk decided he'd had enough with all these Brown people living in his country. From March 1974, the government gave the police permission to raid the homes of 'overstayers', taking them from their families in the middle of the night and sending them back to their country of origin.

Australia saw this and figured it was a good way to solve a problem of their own. Since the abolition of the White Australia policy, more and more Islanders were coming to Australia just like we had, looking for work and a better life. But at some point, the government changed their mind and followed New Zealand's example, stripping honest people from their families and shipping them out of the country like they were damaged goods.

Just like my aunties, thousands of Pasifika people weren't even given the opportunity to say goodbye. They were snatched from their bed and taken to a detention centre, treated like criminals. For what? For wanting to work and support their families.

And do you want to know the really cruel thing? Out of the so-called overstayers in New Zealand, a third were from a Pacific Island, but they made up eighty-six per cent of the prosecutions for overstaying. Meanwhile, people from the US and UK made up another third of the overstayers, but only five per cent of prosecutions. The message was simple: if you're white and overstay, we'll turn a blind eye. If you're Brown, you better be prepared for your house to get raided, your children traumatised and your family ripped apart.

In 2021, the New Zealand government formally apologised for the Dawn Raids. Prime Minister Jacinda Ardern gave the following address:

While these events took place almost fifty years ago, the legacy of the Dawn Raids era lives on today in Pacific communities. It remains vividly etched in the memory of those who were directly impacted; it lives on in the disruption of trust and faith in authorities, and it lives on in the unresolved grievances of Pacific

communities that these events happened and that to this day
they have gone unaddressed . . .

We acknowledge the distress and hurt that these experiences
would have caused.

About bloody time.

BAD

In 1987 I was about to start high school while Mum was finishing studies of her own. She was already a qualified nurse but she went back to college to get a graduate diploma in community nursing. As the end of her course approached, Mum would work during the day and spend the night locked away in her bedroom studying. I never saw her smoke, but at nights I could smell the cigarette fumes wafting through the house, a sign that Mum was buried deep in her books. It was probably because of the stress she was under. I reckon it was also her way of having some alone time. Everything Mum did was for other people, but at night, with her family fed, she was able to lock herself away for just a few hours, light up a cigarette or two and get lost in her studies.

Meanwhile, Dad stepped up like a man. He took over the bulk of the cleaning and the cooking so that Mum could focus on work and her diploma. It was nothing for me to see Dad in an apron, either making our lunch boxes for school or fixing dinner. As I got older I realised how rare that was. In my household, Dad did whatever was asked of him, and he didn't complain. To me, *that's* what makes you a man. Though, if I'm honest, his repertoire in the kitchen wasn't as wide as Mum's. There was a lot of fish and *a lot* of Tongan stew, which is basically corn beef

47

combined with water, flour, curry powder and salt. Whether we were at home or in school, Tongan stew was a staple on the Lātūkefu menu.

There's a story Mum loves telling about Dad from before I was born. When Sabne was a toddler, Mum was in a studying phase, so Dad was doing most of the housework. On Saturdays, both Sabne and Mum would watch Dad play footy, and during the half-time break Sabne would run onto the field with the water bottles.

'Mummy!' she'd cry out as she ran towards Dad. 'Here you go, Mummy.'

Because Dad was doing all the so-called 'mum' jobs, Sabne came to think of him as 'Mummy'. Not sure how much Dad enjoyed the retelling of that story, but Mum and his teammates definitely got a good laugh out of it.

With Mum balancing work, study and family, she became ill from the stress. Or so she thought. A few weeks went by and nothing changed, so when she had a break in her schedule, Dad took the family to Bondi Beach for the weekend to rest and take her mind off things. Even then, with no work to do, Mum felt worse. When we got home, she took herself to the doctor, who confirmed what she'd suspected: she was pregnant.

The news came as a shock. Although Mum and Dad might not have planned to have another child, coming from a family like ours, a new addition was always going to be a blessing. As Sabne and I got on board with the idea of a younger sibling, Mum went to her first meeting with the obstetrician.

During the ultrasound, the nurse went quiet. 'I can't hear anything,' she said before leaving the room to get the doctor. Looking concerned, the doctor checked the monitor. A few minutes went by in silence.

'Lu'isa,' he said gravely, 'there is no sign of the foetus. I'm so sorry.'

That was it. The excitement of gaining a new member of the Lātūkefu family lasted all of a few weeks. Mum was devastated. Meanwhile, I had another entry to the folder of 'Things I Don't Understand'. I could see the impact it had on Mum, but it didn't feel like *my* loss.

That, too, didn't last long. Watching Mum suffer over the following months made clear the significance of what had happened. I watched her closely, trying to distract her or cheer her up if I felt her mood drop. One day, I was playing outside while Mum was in the kitchen washing dishes.

'Hey, Mum,' I called. 'You know what?'

'What, Hau?'

'Maybe it wasn't a bad thing after all what happened,' I told her. 'Because, if you had the baby you wouldn't be able to go back to work, so we'd be very poor, wouldn't we?'

I think she appreciated my practical naivety. I continued to check in on her, but as for my own feelings? They stayed buried in that hidden folder that was steadily getting bigger. It wasn't until I started writing songs that I had the ability to verbalise how these events impacted me. It was like learning a new language, a whole new form of expression. But that was still a few years off.

When I entered high school, I'd been introduced to the sounds of hip hop, but let's get one thing clear: I was still a Queanbeyan boy through and through. So, naturally, I was rocking one glorious mullet on the first day of school. After registration, we were organised into classes for the year. Clearly Mum's fears about me in primary school were misguided because I was assigned the top set, while Patrick and most of my boys were in the bottom set. Thankfully, when I arrived at class, I saw Matt Beckenham, a kid I knew from primary.

'How ya goin', Matt?' I said as I slid into the seat next to him.

We weren't close but at least he was someone familiar. I had got used to primary school; it was near my house, I had my cousins and sister nearby, plus a tight group of friends. That first day at Queanbeyan High felt different. It wasn't just because I was separated from my crew; there were so many students that I started to feel self-conscious, as if people were staring at me.

High school is like a jungle for kids. You show weakness and the pack will hunt you down. It's sink or swim. As a result, you begin to notice all the things that make you different. In primary school, these things are accepted as a part of who you are, but when you enter the arena of high school, they become a weakness, a chink in your armour.

I got the sense some students were looking at my leg. Since the op to fix my club foot, I'd never spent that much time thinking about it – after all, I could still run, play footy and do everything else my friends could do. But the operation cut out half of my calf muscle so the size difference was definitely noticeable. I prickled with embarrassment, as if everyone was about to find out a big secret I'd been hiding.

I got to lunchtime unscathed, and Matt and I went to find some of the others from primary. I sat down next to Patrick, who was digging into his ham sandwich, and opened my lunchbox to find one cold portion of Tongan stew staring back at me.

'Ah man, not again!'

Rock Steady Crew had planted a seed in my brain, but everywhere else was all about new wave and the start of the glam rock era. KISS were kickin' arse and Bon Jovi had just started to pop. The music was okay, but for me it was all about the theatricality. I was always attracted to things that seemed different, and whether it was Jon Bon

Jovi and his massive mullet or Gene Simmons in face paint and a full spandex outfit, these guys were so unique, so far away from anything I saw in Queanbeyan, that I couldn't take my eyes off them. Plus, Sabne was a big fan and, with her being four years older than me, I was always happy to follow her lead.

During that summer at Queanbeyan High, our tastes changed. Sabne had just turned fifteen, and Mum and Dad sent her to Utah to spend time with Mum's family. It's funny to look back on now: my folks were so strict with Sabne that she was barely allowed to walk down to the end of our street on her own, but apparently it was fine to send her halfway across the world!

Sabne was only gone for a few weeks but she returned with a little box of treasures that altered the course of my life. The first thing she did was tell me about Salt-N-Pepa.

'*Everyone* was talking about them, Hau,' she explained with the relish of someone who knows they're in on a secret. 'They're these three women from New York . . .' *I've heard of that place,* I thought. 'And they do all these crazy dance moves when they perform.'

She dumped her stuff on the ground and launched into a rendition of 'Push It', throwing her hands forward while her hips went back, before twisting to each side. She'd obviously been practising. My eyes widened as she danced, but the best was yet to come.

'I got a bunch of tapes from the cousins,' she told me casually as she wrapped up her performance. 'You can check them out if you want.' (Sabne was always better at sharing than I was.)

She dug in her bag and pulled out a handful of cassette tapes. First, there was LL Cool J, *BAD (Bigger And Deffer)*; then *Crushin'* by The Fat Boys; *Licensed to Ill* by the Beastie Boys and *Back in Black* by Whodini.

Before I heard the music, it was the fashion that made me stop and stare. LL Cool J was standing on top of a car like a boss, rocking a red Kangol hat, a black leather tracksuit and red sneakers. I didn't even need to hear him rap to know LL Cool J was *the* man.

Clearly cars on album covers were a big thing back then because the Fat Boys were also on top of one, wearing colourful jackets that I later learned were the handiwork of Harlem fashion designer Dapper Dan. Whodini were more old school in their clothing, wearing head-to-toe black leather, while one had on a black, flat-brimmed sombrero. The Beastie Boys meanwhile . . . well, they were just the Beastie Boys, with their jeans and sneakers.

I inspected the cover art of each of the four tapes like a scientist inspecting the contents of a Petri dish. Looking closely, I could make out the brand names on the clothes; the way Whodini rolled up their sleeves to show off their gold bracelets; the way the Fat Boys' jackets opened just enough to reveal their thick gold chains; even the way LL Cool J stood, leaning back as if to say, *And what? Whatchu lookin' at?*

I loved the grandeur of KISS and Poison, but there was something even more captivating about this crop of artists. You can't take your eyes off Gene Simmons because he forces you to look at him. But with LL Cool J, his outfit said, *I don't care if you look at me or not, I know I'm the shit.*

Finally, I took *BAD* out of its case, placed it carefully in my tape deck, pressed play and went down a rabbit hole from which I would never return.

Over the next year, I went through a personality shift. The punch-happy kid from primary school was steadily replaced by a shy boy who only spoke when there was something to say. It's not like I was fading into the background, but I needed my environment to be comfortable and my family to be close in order for me to be myself.

This change got Mum worried again. She was used to seeing her son get into scraps all the time, now here he was barely speaking. She came to one of my first high school rugby games and, sure enough, a fight broke out. Panicking, Mum surveyed the melee, expecting to find me in the thick of it, dishing out a few right hooks. But my fighting days were behind me. Mum finally found me hands on hips, standing calmly next to the ref, watching the fight with a slight look of bemusement. I let everyone do their thing then I got on with the game.

If there was one place where I came alive, it was creative writing class. If I was quiet on the outside, inside, my brain was in B-boy overload. From Rock Steady to LL Cool J, all I did was think about hip hop and breakdancing. I would write elaborate stories in my notepad about B-boys with their slick moves and Kamikaze head-bands. Saturday mornings watching *Sounds* went from routine to something more akin to an obsession. Staring intently at the screen, I'd wait until the one hip hop song came on for me to practise my moves. I had graduated beyond knee spinning, and moved on to more advanced moves, like top rocking.

As much as I loved my friends at high school, they just didn't get it. And I didn't expect them to. Everywhere you looked, it was all about booners, or westies as some people called them. Booners were into rock'n'roll, wore their hair long and rocked flannel shirts. It wasn't as if hip hop kids were rare, they just weren't a thing, period. So when I was at school I kept my obsession to myself and within the pages of my notepad.

The first time my two worlds collided was during the first high school dance. A guy Sabne knew was DJ'ing, playing all the usual

oh jesus, I don't mean to use your name nuain
but I got maths next up, its gonna drive me insane
Mr.Crispin, my teacher who tells me to listen
to the system, but I piston
him off when I talked, then he walks across the room
talking mathematical crap at a high volume
so tell me, tell me, tell me what I'mma do with trigonometry
I'd rather study arts or maybe some philosophy
30 minutes to go in this class,
I'm dying to get the hell outta here and fast
"GRAB YOUR TEXT BOOK!" HE SLAMS
"NEXT LOOK!" some squares
oh my man whats the gee goin on about
maybe I'll just lounge, and write a song about
the maths class that I'm in

pop and rock tunes by bands like Twisted Sister and AC/DC. Most kids danced away happily while I stayed close to the DJ booth.

'Can you play "I'm Your Pusher" by Ice-T?' I asked.

The DJ laughed. 'Bro, I can't play that here. Besides, how do *you* know Ice-T?'

'He's a rapper,' I explained casually. I'd seen him on *Rage*. 'And he's sick! C'mon man, just play it once!'

Amused by this little hip hop upstart, the DJ chuckled and proceeded to ignore me for the rest of the evening. Disappointed, I went and found Matt and the rest of the guys.

'This DJ sucks,' I announced. The others murmured, not really agreeing or disagreeing; they weren't into music the way I was.

We hung out in that slightly awkward manner typical of prepubescent boys at a party with girls for the first time. Keeping my eyes on the DJ, I saw him look over at me and place a record on his turntable.

'Yo, it's time for me to pump the volume . . .'

'Oh shit! It's Ice-T!' I shouted to my friends, who responded with a look of confusion. Ignoring them, I hit the dance floor, making a beeline straight for the middle. This was my chance to shine. As Ice-T rapped, I pulled out all my best moves while the other kids shuffled back, giving me space to perform. To be honest, I barely noticed – I was totally zoned in on my routine.

I'd only just got into my rhythm when the DJ skipped to the next track. Some corny pop music replaced Ice-T's street shit and order in Queanbeyan was restored. But I'd had my moment, a taste of what was to come.

At class the next day, one of the other students came up to me as we were unpacking our bags. He was a booner and was known for pressing kids around school, rolling them for their lunch money.

'Hey, where'd you learn to dance like that?' he asked, clearly impressed.

At first, I was shocked. *He talking to me?* Quickly, I gathered my composure.

'Just something me and my cousins do,' I said, shrugging.

It's called hip hop.

SABNE

Did he tell you about his Star Wars figures yet?

Okay, so when the first Star Wars film was released, all the family was there. When Hau is into something, he gets really into it, and at this time it was Star Wars. He always had the action figures, then for Christmas he got two Luke Skywalker figures, and a Darth Vader – they were special ones, too, about 30 to 40 centimetres tall. He got those kinds of gifts while everyone else got T-shirts and things like that. I know the cousins were always looking at him like, 'Yeah, he's spoiled!'

He used to set things on fire, too. I had a Barbie doll with long blonde hair. I remember coming home from school one day and her hair was gone. He'd burned it all off! But the biggest fire he caused was at Uncle Maile's house. The extended family was there and I remember everybody running out, shouting. There were boxes of clothes my uncle kept under the house, and Hau had set the whole thing on fire. It was pretty big, actually.

He can get nasty when he gets mad. I remember one time, I had just broken up with my daughter's father, and Hau turned around and was like, 'Just cause you're not happy doesn't mean you have to make everyone else unhappy too.' He threw that at me, and I was like, 'How dare you! I'm your big sister, you don't talk to me like that!' Yeah, he can be very strong with his words.

THE FAI LOTU

The first time I saw a dead body I was five years old. We were at a funeral for a friend of my folks, and Tongan services often have an open casket. You could tell it was a Tongan funeral just by the sight of it: cars lining the entire street and spilling out of the driveway. When anyone Tongan in Canberra died, the entire community showed out to pay their respects. Approaching the casket that day, I watched as Mum and Dad kissed the dead body. When they'd said a few words to the family, Mum nudged me towards the casket. On tiptoes, I closed my eyes, held my breath and kissed the cheek of the dead man. It was cold and a bit eerie, but because everyone was doing it I didn't think much of it. Five minutes later, I was playing touch footy outside with the other kids.

It's one thing to be in the presence of death, but when it visits your immediate family it's something else altogether.

The next time around I was thirteen. I was home alone after school one day when a friend of Uncle Maile called.

'I'm so sorry to hear what happened to your uncle, Hau,' came the voice on the other end.

'What do you mean?' I asked. *Nothing's happened, I just saw him yesterday*. 'What's wrong?'

'Oh . . . *er*, nothing,' he responded. 'Is your dad there?'

'No, he's not home from work yet.'

'Okay, don't worry. I'll . . . *er*, I'll call you back.' The phone line went dead.

What does he mean? I started to panic. *What's happened to Uncle Maile?*

I only had to wait a few minutes for my fears to be confirmed. Looking out the window, I saw Dad park his car, then slowly get out and walk towards the house. He'd been crying. It was normal to see my dad cry, but something about this felt off. He looked scared, too. Lost.

I ran to the door to meet him. 'Dad, is everything okay?'

He put his arm around me and led me to the couch. I sat there waiting as Dad looked vacantly out the window, his eyes red from the tears.

'Hau, Maile died this afternoon,' he said simply.

Uncle Maile died of an asthma attack. Not a car crash, not cancer, not old age – an asthma attack. He was only in his sixties. Even at thirteen, I knew that was too young an age to die.

He was like a second father to me, so his death came as a real shock. When I'd had my first day of school, it was Uncle Maile who'd taken me. He was also over at our house all the time, and because he travelled a lot for work, he'd come back armed with gifts for me and Sabne. Once, he returned with huge figurines of the wrestlers Hulk Hogan and Junkyard Dog, just as I'd asked. Little did I know at the time that he'd spent hours hitting a dozen different stores to find them. But Maile would have tried a dozen more if it meant putting a smile on my face. He lived for us kids.

Before Maile passed away, I thought of my uncles as invincible. I watched in awe as they ploughed through guys on the rugby field;

I giggled as they casually picked me up with one hand and tossed me onto their shoulders; and I stopped dead in my tracks whenever they told me off. They made me feel safe and provided a layer of protection between me and the world. When my uncles were around, nothing could touch me.

Maile's death changed that. It was a pain I hadn't felt before, one of those moments that you instantly know will be significant. The tectonic plates of my childhood were shifting, with the innocence and joy slowly making way for something harder, more brittle. And once those plates shift, there's no turning back.

The next few weeks went by slowly. Uncle Talia'uli had the biggest house, so each night we would gather there for the *fai lotu*, a Tongan ritual that acts as a memorial service until the actual funeral, known as the *putu*. As usual, the whole community showed out. I'd been to this sort of thing a hundred times before but never for my own family. My dad and all his brothers were in the living room, with Sione holding court. Families arrived and paid their respects to my uncles before taking a seat. In that room was one of the most intense displays of emotion I have ever witnessed; Tongans don't do the whole stoic thing. I watched as grown men and women cried out in grief, their emotions spilling over into the garden where my cousins and I sat. I'd never seen people cry like that, not even on TV. It seemed almost performative to me, as if they were *making* themselves cry, but that was only because I wasn't used to it. In Australia, you hide your emotions. You grit your teeth and carry on. Tongans do the opposite; they allow themselves to feel, and therefore to heal.

Each family brings a gift to the *fai lotu* – sometimes food, sometimes money, sometimes traditional Tongan ceremonial items, like *ngatu*, which is similar to a rug, made by flattening the bark from *hiapo* (paper mulberry tree) then decorating it with natural dyes and pigments. No Tongan occasion is complete without *ngatu*. They're often used to tell stories from Tongan history or simply mark an important occasion. Because they're made from bark they need to be kept flat, so in our house they were kept under the bed – *my* bed – which explains why I always had a lumpy mattress.

The garden had a different vibe. After families had paid their respects, they continued outside where there was a gazebo set up for everyone. If the living room was where you went to mark the tragedy of Maile's death, you went outside to honour his life. It wasn't a party, but we laughed and joked, recalling stories about our uncle, brother and friend. By allowing ourselves to feel the pain of this tragedy, we could also recognise the beauty of our time together. That's the thing about life: you need both.

This went on for two weeks. We'd go from school to Uncle Talia'uli's then, when it was late, we'd drive quietly home, everyone exhausted from the emotion, before it was back to school the next day. It took its toll on Mum and Dad, both emotionally and financially. All the family arriving from Tonga needed their plane tickets paid for and accommodation sorted. That doesn't come cheap. Having to manage these things while dealing with the death of your brother is no easy task.

As for me, I'm not sure I've ever really gotten over the loss. It just seemed so unfair, so premature, that it's stayed with me ever since, like a knot in my heart that won't go away. But it was nothing compared to the grief of Maile's immediate family. 'Uli was five years old when his dad died, while his mum, Aunt Lesieli, was pregnant with their second child. Named after his dad, Maile was born a few months later. From then on they became my little brothers, and it kills me that they didn't get to grow up being spoiled by Uncle Maile the way Sabne and I were. He would have been so proud watching his boys grow up.

HIGH ROLLER

I was ready.

I'd been listening to the tapes Sabne had brought back from the US so often I could recite them from heart. I wasn't just listening; I was *studying*. LL Cool J emphasised every syllable with B-boy energy; his presence on the mic smacked you round the face as soon as he rapped his first bars. Meanwhile, the Fat Boys were more playful with it, riffing off each other and finishing each other's lines with funny remarks. It was all about timing and saying the coolest shit you could think of. And we must not forget the amazing beatboxing from Buffy.

After a few months I started playing around with my own rhymes, taking an exercise book from school and dedicating it to writing anything that came into my head. A lot of it was influenced by gangsta shit, so I was talking about gats I didn't own and drugs I didn't sell. It was mad cringe, but it was a start.

When we got an assignment in English class to write a poem, I knew it was time to show off my newly acquired rap skills. I rehearsed for days, figuring out which sections to emphasise most and learning every word so I wouldn't have to look at my pad. After a week of preparing, I was ready.

gangsteR stroll on, gangster roll on
as we hold on, police patRol on
with the bad-ass gangsteR limp
grab the bit hox to play the pRanksteR pimp
rollin' with the homeboyz on the street
strate-up ganxsta step up u might git beat
oR blown-down, ya shouldn't of step up for the show-down
cos u know you would go-down
cos I'm the gangster of streets, the stalker of nightmares
I pack the 12 gauge & set the right-where
I want to, and blow the fuckin smoke and peel the cap
into your face, your leg and even in your back &
for this gangster is hard, a 9mm is my calling card
call me a sucker-punk your face will get be scard
gangster-flowin' where ever I go
always with 2° or moRe brother so I show...
up with a posse, and know one can stop me
fROntin up hard killin' niggaz like nazis
pushin my luck but I don't give a fuck
this nigga is bold, fuck the five-o .
cos when your a gangsteR, u go all out
bullets flyin', mothers cryin' it's all clout
I'm strait-up hart, I'm never a pRanksteR
never slippin' or trippin because Im a gangsTER

***

When I got to class that day, I'm not gonna lie – I was shitting myself. It was the first time I would perform in public, so I was nervous how everyone would react. *What if they laugh?* I pushed the thoughts to one side and took my seat in the middle of the classroom. This was the same for me in every class: I'd stay close enough to the teacher so I could listen but near to the back so I was still in on the jokes. Remember what I said earlier? It's all about balance.

While the first few students got through their performances, I was going over my rhymes in my head to ensure they were rock-solid and ready to go. Staring out the window, I was mouthing the lyrics when the teacher called my name.

'Hau,' Mr Stevens called out again. 'Are you ready, Hau?'

'Ah . . . yes, Sir.'

My heart was racing as I slowly made my way to the front of class, skimming over the performance in my head one last time. The poem was all about the lifestyle of those living on the edge of society. Those people who throw their two fingers to the law and live life at a hundred miles an hour. They don't care about consequences or what other people think. It was called 'High Rollers'. I took a deep breath and started.

'Speed of life . . . fast, it's like walkin' barefoot over broken glass . . .'

Okay, at this point it's probably worth mentioning that I didn't actually write these lyrics – Ice-T did. I know, I know, it was a risk, but it was a calculated one. I figured the chances that anyone in that classroom had heard of Ice-T were slim, and the chances they knew his song 'High Rollers' were even slimmer. But as I worked my way through the first verse, I began to sweat. Surely Sir will realise I didn't write this? How could a fourteen-year-old from Queanbeyan know about the lifestyle of street criminals? *Keep it together man!* I gathered myself for my – sorry – *Ice-T's* final line:

'Definition: street player, you know who I mean . . . high rollers.'

As if emerging from a trance, I came to before scanning the class-room to see if anyone knew what I had just done. Nothing. Relieved,

I quickly took my seat, praying for the bell to announce the next class and save me from my shame. Sir had other ideas.

'Hau, that was fantastic!' he enthused.

I went red. *What? Is he serious?*

'The metaphor of broken glass is a brilliant way to open,' he continued. 'It signifies a trap, as if the lifestyle of these "high rollers" comes with a lot of risk. They must dodge the broken glass if they are going to survive. And to continue that metaphor into the second line where you . . . What was the line again, Hau? "It's like . . ."'

Oh God. Please make it stop. 'It's like, jumpin' rope on a razor blade,' I mumbled.

'Exactly! The razor blade is another hazard they must avoid. After just two lines we already know the dangers inherent in this lifestyle. Really impressive work, Hau.'

I sank a few inches in my seat.

'Okay, who's next?'

Thank God. Sir switched his attention elsewhere, allowing me the freedom to self-combust with embarrassment. I started wondering if Sir was baiting me, seeing how far I would go with the lie. *Surely, he knows? I mean, we don't even say 'jump rope' in Australia; we call it a 'skipping rope'. Should I say something now and own up? Mum always says it's better to be honest.*

Fuck it. You've made your bed, I told myself. *Too late to come clean now.*

The bell finally announced the end of class. On my way out, Sir tapped me on the shoulder.

'Nice work today, Hau,' he said, smiling. I still couldn't figure out if he was being genuine or not, but I no longer cared.

'Thanks, Sir!' With a grin on my face, I made my way to my next class.

***

That weekend, we were at a fundraising event for one of the churches back in Tonga. It was at the Croatian Club in Canberra, where all the functions were. Don't quote me on this, but I'm pretty sure that was because the Croatian Club was the only place that would allow Tongans to host their boisterous events. This was 1989, nearly twenty years after Uncle Sione first arrived in Canberra, so by this point we were far from the only Tongan family in the area. Still, it was a tight-knit community; everyone knew everyone. I'd leave the folks to do their thing while I hung out with the other kids, talking shit and playing touch footy if there was space. It was supposed to just be a bit of fun, but things would always get heated. Any kid knows how this goes: touch turns to full-blown tackles which turns to scuffles. The next thing you know, the parents are being called and the game's over.

I always looked out for JJ, who was around my age and grew up with me like a cousin. You know how it is in the Tongan community; everyone's cousins. Big fella spoke with a slight lisp and loved a good yarn. He was one loud kid, JJ – his voice, his laugh, his presence. Nothing about him was subtle. It was a joyous loudness, though, rather than an obnoxious one. He lived in Canberra so we went to different schools, but at the community functions it was always me and JJ. We'd been hanging out since we were kids, but our friendship was isolated to these fundraising events until one day JJ invited me to Canberra with him.

'Come hang, bro,' he said. 'We're going to the Happy Days arcade on Friday night. You should come.'

Because JJ went to school in Canberra, he was tapped in to what was going on far more than I was out in Queanbeyan. I didn't know what Happy Days was, but I was down to find out.

'Yeah, easy,' I replied. 'I'll see you there.'

***

When Friday rolled around, I was planning my outfit from the moment I left school. Everyone knows first impressions are important, but for a fourteen-year-old kid on his first solo trip to town? It's a matter of life and death. I knew I had to be on point. The only thing was, Mum was still buying my clothes. I didn't have a Kangol like LL, and I *certainly* didn't have any Dapper Dan. But you know what they say, a bad tradie blames his tools. Besides, style's all about confidence anyway.

Other than confidence, there was one thing I *did* have: my Adidas. Earlier that year Mum had bought me a pair of high-top Adidas sneakers. They were white with blue and yellow detailing, but more importantly, they were the sickest thing I had ever owned. I felt like Run-DMC every time I put those things on, instantly transforming from a Queanbeyan lad to a fully-fledged B-boy from Hollis, Queens. I wore them so often they started to get holes in the sole, but I didn't care. Each time a new hole appeared, I'd touch them up with some glue and whatever material I had at arm's length, then chuck them right back on.

With my Adidas on my feet and some change Mum lent me in my pocket, I took the bus to Canberra and met JJ outside Happy Days.

'Yeah boyeee!' I dapped him up and we walked upstairs to the arcade. JJ knew the place, so I followed a few paces behind, not quite familiar with my surroundings yet.

'Yo, Talo!' he called out to a kid a few years older than me, who I'd seen around at different functions. Talo was Tongan but he had his own swag. I'd grown out of my mullet and was rocking a fade by this point – the same with JJ – but Talo had a mane of wavy, long black hair with an undercut. That was a first for me. He was leaning on a pool cue, halfway through a game, when we arrived.

'What up, JJ?' They shook hands as I stood there, waiting for an introduction. 'This is Hau,' JJ said finally, pointing to where I was standing.

Talo greeted me with a big smile. He had a kind, gentle manner when he spoke that showed off a quiet confidence. It was probably because he was older; Talo had less of the adolescent awkwardness young teenage boys have.

We joined Talo and a mate of his who was around the same age but had a full moustache and a long rat's tail trailing down to the top of his spine. *What a look.* The four of us went and found somewhere to sit. On the way, Talo wandered up to the jukebox and put on 'Smooth Operator' by Big Daddy Kane. I kept it cool but inside I was impressed with his choice. If it was anywhere else in Canberra, the jukebox would have been full of rock'n'roll, but Happy Days wasn't like anywhere else in Canberra.

For the next few hours, all we did was talk – about hip hop, girls, school, anything. From the outside it would have seemed like nothing special – just four teenagers talking shit in an arcade – but on the inside it was exhilarating. I had a good crew of friends at school, but between Patrick and Matt and the rest of the guys, we were mainly friends through circumstance. We didn't really have similar interests, which is why I was always with my cousins on the weekend. But with JJ and Talo, it was like meeting my tribe. I was only fourteen, but I took one step closer to being an adult that day. My place in the world started to make sense. *These are my people,* I realised. *This is where I belong.*

At nine o'clock that evening, I had a bus to catch. Walking out, I scanned the room and realised it wasn't just Talo with his undercut and his mate with his rat's tail who had a unique style. *Everyone* had something going on. I looked down at my Adidas. The colour was fading and the holes were only getting bigger. *Yeah*, I said to myself, *it's time to step my game up.*

First, I needed a job. If I was going to stand out like the rest of the crew at Happy Days, I needed to be able to buy my own clothes and not rely on Mum. I had some pocket change saved up from when elders would come round to see my folks, but it never amounted to much. On the way out they'd often slip me five dollars and tell me to buy some lollies. Sometimes I would, but more often than not I'd save up the money until I could buy a cassette tape from Impact Records in Canberra. But this was a painful process; I needed cash and I needed it now.

My boy Craig Mather at school was the first of our group to get a job. He was working at KFC, so after an opening came up he put in a good word for me. This was before mobiles, and even emails, so I sent my application in by post and waited for a reply. A few weeks later, Craig told me his boss had been trying to reach me.

'He said, "Tell your Māori mate I left a message for him",' Craig relayed to me one morning at school.

Māori? To be honest, I wasn't surprised. Māoris came to Australia before Islanders did, so for a long time Australians saw any Brown person as Māori. I wasn't offended; instances like this always seemed a bit dumb to me more than anything. To be fair to Craig's boss and, let's be honest, almost any other Aussie bloke in the '80s and '90s, they didn't know. But at the same time they didn't *try* to know. I mean, I could see there was a big difference between Māoris and Tongans, but maybe that's just me. Either way, I never heard from Craig's boss again.

Soon Craig had himself another job, this time delivering pamphlets from local businesses to houses in Queanbeyan. He hooked me up and the two of us would cruise around the neighbourhood on our BMXs flinging pamphlets into letterboxes. I was stoked to have my first job and would spend most of the shift daydreaming about different things I would buy: clothes, records, Adidas sneakers with no holes.

After I got my first pay cheque, Craig and I went to Riverside Plaza to spend some of our hard-earned cash. For anyone not up to date on the intricacies of the pamphlet industry, we're hardly talking big money. In other words, I had to be frugal. For the first hour or two, we just window-shopped. I wasn't about to drop my first pay cheque on just anything.

After a while we hit a sports store, which I'd walked past with Mum a bunch of times before but had never been inside. I studied album covers for fashion inspiration, so I knew the sort of thing I was looking for. I wasn't a booner with their flannel shirts and boots, and I wanted to stand out from every other kid in Queanbeyan who just wore whatever shirt-and-shorts combo was put in front of them. I did a few laps, savouring the fact I had money in my pocket for the first time in my life before honing in on something I liked: a long-sleeve crew-neck Puma shirt with a brown patch on the front. *Thiiiiiis is what I'm talking about.*

'Craig,' I called out across the store to where he was checking out the sneaker collection. 'What do ya reckon?'

'Yeah, bloody oaf! How much is it?'

I looked at the label and realised I could afford it . . . just. Plus, it fit perfectly. The style – or lack of – in Queanbeyan was baggy clothes that hung off your body without much shape. But this shirt was fitted; it was snug around my shoulders and the crew neck sat high on my collarbone, almost like a turtleneck. It was a vibe.

But as I looked in the changing room mirror, I started to feel anxious. I'd seen my older cousins give their first pay cheques to their family – it was like an unofficial tradition – and here I was about to blow mine on some fresh Puma gear. Unsure what to do, I knew I had to call Mum. Putting the shirt back, I left the store to find the nearest payphone. Craig waited outside while I slipped thirty cents in and called home.

'Hey Mum, I'm at Riverside with Craig and I've found a top I really like,' I explained. 'I have enough money – can I buy it?'

'Of course, Hau. This is your first pay cheque; you should be proud of yourself.'

'Yeah, you're right – okay, thanks, Mum.' Before hanging up, I asked, 'Hey, what's for dinner? I'll be home soon.'

'Your dad's doing Tongan stew,' Mum replied.

Of course. I hung up the phone and went straight to the cashier.

HAPPY DAYS

Before the internet, keeping up to date with hip hop news wasn't easy. You had to stay glued to shows like *Rage* and *Sounds*, and make sure you had the latest copy of *The Source*. Growing up, *The Source* was like my Bible. And just like the Book of Revelations, it was full of stories that blew my mind. While flicking through an issue one afternoon, I read that Ice Cube was leaving NWA. I couldn't believe it – Cube was the backbone of the group. *What are they going to do without him?*

After school the next day, I got invited to Alvin's house. Alvin was mates with some of my friends from school but he lived in Tasmania with his dad. When he was back visiting his mum in Queanbeyan, his friend Steve Coulton told him he should meet me.

'Hau's mad into hip hop, just like you,' he told Alvin. 'You guys should hang out.'

'Yeah, sounds good. Tell him to come over.'

When I arrived, Alvin was in his room listening to music.

'What's up, man?' I asked.

'Not much,' he replied. 'Just checking out that new Ice Cube album.' Alvin pointed to his music collection, where I could see

Cube's trademark frown staring back at me. Confused, I stepped closer and read the title, *AmeriKKKa's Most Wanted*. I didn't understand.

'But I thought he only just left NWA?' I asked.

'Yeah, not long ago,' he said casually. 'This is his first solo album.'

I don't know what was more shocking: the fact Ice Cube had left NWA or the fact I was being schooled on hip hop by this white boy from Tasmania. I couldn't help but be impressed. Alvin showed me the rest of his collection. This kid was no joke. He had Eric B. & Rakim's *Follow the Leader*; *Road to the Riches* by Kool G Rap & DJ Polo as well as some MC Shan and the new Fat Boys tape. I was almost speechless. *I thought I was the only one around here who knew about this stuff?*

Although hip hop was my new love, footy still held a special place in my heart. My week was punctuated by training sessions (which I hated) and games (which I loved). Australia is all about League, but Union is more popular in the Islands. Considering my dad and uncles played Union, I wanted to play that code too. But as an Under 14, I played both – for the Queanbeyan Whites in Union and the Kangaroos in League. That year, we got to the grand final in each code.

Sport at that age is hardly strategic; you rely on the natural athleticism of a few kids and hope for the best. It's not 'til later that you start to experiment with different plays and tactics. When it came to star players, Matt Beckenham was our guy on the Roos. He was so quick that he went on to compete at the 2000 Sydney Olympics in the 400m hurdles. I wasn't one of the stars but I was solid. All about crash and bang, I was a workhorse but I was also good with my hands, especially for a prop, a position not known for its deftness of touch. My speciality was my ball-handling skills; if someone was taking me down, I'd look for the one-handed pass to get the ball moving before I was tackled. Off the back of Matt's tries, we went undefeated that season and won the final with ease.

The Union final with the Whites was a different story. We were facing St Edmund's College, a private school in Canberra that played in the weekend club competition as well. They had the facilities, the resources and the pick of the players in the local area. But we had heart. Our star player was Afa Gafa, a Samoan kid who came over from New Zealand. You know those kids who are already knee-deep into puberty by the time they enter high school? That was Afa Gafa. The kid was a beast. It would take at least two or three of the opposing team's players to bring him down.

The game was played at Phillip Oval in Canberra's south-west, my first time playing in front of a grandstand. Knowing it was going to be a tough game, I was sure to go about my pre-match routine with purpose, starting with the breakfast of champions: a bowl of cornflakes. With Mum and Dad watching, we got there early to soak up the experience. It felt like a grudge match. St Eddies wasn't far from my school, but it was a different world altogether. If you had money, you sent your kid to St Eddies; if not, you sent them to Queanbeyan High.

The game was tied going into the final five minutes. A low-scoring match, there was little separating us until Afa Gafa received the ball out wide, a few yards into the opposition half. He had space to run, which meant St Eddies were in trouble. Ball in one hand, Afa dodged the first tackle like a gazelle elegantly sidestepping a clumsy predator. The crowd rose to their feet: 'GOOOOOOOOO!' Exhausted by this point, I was trailing behind play, but it didn't matter. The game was in Afa's hands now.

He didn't bother dodging another tackle. Instead, Afa put his head down and raced for the corner, powering through three more defenders along the way. *Oh shit, he's gonna do it. We're gonna win!*

Leaving a trail of players strewn across the turf, Afa Gafa reached the tryline and sealed the game. The underdogs had come out on top: two grand-final victories in one weekend.

Alvin was back in Queanbeyan in December. Realising we both loved hip hop as much as the other, he began hitting me up whenever he was in town. His mum only lived down the hill from us, so we spent most of the Christmas holidays in his bedroom writing rhymes and listening to records.

Alvin wasn't only up on his rap but he was also one hell of a talented artist. One of his favourite things to do was redesign album covers, coming up with his own take. I was at his place, sitting beneath the massive Geto Boys poster he had in his bedroom, when he showed me one he'd been working on.

'This one is for Schoolly D,' he said, holding up his notepad.

I immediately started cracking up: 'HAHAHA! Yeah, that sounds like him!'

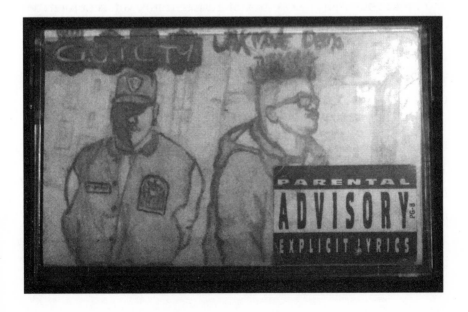

Schoolly D repped Philadelphia and was one of the very first gangsta rappers, talking in detail about drugs, guns and sex. He was the one who'd inspired Ice-T to go down the path he did. The album Alvin was redesigning was called *Am I Black Enough for You?* but I reckon Al's title was better: *I Keep My Dick in My Hand and Smoke Weed.* Can't tell me that ain't catchy.

'You know,' Alvin said, laughing, 'because he's always talking about holding his nuts and smoking weed.'

'Let's write a verse to it,' I replied. This was our routine. Before we could write to an actual beat, we made up verses based on songs we liked or album covers that Alvin had designed. As I took out my notepad, a shout came from outside the room.

'Oi, Alvin!' came the booming voice of his stepdad, Simon. 'Get outside and mow that lawn! I'm not telling you again.'

I looked at Alvin. Simon – or 'Simo' as everyone but Alvin called him – was Māori and one staunch dude. He was not the sort of guy you ignored. Luckily for us, he was also a massive hip hop fan. He poked his head into Alvin's room.

'I told you . . .' his boom box of a voice trailed off as he saw me. 'Oh, didn't know you had company. What youse boys up to?'

'Just working on some music,' Alvin told him. 'Can I do the lawn after?'

'Chur,' he said, nodding. 'You boys have fun.'

Simon closed the door and we got back to rewriting Schoolly D's lyrics. A few minutes later, I had something. Putting my notepad down, I gave Alvin a quick rendition.

'These girls are all in my bag like a testicle,' I rapped. 'My balls are so big, they're gonna be historical.'

'Haha! That's dope,' Alvin said. 'Oh shit, that reminds me – you remember that DJ I was telling you about in Tassie, Dope DJ DD?'

'The one who spins the rap records?'

'Yeah, that's him. He said if we record an intro for him, he'd use it on his show.'

'Mad, let's do it!'

Putting away our notepads, Alvin took out his tape decks. He used one to play a beat he'd found, and I used the other to record the intro.

'What should I say?' I asked.

'Just a line saying welcome to the show or whatever.'

'Cool.'

Alvin played the beat and I adopted my best American DJ persona – despite DD being from Tasmania – lowering my voice as far as it would go.

'Yo, this is Dope DJ DD, and you're listening to "Live From The Terrordome".'

'Mad,' Alvin responded. 'Let's do it one more time.'

This time I slowed my voice down to a sultry drawl, lengthened the 'yo' and added some inflections so it didn't all sound like the same tone.

'Yooooooooo, this is Dope DJ DD . . . and *you're* listening to "Live From The Terrordome".'

Alvin stopped the recorder. 'Bro, we're gonna be on the radio!'

I was living a double life. There was the school version of me: shy but popular, I got on with everybody and was able to float between the different groups like a neutral. Being good at sport always helps you do that at school. But outside of Queanbeyan High I was becoming the true version of myself. That first visit to Happy Days ignited in me a desire to seek out more opportunities to live out the music, style and culture that I had come to love. I've never done hard drugs but I reckon it's similar to the way drug addicts chase that high after their first hit. If I wasn't daydreaming through class or playing footy, I was seeking out my next hip hop high.

Happy Days became a habit for me, JJ and Talo. After that first visit, I kept going back every Friday night until even that wasn't enough. So we started wagging. Sabne casually dropped into conversation one day that she could mimic Mum's handwriting, and I just knew that information would come in handy. It must have been a whole year or two later that I brought it up. I waited 'til I caught sis in a good mood.

'Yo, Sab, can you do me a favour?'

'Depends what it is,' she said without looking up from what she was doing.

'Can you write me an absent note tomorrow if I skip school?'

She turned to face me. Now I had her attention.

'C'mon, sis – I know you used to do it all the time!'

'First, I didn't do it all the time. And second, that doesn't make it right.' Sab might have been the rebel, but she was also my big sister – and she took that role very seriously.

'Look, I'll do it, but I don't want you to make it a habit. Okay?'

'For sure! Thanks, Sab. It won't happen a lot, I promise.'

Spoiler alert – it did happen *a lot*. Maybe Sab lost the nerve to tell Mum, or maybe she trusted me, but from that day on wagging became a habit. Not every morning – I wasn't that dumb – but during most weeks in Year 10 you'd be just as likely to find me in the Happy Days arcade, slotting money into the jukebox, as you would find me in school. Considering Dad's history of wagging, it was almost like a rite of passage. And, like Dad, I had my routine perfected like an art form.

I woke up and got ready for school like any other day. I dressed in our school colours – white, grey and maroon – had my breakfast and waved goodbye to Mum and Dad as they left for work. *Nothing suspicious here, folks.* Then I changed out of my school colours and into my Happy Days gear, aka the freshest outfit I could find, before taking a bus to Civic in Canberra to meet JJ and Talo.

I was at home watching TV when Alvin called from Tasmania.

'How'd it go?' I asked immediately.

'Yeah . . . not great.' He sounded disappointed. 'Dope DJ DD let me spit a few bars live on air—'

'*What?* That's awesome!' Before I could say anything else, Alvin jumped in.

'Yeah, but he cut me off! I rapped our verses from the Schoolly D song we made, and I was careful to swap out all the swearwords and everything. But I kept in your line about testicles. Bro, I didn't even know "testicles" was a curse. As soon as I said it he cut me off and told me I couldn't go up there anymore.'

'Ah really? Man, fuck that guy,' I said. 'How you meant to rap and not swear at all?'

'That's what I told him. After that I didn't bother giving him the intro. Sorry, bro.'

'Nah, all good, man,' I reassured Alvin. 'We're too advanced for him anyway!'

'Exactly. Okay, Simon needs the phone. I'll be back at Easter. See you then.'

'I got next!'

I'd worked my way up the unofficial Happy Days pecking order, so I no longer felt timid about securing the pool table. It helped that there were a lot of Islanders who went there that I knew from the community, so I was never a complete outsider. As I racked up the balls, two girls walked past the table, leaving a trail of sweet perfume behind them. I stopped what I was doing and gave JJ a look.

'*Damn!*'

Even the girls at Happy Days were better. At school, there were a few who'd caught my eye, but it never seemed like we had much in common, like we were speaking a different language. At Happy Days, the girls were bad *and* cool. I hadn't really developed any game yet but Talo, being a few years older, knew the go. He left me and JJ to play pool while he followed the perfume.

I broke and drained a few stripes.

'Lucky bugger,' JJ laughed.

'Man, you don't need luck when you have talent like this,' I told him. 'Hey, you heard that new album by A Tribe Called Quest? *People's Instinctive Travels*, or something like that. *The Source* gave it five mics – first time they've ever done that.'

I drained another.

'No shit? Five mics?' JJ said, happy to divert attention from his impending defeat. 'I'll have to check it out.'

As he chalked his cue, Mac and Errol, who we knew from around Canberra approached the table.

'Yo, what's up?' said Mac, dapping me up.

'Not much, man, just giving JJ a lesson here in pool.' I smirked.

'Ah yeah? You need a real teacher, come see me,' said Errol. 'You boys going Firehouse this weekend?'

Firehouse was an underage nightclub and, like Happy Days, it was a hip hop haunt where you went if you wanted to stand out from the rest of the Canberra crowd.

'Yeah, no doubt,' I told Errol. 'We'll be there.'

When it came to the Happy Days hierarchy, Mac and Errol were at the top. A good few years older than me, they were the best dancers, the best dressers and, of course, the girls loved them. Even their names were cool; 'Mac and Errol' made them seem like they were some rap duo from the States. If they were born in Atlanta instead of Canberra, they probably would've been. You can't teach that sort of funk.

Like me, everyone inside Happy Days was on a journey to self-discovery. Among the pool marathons and arcade games, we stole glances at each other, picking up on the fashion and the slang to make sure that at any point we always knew what was hot. To be out of touch meant risking being left behind. When we trotted upstairs to where the action was, it was like walking through the mythical wardrobe into Narnia; we left Canberra behind and entered a place we had only read about in *The Source* and seen on *Rage*. It was where we were free to be the people we wanted to be – not what white Australia projected onto us.

Adjacent to Mac and Errol at the top of the hierarchy were the Asian kids. I'd thought they were all from Vietnam and Thailand until Talo explained that most of them were from Laos.

'Where's that?' I'd asked.

'Right next to Cambodia.'

Huh. I was getting an education in hip hop culture *and* geography. Because Happy Days was one of Canberra's most diverse hangouts – there were Islanders, Africans, Asians and a handful of whites who wanted to be any of the aforementioned three. Most of the time everyone mixed with each other, but when fights broke out it was like prison, with each ethnicity sticking together.

While the Islanders could fight, it was the Asians who had the sauce. Maybe it was because fashion tends to fit their body shape better than us, or maybe it was because they had more money. A lot of them had decent jobs working in restaurants or their families owned bakeries, and the rest were getting into street shit so they had cash in their pockets. For them, entry-level fashion meant Country Road jumpers on top of a turtleneck with golden hoop earrings.

A lot of them veered towards punk vibes and had long straight hair styled into a ponytail or tall, jagged spikes held together by industrial amounts of gel. The next level was reserved for the street dudes who modelled their aesthetic around Hong Kong gangsters in the movies. These guys were rocking full suits with silk shirts and shiny black loafers. Okay, sometimes it was a bit much, especially for a group of teenagers, but you could never deny they dressed to impress each and every time. If LL and Whodini introduced me to fashion, the Asian kids in Happy Days turned it into an obsession.

Talo returned empty-handed just as I was down to the black. I lined up the shot, paused and executed.

'And that, boys,' I said with a smile, 'is how it's done.'

GUILTY

Rap taught me a lot. Listening to Public Enemy's 'Night of the Living Baseheads' I learned about crack and drug addicts. And it was NWA's '100 Miles and Runnin'' that taught me about stereotypes and police brutality. MC Ren raps, 'Since I'm stereotyped to kill and destruct / Is one of the main reasons, I don't give a fuck.' As soon as I heard that line, I had a word for a feeling I knew to be true. Growing up, I'd often overhear people saying rude things about Islanders, and if they noticed me, they were always quick to say, 'Not you, Hau – you're not like them.'

Not like them? At first, I wasn't sure if that was a good or a bad thing. Is it good I'm not like the others, or bad that you think we're all the same? NWA gave me the confidence to understand that there was no two ways about it: stereotyping was bad. It's also just plain lazy. How are you going to reduce a whole race to the actions of a few people?

In English class one day we were given the task of making a presentation about a film, and I chose John Singleton's *Boyz N the Hood*. The presentation was about responsibility, and the section I wanted to talk about was when Jason 'Furious' Styles (Laurence Fishburne) is fishing with his son, Tre (Cuba Gooding Jr with a young Tre played by Desi Arnez Hines II). Furious tells him, 'Anyone with a dick can make a baby; it takes a man to raise one.' But when I told Miss the topic of my presentation, she seemed hesitant.

'I've heard that's a very violent film, Hau,' she told me. Miss wasn't necessarily saying I couldn't do it, though she clearly wanted to see where I was going with it. But when she questioned me, MC Ren popped into my head. *You only think that because the film is about Black people: that's a stereotype.*

'Yeah.' I shrugged. 'So's *The Godfather.*'

With that, I had her. She let me do my *Boyz N the Hood* presentation with no further questions.

It's a beautiful thing to find something you love so young because – not only do you have a passion to build your identity around and give you purpose – it puts a battery in your back to get out there and claim your place in the world. It makes you hungry to learn new things so you can get better at whatever it is that's driving you. For me, rap wasn't only helping me make sense of the world and my place in it, it was helping me develop new skills.

Since Alvin and I started trading tapes back and forth, I got handy with cassettes. The Walkman I had didn't come with a rewind button, so I figured out how to use a pencil to rewind them after listening. Then I started using a method called 'pause-stop recording' that allowed me to record loops of instrumentals to rap over. Using a tape deck, I'd play part of a beat and record it before pausing the beat and stopping the recording. After that I'd rewind and repeat the process until I had a loop of the beat. Then I would rap over the beat and use a second tape deck to record everything. Later, my cousin Hounga got a dual cassette player that meant we could play the loop and record our raps with one machine. I quickly learned about tempo, and when I found tracks that had the same BPM (beats per minute), I was able to mix them. But the real game-changer came when another cousin of mine, Sione, got a four-track recorder. You could play a beat on one track, have a few different vocals on the others, and then record straight to cassette. It also had pitch control that allowed me to get creative, pitching my vocals up and down, and even doing the same for samples.

The more I did things like this, the hungrier I got to actually start performing. But there was one more thing I needed before I could officially take that leap: a rap name. In between our Happy Days visits, JJ, Talo and I would hang out at each other's houses and write lyrics in our notepads or practise our dance routines for Firehouse. One afternoon, I came to them with an idea.

'We should start a rap group like NWA,' I told them. I had it all mapped out. 'No one's doing that in Australia – we could be the first!'

As they were sounding their approval, I kept going.

'We should call ourselves GUILTY,' I proclaimed. 'Guys Unlimited in Looks, Talent and Youth.'

'Oh shit!' replied Talo. 'That's sick!'

Pleased, I said we also needed our own individual names. Of course, I already had an idea for mine. A lot of rappers in the early '90s based their names around letters and syllables: Kool Moe Dee, Chuck D, Heavy D, Ice-T and so on. Mine was going to be the same.

'I'm gonna be Cruel-T,' I told JJ and Talo. 'You guys have a think about your names.'

MC Hammer changed the game. With his song 'U Can't Touch This' he found a way to turn rap into pop music, becoming a household name overnight. His records were catchy, his outfits were dope and

the mental assassins back, I bet you thought I had left ya
but true known fact is that I had crept ta
all those opposed to the kang, to be so now I'm back
but it aint no thang to me
I just grab the microphone and bein' guilty to the bone
I smoke the mic just like a homegrown
toke a pull... don't it make ya feel dizy
sit back and loung and let the music git buzzl
and let the aroma just hang,
heart to soul the tribe and guilty is the gang
or exploding like dynomite, and you'll find I mite

his dance moves, well, no one could dance like Hammer. He became one of the first hip hop megastars, and with that status comes a lot of hate. But in 1991, before Q-Tip and others started dissing him in songs, he was still the man.

If you wanted to dance like Hammer – which I did – you needed a pair of Hammer pants. And the only place in Canberra deserving of Hammer pants was Firehouse. Each Saturday night, come rain or shine, we were there. If Happy Days was where we went to learn about the culture, Firehouse was where we went to *live* it. When JJ, Talo and I began going regularly, I asked one of my cousin's grandmothers to sew me a few pairs. She went above and beyond, giving me three options, all in different colours. That way, I could cycle through them and not have to wear the same thing two weeks in a row.

One Saturday evening, I faced my bedroom mirror rocking my best B-boy pose. We'd been practising our routines all week, so I wanted everything to be on point. I had on these shiny black leather shoes with metallic lacing hooks, an oversized long-sleeve black turtleneck and my shiny Hammer pants that made me look like a human disco ball whenever I hit a spin. Bro, I was g'd up from the feet up.

With nobody watching, I went through our routine in front of the mirror one last time. That year, the young rap duo Kid 'n Play were the shit, and their movie *House Party* was everywhere. There's a scene in the film where Kid 'n Play bust out this crazy dance routine where they face each other doing a move called the running man, which is basically an exaggerated run on the spot. After two beats, they come together and theatrically tap each other's opposing foot. May sound kinda weird, but trust me, it was wild. You just needed to make sure you didn't fall on your arse while you did it.

As I went to leave, I noticed the fruits of last week's labours on the back of the bedroom door. It read 'Herpies'. Hear me out. I was getting into graffiti, and just like a rap group isn't a group without a name, a graffiti artist isn't shit without a tag. I wanted something that would shock people immediately, and I needed a word with letters that flowed effortlessly so that it would appear fresh and smooth when I tagged it. So, naturally, Herpies was the obvious choice. I used my bedroom door to test it out before taking it around town.

Yeah, you heard me, I was going round Queanbeyan spreading Herpies.

I turned up and ordered a Coke. Some of the other kids had started getting into alcohol already, but I wasn't bothered by all that. I was fine with the hip hop. The bar was to the left of the entrance, with the dance floor on a raised platform in the middle. With drinks in our hands, JJ, Talo and I stood on the sidelines and waited. It was all about timing. The right song will get the crowd in the right mood, leaving them ripe for the taking. That's when GUILTY makes its entrance.

I noticed Mac and Errol on the other side of the club. They weren't waiting for anyone or anything. With moves like theirs, they could do whatever they wanted. They had a magnetism to them wherever they went; girls followed and guys watched on in awe. Like Hammer, they were untouchable.

The ice cubes in my drink began to melt. I only had enough money for a few Cokes, so I didn't want to spend all of it in the first hour (a trick I would carry into my later years of clubbing). Talo and JJ started talking to a group of nearby girls but I ignored them, keeping my eye on the dance floor. Tonight, I was all business.

After a while, the DJ picked up the energy, replacing the more down-tempo stuff with some New Jack Swing. As I took a final sip of my Coke, I heard it: the first few seconds of 'Gonna Make You Sweat' by C+C Music Factory. This was one in a handful of our go-to songs. It had the rawness of hip hop, but it also had a hypnotic bassline you could dance to. I looked at JJ and Talo; they already knew what time it was.

Dance battles in the club aren't like what you see in the movies. There are no judges or scorecards – the only thing that matters is the crowd's reaction. If a song comes on and you're feeling it, you jump in the middle and start doing your thing. If the crowd likes it, they'll make space. If not, you better keep practising. The Firehouse dance floor was like our Colosseum; our reputation was built off the crowd's approval. And, man, we lived for that shit.

Talo took to the centre of the dance floor straightaway. He was the oldest but he was also the best dancer. Because he was double-jointed and had a long, wiry frame, he could move his body in ways JJ and I, who were more heavy-set, could only dream of. We were coordinated but not as agile as Talo, so we tended to keep our moves simple.

After Talo did his thing, JJ and I took the centre to let him get his breath back. Facing each other, we pulled out our rendition of Kid 'n Play that we'd been practising. *Running man, one step forward, foot tap, then back, one, two.* The crowd showered us with their approval, but Talo wasn't done. Sensing we had the crowd where we wanted them, he decided it was time for one of his signature moves. Standing upright, Talo grabbed his right foot with his left hand and jumped his left leg through like he was a human skipping rope. The crowd, including Mac and Errol, went crazy.

At that point, it was a wrap. GUILTY was officially in the building.

X-KWIZIT

It's 13 October 1991, and history is being made. No, I'm not talking about the shitstorm brewing in federal politics that would eventually see Bob Hawke replaced as PM by Paul Keating. Nor am I talking about the impending fall of the Soviet Union. This is far more important. From Strong Island, New York, the trio of Posdnuos, Trugoy and Maseo, officially known as De La Soul, are in Australia and tonight they're playing a sold-out show in Queanbeyan. Not Sydney, not Melbourne, not even Canberra – they're in the fkn 2620!

There's only one problem. I'm stuck outside. It's an over-eighteen event, and I can't get my hands on a ticket, but if you think I'm missing this opportunity you must've knocked back more beers than Bob Hawke on a Friday night bender. (Allegedly.) Sabne and Sione got tickets, and I hitched a ride with them, hoping to find a moment throughout the evening to sneak in.

Now here, I'm not so hopeful. The bouncers guard the entrance like God Himself has enlisted them to defend the gates of heaven. Drunk off the power provided by a walkie-talkie and a clipboard, they stand with their arms crossed and legs wide, to make themselves more physically intimidating. Whatever vibes they're trying to give off, it appears to be working because my chances of sneaking through undetected just went from 'hopeful' to 'you're dreaming'. Still, I wait.

A few latecomers arrive, show their tickets to the bouncers and are let in, which means the venue doors open for a brief second, letting out a few notes of De La Soul's hit song 'Ring Ring Ring'. My stomach leaps with excitement, like a life-long smoker getting their first whiff of tobacco smoke after a long-haul flight. I stand on tiptoes, hoping for a glimpse of the stage. As if toying with me, one of the bouncers quickly slams the door shut, and I have to settle for the faint bass now seeping through the auditorium doors.

With the show reaching the halfway point, it's time to call the Hail Mary. I puff my chest out proudly and approach the bouncers.

'Sorry, mate, I'm running late and can't seem to find my ticket,' I tell them, patting my pockets, as if that would somehow make the lie more convincing. I can't tell if they saw me sneaking around the entrance a few minutes ago or if my attempt isn't quite as watertight as I'd hoped, but both men look completely unimpressed.

'No ticket, no entrance,' they say defiantly. Dejected, I find a nearby bench and wait for Sabne and Sione to take me home.

We've all been there. That feeling of being excluded, of having to watch from the sidelines because you don't fit the criteria. Maybe you're too young, too small, or perhaps they've decided you're not the right colour or gender. Sometimes you can fight it, other times there's an immovable object, like two staunch bouncers and their swollen guts, standing in your way. The thing is, if you want something bad enough, whatever obstacle they throw at you, you'll be able to overcome. Because no matter how hard they try, they can't keep you outside forever.

That De La Soul gig summed up my start in hip hop. Living in Queanbeyan, a town whose radio stations proudly proclaimed they didn't play any 'rap crap', I was born an outsider. As frustrating as that was, I knew that Queanbeyan wouldn't be able to contain me forever. And I was right – fast-forward several years and I would be opening for De La Soul when they toured Australia, where I was able to swap catching a brief glimpse of the hip hop icons for actually meeting them in person.

But that didn't happen overnight. So, let's get one thing clear: you have to do the work. These things don't just land at your feet, especially not for us Brown folk. To complement your passion, you need focus. You need to rid yourself of any and all distractions so your mind can dedicate itself to the task at hand. A lot of times, this means understanding that not everyone is supposed to join you on your journey.

For me, this involved cutting ties with GUILTY. JJ and Talo were still my boys, but I started to see that they didn't share my drive. For them, forming a hip hop group was a cool idea, nothing more. They always *said* they wanted to do it, but actions speak louder than words. And I wasn't seeing any proof they wanted it as bad as I did.

We carried on hanging out, hitting Happy Days and Firehouse as often as before, but I realised that if I wanted to make it as a rapper, I was going to have to make it happen myself. Fate works in mysterious ways because it wasn't long after De La Soul left town that I had my first real opportunity as an MC. The Disco Mix Club World DJ Championships (DMCs for short) were coming to Canberra, and one of the local DJs we knew from around town, DJ Ken, asked me and Sione to join him on stage and rap a few verses so he had an extra element to his set. I was still underage, but no one was blocking my entry this time.

In the early '90s, hop hop was still all about DJ culture, and there was no stage more prestigious than the DMCs. It may sound strange now, but in the early days of hip hop, rapping was an afterthought.

When the first hip hop parties were thrown in the Bronx in the late '70s, the 'rapper' was usually just a mate who spoke over the beat; it was the DJ who got the party poppin'.

When it came to the DMCs, each participating country had a local competition to crown their best DJ before the winners came together to battle it out for the global crown. Each DJ got around five minutes to complete their set, bringing out all their best tricks to impress the crowd. In the '70s and '80s, DJ culture was based on the likes of Grand Wizzard Theodore, Grandmaster Flash and DJ Kool Herc, who'd perfected the art of scratching, turning DJing into a performance where you did more than simply play records. The next step in the evolution was with Run-DMC's Jam Master Jay, who had the same technique as the older gen but brought more charisma to the table. By the late '80s, early '90s, it was the likes of DJ Jazzy Jeff and DJ Cash Money, both out of Philadelphia, who were taking things to a whole other level, making DJing more technical and innovative. Jazzy Jeff had a move called the 'transformer scratch', which sounded like the robots in the '80s cartoon *Transformers*.

DJ Ken was no Jazzy Jeff, but he was a ticket to my first stage performance. By the time he reached out, I had dropped Cruel-T and was going by X-Kwizit, a reflection of the fact that I was developing a love for more avant-garde groups like De La Soul, A Tribe Called Quest and the other artists who made up the Native Tongues collective, whose Afrocentric lyrics started moving rap in a more conscious direction. Their raps tackled a wide range of themes with a playful creativity, and musically their samples were eclectic, borrowing heavily from jazz. It was less about making listeners fear you and more about making them think. And let's be honest, I was never all that cruel in the first place, anyway.

On the night of the battle, we arranged to meet DJ Ken in the foyer. As I waited, I saw one of the other DJs, a lanky white kid, who was sitting on the floor with his entire record collection spread out around him while he frantically tried to organise them in time for his set. *Thank God I'm not working with this guy,* I thought. He was blocking the entrance but was so engrossed in organising his records that he barely seemed to notice. *He's doing this on the night of the battle?*

Thankfully DJ Ken was more prepared. As we waited backstage, he explained his set to me and Sione and when he wanted us to join in. I knew I wasn't the star of the show, but I had my verses ready to go and was confident I could freestyle a few bars if needed. If it were a rugby match, I would have been up all night worrying, going through my preparation in my head over and over again. But on the footy field the list of variables is endless – the weather, your opponents, the referee, etc. – whereas on the stage you're the one in control. Sure, the crowd gave me a few butterflies, but I knew what I had to do, and I felt comfortable doing it. My preparation turned out to be in vain, though, because the experience was over as quickly as it started. DJ Ken was knocked out in the early heats, but I'd got a brief taste of what it was like to perform – a taste I could easily get used to.

On the way out, I caught the kid from the entrance performing his set. After watching him flail around in the foyer, I was expecting a train wreck, but, to my surprise, he was incredible. Part style, part technical, the way his whole body moved with each scratch looked funny as hell, but funky at the same time. I knew this kid must've been from the school of Jam Master Jay, but there was something fresh about him too.

The kid wasn't only talented, he was also the same age as me; his adolescent acne lit up by the stage lighting was a clear giveaway. Even though neither of us got anywhere close to winning, something about the experience gave me hope. It was proof there were other teenagers like me coming up who had made this their world. The winners, DJ LD Glove, Ea$y Money and MC Rhyme, had way more experience, and while they were good, I knew we would be better.

For now, revolutionising hip hop would have to wait. After all, I was still in school – annoying things like that always get in the way. In my final two years I went through another mini personality shift and started hanging with the rough-around-the-edges kids. Every school has a group of them, and in those times they were usually immigrants or kids of immigrants. Something about me growing in confidence as a rapper helped grow my confidence as a person; I was no longer the shy boy who'd entered high school. I was one of the few kids who fit in whether I was surrounded by the rugby crew, the bad boys sneaking darts behind the portables or the nerds who made up a lot of my top-set classes.

Meanwhile, Alvin and I got a reputation as the school rappers. We were always passing tapes back and forth in the hallway or free-styling during lunch hour, so we stood out like sore thumbs in a school full of metalheads. We started to be referred to as 'the House Rappers', which was neither an insult nor a compliment. The booners who bestowed this title upon us were – I *think* – combining house music, which was also a new phenomenon in the early '90s, with rap to get one rather underwhelming nickname. At the very least, you had to admire the effort.

Of course, they had a point. Hip hop was *always* on my mind, so much so that when I had to pick the topic for my HSC music class, I chose rap. When the principal, Mr Marks, heard this, he wasn't impressed. Mr Marks was married to one of the music teachers, and they were massively into their jazz music. And not the cool Miles Davis/John Coltrane kind of jazz, either. So it was hardly surprising

trippin' the lyrics like a basketball
try to dis the x. you'll end up in the casket...all
n' all, the rime continuals
play me on your audio and visual
set-up, let up git off your ass and get-up
dance to the ministry in this gee but don't get fed-up
with how drop bass and cause a lot of damage
the beats savage and ravage but yo o i still can manage
with the melodial massacre, the grand finale crescendo
strate from the git-go rollin' in the benzo
pump it in the jeep, feel the thumpin' beat
dance up in your seat, and feel the beat go...
uh, can you feal it like the Afro's
feel the mic blow... and the x-perience

-peace-

positive.education.always.corrects.errors

.x.kwikit

he wasn't a fan, but I didn't expect him to kick up such a fuss. If anything, I assumed he would encourage a student trying something new. But in an effort to dissuade me, he called my mum in for a meeting.

'Rap music isn't a real thing,' he explained. 'There's no future in it, Mrs Lātūkefu. I strongly recommend Hau picks another topic.'

He probably assumed Mum would agree with him, but Mr Marks didn't know my mum. In that gentle-but-firm manner, she told him where he could stick it.

'I'm sorry, Mr Marks, but I don't know anything about music,' she said. 'Hau is the one in our family who understands music, so I think he knows what he wants.'

With that, she stood up, smiled and left. Meeting adjourned.

A few months later, I was back at Firehouse, this time with my cousins Sione and Hounga after we'd signed up to compete in a mini rap battle. Like the dance battles at Firehouse, it was a thrown-together affair; they cleared out the dance floor to make way for a small stage and had the crowd surrounding us. The floors were sticky from last night's spilled drinks and the smell of teenagers' cheap cologne filled the room. It was grimey, which, for a rap battle, seemed only right.

Sione put us at a massive advantage. He was four years older but he was also a natural when it came to music. On top of his hip hop background, he was a massive Prince fan, so his reference pool was broad and eclectic. His lyrics were more complex than your average teen rapper but, most importantly, he just had that flavour. When Sione held a mic, it was like an extension of his arm: it looked like he was born to perform. A lot of people – okay, *white* people – think of rapping like it's a trade. Once you master the technicalities, you're basically there. And while technique, rhythm, flow and all the rest are important, all of that only gets you so far. The crowd has to *want* to see you perform; and the crowd is a notoriously fickle beast. So, you have to captivate them before you even open your mouth. That flavour, that funk, that sauce – whatever you want to call it – is something that can't be taught or bought. And Sione had it for days.

We were facing off against two MCs and a DJ who had come armed with his own beat. If rap was a science and not an art form, that in itself should have put them in the winning seat, because we just brought along someone else's instrumental to rap over. But you heard what I said about flavour, right? That shit was over as soon as we hit the stage.

They did all the right things: their bars were solid and the beat in particular was really impressive, but when it came to stage presence, they were out of their depth. Sione was in full control while Hounga and I focussed on working the crowd, adding a slice of youthful energy to Sione's advanced rhymes. We were a trio of funky Islanders against three nerdy-looking white boys. Man, they never stood a chance.

THE X-KWIZIT E.P.:

production: Alofi LATUKEFU · ARRANGEMENT: X-KWIZIT · LYRICS LL LATUKEFU

• JUST KICKIN' 'EM: music: tone Léc • vocals: X-KWIZIT

• MONKEE PHRYIN' EM: music: tone LEc vocals: X-KWIZIT

• WHAT I SEE: music: Roger Troutman vocals X-KWIZIT

• TELL ME THAT U FEEL THE SAME: music: PRINCE · vocals: X-KWIZIT

• KISS OF AFFECTION: music: earth, wind + FIRE · vocals: X-KWIZIT

• WARNING!: music: earth, wind + FIRE · vocals: X-KWIZIT

• SIMPIN': music: TOO SHORT · vocals: X-KWIZIT

• THE INTELLECTUAL VALUE (FROM A STUDENT'S PINT OF VIEW): music: TON LEc · vocals: X-KWIZIT

• JAZZY MOVEMENT: music: FRESH PRINCE · vocals: X-KWIZIT

• PHRZY PHONKITE: music: PROFESSOR X vocals: XWIZIT

THESE FRONT DOOR KEYS

Queanbeyan is not known for many things. Yes, it's the birthplace of Rugby Union legend David Campese, and then there's George Lazenby, the only non-Brit to play James Bond, as well as my mate and award-winning author Omar Musa. If you're after some nature, the Queanbeyan River can hold its own against any in the country, and back in the days of Prohibition, Queanbeyan got a reputation as the go-to watering hole for Canberra residents looking to skirt the capital's alcohol ban.

All these things are great, but if you want to know the *real* Queanbeyan, there's one place you need to visit: Kingsley's Chicken. On the surface it's a local fried chicken joint like any other, but trust me, nowhere does it like Kingsley's. The quality of the meat is way better than what you'll find at KFC, but it's the chips and gravy that really steal the show. In my teenage years, a two-piece meal with chips and gravy was a weekly affair.

In my final year of high school, after a few small shows with Hounga and Sione, I was getting something of a reputation as a local rapper – which, let's be honest, was more of a process of elimination as I was one of the *only* local rappers. Either way, when Kingsley's wanted someone to record a rap to feature in their radio advert, they turned to none other than X-Kwizit himself.

I was buzzing. I had a footy match immediately after the recording, so I arrived in my tracksuit, ready to work. The sound engineer, who looked like he'd rather be anywhere in the world than in a recording studio with a seventeen-year-old, handed me a piece of paper with the rap on it and led me straight to the booth. He wasn't messing around. Unsure what they wanted from me, I put on a fake American accent, as if we were advertising some chicken joint in the Bronx. The engineer didn't seem phased by the accent, but he didn't appreciate my flow. Without looking at me, he cut me off halfway through.

'From the top please, and this time just read the lines as they come,' he instructed.

I did it again. And again, he stopped me. He clearly wanted a straight read, but that just wasn't me. *Why get a rapper to do this if you don't want it with any added flavour?* Ignoring the engineer, I continued doing it my way, inserting some funk into their corny lines.

Each time, I was met with the same weary look. 'One more time please.'

After a while, he gave up, handed me my $200 fee and sent me on my way. I never did hear it on the radio, but then again I never listened. To be honest, I didn't care either way. X-Kwizit was now, *technically,* a professional rapper.

Meanwhile, the early signs of growth within the Australian hip hop scene were finally starting to show. The first ones to really leave an impression was Sound Unlimited, formerly known as Westside Posse, who became the first Australian act signed to a major label.

Of Russian, Spanish and Filipino origins, they released their debut album *A Postcard from the Edge of the Underside* in 1992. It's gritty and dark, with that American East Coast energy to it.

These were impressive domestic milestones, but for me, along with pretty much everyone else on the planet, rap was still an American thing. The so-called Golden Age of the late '80s, early '90s, defined by the political activism of groups like Public Enemy and Run-DMC, was starting to make way for a new era led by artists like Dr. Dre and Snoop Dogg. Dre's classic *The Chronic* was everywhere, the G-funk scene was beginning to take over the West Coast, and the Native Tongues collective were starting to dominate the East. Even the South was making its mark with groups like Geto Boys going platinum.

Despite what was going on in the States, when I saw the video to Sound Unlimited's 'Kickin' to the Undersound', a switch flicked within me. It wasn't even about the music; it was more their wardrobe. In one of the scenes, you can see the MC, Rosano, wearing a Sydney Kings jersey and cap. Not a Lakers jersey, not a New York Giants NFL jumper – he was repping Sydney, Australia. His hometown. In that moment, it was like the hip hop blueprint for success I'd grown up on was blown straight out the water. Having been raised on a steady diet of US releases, I thought you *had* to appear American if you wanted to make it in hip hop. Just as I did for Kingsley's, you *had* to imitate a fake American accent when you rapped, and when it came to fashion, you *had* to rock trends ripped straight from New York or LA. That was just the way things were. But here was the most successful rap group in the country, and they're embracing *Australia*?

The final year of school was a write-off. I'd grown used to seeing my report cards littered with the same comment: 'Hau's an intelligent boy if he could apply himself more.' What my teachers didn't appreciate was that I *was* applying myself, just not necessarily at school. Art was one of my favourite classes, but even there I was coasting. We were supposed to spend the final two years working on a project that would be our school career's defining achievement, but I left it to the last minute. And I mean literally: I stayed up all night working so I at least had something to submit the next morning when it was due.

I was talented but not talented enough that I could afford not to do the work. The grade came back poor, and I no longer had the luxury of tomorrow. Before my HSC I was always able to brush off my teachers' comments, claiming I would start applying myself when it mattered. But I'd run out of time. I sent off some last-minute applications to design school but unsurprisingly didn't hear back.

Fortunately for me, my life was about to take a very different course.

After some successful local performances with my cousins, Hounga decided to go in a another direction. I made the mistake of introducing him to Jodeci and Boyz II Men, and after that he wanted to become a R&B singer, claiming there was more chance of meeting girls that way. To be fair, I couldn't blame him. So, it was left to me and Sione.

The term 'fake it 'til you make it' comes to mind when I think of my time with Sione. We'd appeared on a few stages, but aside from my fledgling career as a jingle performer for Queanbeyan's fast-food joints, we'd never set foot inside a professional studio. Regardless, we somehow warranted getting a manager. More than anything, it sounded cool. We weren't just rappers, we were rappers *with a manager*.

We met James through a mutual friend. He mentioned he knew Sound Unlimited, so we figured that was a good sign. Despite not doing any other research on him, we handed over the reins, and very quickly it started paying dividends. Unbeknown to us, he applied for, and won, a local government grant to record an EP. Sione and I were finally going to hit a studio together.

We just had one thing to sort out before we did: we needed a DJ. This wasn't Firehouse; we couldn't just throw on someone else's instrumental and hope for the best. We needed our own beats. Again, James earned his non-existent pay cheque, bringing us a tape of a local producer he'd come across. At first I couldn't believe what I was hearing.

'This guy is from Canberra?' I asked. The beats were way more advanced than anything I'd heard locally, and there wasn't just one or two – there were stacks of them piled up, ready to go. We told James to find this guy and bring him to us; we had work to do.

We met at the Woden Youth Centre in Canberra. He arrived carrying an entire desktop computer. Imagine this for a second. This is 1992, when desktop computers were the size of small cars. And to clarify, no one asked him to bring any hardware. Nonetheless, our new DJ walked in lugging a massive suitcase and a stack of records. Wearing a chequered shirt buttoned right to the top, he was tall and skinny with big, round eyes and a long, thin neck that almost made him resemble a meerkat. I couldn't place him but he seemed familiar.

'My name's Daniel,' he said. 'We've actually met before.'

Sione and I replied with blank faces.

'We battled each other at Firehouse,' he continued. 'It was me and two of my mates against you two, and there was one more, a younger kid.'

That's when it hit me. He was the DJ! No wonder his beats left an impression; I'd heard them before. We carried on talking and realised this wasn't the only time we'd crossed paths.

'I was at the DMCs last year as well,' Daniel explained. 'I think I saw you then.'

The kid in the foyer! Now it was all coming back. The DJ who decided to organise his records on the night of the battle was standing in front of me. It was like the hip hop gods had led us to one another. While Daniel unpacked his records, he explained to me and Sione that he originally wanted to make music for video games. He'd even taught himself to code, he said, but after discovering the group Boogie Down Productions and Run-DMC, he started making hip hop instead.

A representative of the local government was there to officially hand over the grant money and, curious about Daniel's giant computer, began asking questions about what he did with it. It was immediately clear that Daniel was *very* socially awkward, but as soon as he got in front of that computer he made sense. He was in his element. With us watching on in amazement, Daniel took the guy through his beat-making process, which went way over all of our heads. He made me and Sione, with our pause-stop recording, look like total amateurs.

After a mini performance to officially seal the grant, Daniel packed up his records and his computer and left. I was speechless. It would be an understatement to say I'd never met anyone like him. I don't think *anyone* has ever met anyone like Daniel. Like his beats, the man is truly one of a kind.

A new crew meant a new name. Again. As a trio, we decided to call ourselves Tribe Ledda L. The tribe was a nod to us being a family as well as to A Tribe Called Quest, and the L stood for our surnames, Lātūkefu, as well as Daniel's, which is Elleson. Recognising we were embarking on a new era, I also took the opportunity to come up with a new rap name for myself. This time I went with Fatty Boomstix. Sabne said it to me as an insult one day and it stuck. I just liked the way it rolled off the tongue. Meanwhile, Sione became JJ Tix. Sione is Tongan for John, so a lot of people called him JJ, and he added the Tix for effect. With that, Tribe Ledda L was assembled: JJ Stix and Fatty Boomstix on vocals and DJ Danielsan on production.

When Tribe Ledda L arrived at Studio C in ANU's Drill Hall Gallery, there was frost on the ground and a vibrancy in the air. Just as winter made its retreat, you could feel a new energy building. Like a bird slowly hatching, Australian hip hop was finding its feet. Unsure and unsteady, it staggered slightly but, make no mistake about it, it had arrived.

Sydney was the epicentre. As well as Sound Unlimited and Def Wish Cast making straight hip hop, there were groups like Skunk-hour that started out as an urban funk band before adding a rapper on vocals. It had all the hallmarks of hip hop, just with different packaging. This was becoming common, as if hip hop was entering through the back door. Whether Australia liked it or not, the flood-gates were soon to open.

The grant gave us three studio sessions to record our EP. We arrived like three kids entering a candy store without their parents. There were records lining the walls from floor to ceiling, boasting a collection more extensive than most of the record stores in town. We spent the first hour flicking through albums, quickly realising that Daniel had grown up on the same artists Sione and I obsessed over.

Daniel picked out Gil Scott-Heron's *The Revolution Will Not Be Televised* and quietly inspected the liner notes before putting the record on. A mixture of spoken word and jazz, it had the raw intensity of rap but was released way back in '74. Daniel was blown away.

This was my first time witnessing his intense curiosity. He could be quiet and detached, but give him something that makes him think and, like a kitten who's just got hold of your favourite jumper, he'd pick away at it until there was nothing left. When Daniel's mind latched onto something, there was nothing that could deviate his attention. As I would find out over the next twenty years, this could be both a gift and a curse.

When we managed to get Daniel's focus back on Tribe, we got to work. Most of our time was spent recording a solo song Sione had written called "Cause It's Enough". It was a tough track to nail because Sione raps, sings *and* plays the guitar, another testament to his supreme talent as a musician. Then we did a remix version of a song Sione and I had written called 'Let Us Get On With the Biz'. We found one of Daniel's beats that seemed to fit and chopped it together into a song. It was raw and imperfect, but then again, so were we.

After the three sessions were up, we had four songs recorded and an EP named *These Front Door Keys*. Five hundred copies were pressed and sent to Impact Records to be sold next to Eric B. & Rakim. Our journey had officially begun.

DANIEL

I'll tell you my main recollection of the first time I saw Hau. When Hau, Sione and Hounga got up and did their thing at Firehouse, it just blew me away. That was the first time I had a perspective on how much better someone could be than me and my friends. If you were in the crowd that night, there's no way you were cheering for us. You were cheering for those guys. It was that obvious.

Let's put it this way. It's clear to me now in retrospect, having spent many years since then with Hau and his family, that they had a far deeper culture of music, dance and stuff, you know? And, I was like a kid sifting through the trash on the side of the road, who got into old records.

I'd always been trying to make music. When I was ten, I was doing weird stuff with an old RadioShack computer. Sort of programming things and hooking things up to get them to make weird electronic music. That was more just about the sounds and playing things and accomplishing something. I was always busying myself as a kid. I was on my own all the time. And so I did all kinds of things. I painted. I built things. And music was just one of those things.

After we recorded These Front Door Keys, *we started doing live shows. We did a set for the National Multicultural Festival in Canberra in '93, which I remember being absolute fire. We were kind of winging it. From the get-go we would pretty much get on stage and be like, 'Oh, let's do this song. And then let's do that song.' I'd pull some record out of a paper bag or something and go, 'I'll play this!' It was pretty thrown-together stuff. But I do remember we had a decent crowd around us, and Hau and Sione were rhyming over the Tribe Called Quest 'Scenario (Remix)' that had just come out. And then halfway through the track, I cut in the instrumental of 'Buck Whylin'' by Terminator X. It just went off. We all felt like we were ripping it. And that – that right there – is probably the first moment in my entire life where I felt that* thing.

That really was a moment for me and Hau, from that day forward and all of those years that we performed together. Because I have different feelings about a lot of the music that we did. At times we did some great things, and at times we were doing some pretty mediocre things. But we had some crazy chemistry on stage. I've done a lot of different performances and been a part of a lot of different things, but that chemistry is a rare thing.

That was the main reason we did well as a team: you could listen to our tapes or our CDs or whatever and be into it, but the reason we had respect and kind of like this cult following was because when people saw us live they couldn't deny that we shat all over everyone else.

Hau could freestyle his arse off, and I would just rinse it on the turntables. It was stuff that none of the other people in our circle did. And so that kept escalating us. And that's why we were doing festivals and things like that. Every time we went out, we'd do an incredible show, people saw, and they were calling our agent and saying, 'Can we book Koolism?'

PART 2
CHURN
1993–2003

Yous must be comedians coz you make me wanna laugh
You didn't know good hip hop
Hau put you on the path
With more skills than Mark Ella
The lip sweller
The number one box office seller
Winning the Quinella
Big fellaaaa!!!

– 'Big Fella', Koolism, 1998

93 'TIL INFINITY

Everyone knew Tunks. Canberra's a small city so news spreads fast and reputations get built off hearsay. And no one had a rep like Tunks. He was hardly a big guy, but with a background in martial arts, he knew how to handle himself. Plus, he was a graffiti artist so his name, or at least his tag, 'Seth', was emblazoned all across the city. Way before I'd even met him, I'd heard the rumours. Apparently, he was running with some guys from Sydney who were into some serious shit. Canberra wasn't like that back then. It wasn't Melbourne, and it certainly wasn't Sydney. It was clean, quiet and kinda boring. Tunks was doing his best to change that.

I'd heard of guys getting bashed left and right for various graffiti beefs with him. If you capped one of Tunks' pieces or bit his style, you were bound to cop it. I nearly found this out first-hand. A few years back, I was waiting outside one of the arcades in Canberra when he stormed up to me, looking mad g'd up.

'Oi, are you Siaosi?' he barked, holding a car windshield reflector with what looked like something wrapped inside.

'Nah, I'm Hau,' I explained.

He thought I was part of a crew of Tongan boys who'd recently come from Sydney and had been making some noise across Canberra. But, like I said, I didn't know those guys, and I definitely wasn't one of them.

'Alright. So you're not with them?'

'Nah man, fuck those guys,' I said. This seemed to calm him down. We spoke for a few minutes before my curiosity got the better of me. 'What's that?' I asked, pointing at the windscreen reflector.

'Ah, it's nothing,' he mumbled, walking off.

You're probably wondering if Tunks found those guys. Well, I'll leave him to tell his own stories but, he wasn't someone to mess with. All this to say, when he called my house phone one day, I'm not gonna lie – my heart skipped a beat. Mum answered and shouted for me in my bedroom. Thankfully, he seemed in a good mood.

'You alright, Hau?' he asked, his usual sharp, abrasive tone giving off just enough warmth to let me know this wasn't about any beef.

'Uhh . . . yeah, good. Just chilling. What's up?'

'I heard your tape and wanna interview you,' he told me. Outside of graffiti and bashing cunts, Tunks was an aspiring journo and did a bunch of writing for a street press publication called *BMA (Bands Music Action)*, mainly reporting on hip hop. And by reporting, I mean he wrote lengthy editorials explaining how any and every rapper coming up in Australia at the time was shit. (Yeah, the big fella had some strong opinions.) To be fair, he had a point. The scene was pretty bland, and there were more than a few wannabes, but to paint the whole country like that was taking it a bit far. Besides, there was Daniel and me.

'Yeah, mad. Let's do it.' We arranged for him to come pick us up and we'd do the interview out near Canberra's Mount Ainslie Lookout.

Sweet, I thought, *our first bit of press!*

***

A few days later, he arrived at my house as planned. With Daniel in the back, I sat up front next to Tunks, and we immediately hit it off. Turned out he had grown up with Tongans, and his best mate was related to some of my cousins. He felt familiar. Like me, he was obsessed with hip hop and seemed to know what he was talking about. Which was rare for a guy from Canberra in the early '90s. Especially a white guy.

The only thing faster than his talking was his driving. The bloke was flying down the road like a fucking lunatic! Speeding around corners in his old blue Chrysler, Tunks barely seemed to notice as I watched the number on the speedometer creep up and up. Near misses with oncoming traffic didn't appear to faze him as he continued grilling me and Daniel about hip hop – who we liked, who we didn't. Despite the reckless driving, I was enjoying myself. I'm not sure Daniel, who by this point was sliding from one side of the backseat to the other, would have said the same.

We arrived at the lookout, with a view that swept across the entire city, and began the formal interview. To this day, it has got to be the weirdest one I have ever been a part of. It started pretty straightforward, with me and Daniel discussing our musical influences and the sorts of artists, from Ice-T and Public Enemy to Tribe and De La Soul, who had shaped our sound. Then things got strange.

Daniel was explaining how much time he spent in his room working on beats, which prompted Tunks to ask if what he was really doing was masturbating.

'Errr . . . no!' Daniel replied, confused and more than a little awkward.

Clearly taking the piss, Tunks moved on to me. He was saying something about how he has a different way of seeing things to most people. *Yeah, no shit.*

'Like, that bin for example,' he said, pointing to a nearby trash can. 'If you were to rap about it, you'd probably say how it's big and red and whatever. Me, I'd rap about how I was gonna pick it up and smash it over your head!'

Daniel and I looked at each other. *What the fuck? This guy is on another level.*

But, as bizarre as the whole exchange was, I couldn't help but like him. You see, as I just mentioned, Canberra was a little bland, and here was this guy talking about Ultramagnetic MCs and smashing bins over people's heads. He didn't give a fuck. I'd spent most of my childhood moving towards those who were different – the ones who went against the grain. I was a hip hop fanatic in a city full of metal-heads. And as it turned out, I wasn't the only one.

A few days later, the house phone rang again. It was Tunks. 'You wanna come to a party tonight?' he asked. 'Meeting a few mates out in Tuggeranong. You in?'

'Yeah, sweet. Sounds good!'

This, of course, meant another trip in the deathmobile. Tunks picked me up and we headed south-west to Tuggeranong. His mates Bain and Andrew were in the car and the three of them were bumping Souls of Mischief's *93 'til Infinity*. I was impressed. I was already a big fan of Souls and had just copped a flat cap earlier in the year, inspired by their signature style. Plus, the record had only recently been released. Things usually took a lot longer to make their way to Canberra.

On the way, Tunks told me he was gonna stop at a few spots to do some throw-ups. Fine by me. I still kept my pen on me for the occasional 'Herpies' tag, but Tunks and them were into proper bombing – big, colourful letters on walls or trains. His characters were always next level and were never your generic B-boy/graffiti ones either. One of my favourites was Murder Mouse – a picture of Mickey Mouse crossed with Freddy Krueger. It was crazy.

One of the places they wanted to hit was along the main road, so Tunks and I chatted while he got to work with his cans. The hip hop inquisition from the other day continued, but this time there was more of a mutual respect than Tunks trying to suss out if I was legit or not. He was explaining to anyone who'd listen the impact of Chinese martial arts on the current state of hip hop. Wu-Tang's debut album *Enter the Wu-Tang (36 Chambers)* had just come out, and considering RZA's sampling of old kung-fu movies throughout the record, it was hard to disagree.

Tunks had listened to everything and had opinions on *everything*. To his mind, if you weren't into EPMD, Boogie Down Productions and early Rhyme Syndicate, you were a fuckwit who wasn't worth the time of day. Fortunately for me, I was. He was even talking about groups like Mob Style, fronted by the notorious New York drug dealer Azie 'AZ' Faison. Most of the records Tunks was into were rare, but Mob Style was a different story altogether. As far as I knew, nobody in Australia even *had* that record. Nobody but Tunks, this fast-talking white boy from the suburbs of Canberra.

When Tunks had done his thing we made our way back to the car, which was parked on a verge just off the main road. Tunks was about to get in when a cop car pulled up.

'What are you boys up to?' asked one of the approaching officers. It was here I first witnessed Tunks' ability to talk himself out of any situation. Speaking a mile a minute, he made up some story about needing a piss and convincing us to pull over for just a second. I'm not sure if the cops believed him or were too confused by his manner – an odd mixture of confidence, aggression and respect – that they let us go.

With the sounds of Souls of Mischief turned back up, we drove to the party. I can't remember what happened, but I do know Tunks and I have been best mates ever since. And it wouldn't be the last time we'd be ducking cops together.

TUNKS

I'm a first-generation B-boy. So, I was a B-boy since, like, the early-mid '80s, during its peak years, around '83–'86. It exploded and then sorta died. The type of people who were breaking usually went on to become graffiti writers. So I stopped breaking – unless I was wasted – and went on to graffiti.

People here in Canberra started breaking at the same time as people in Sydney and Melbourne. They were better in places like Sydney because they had American military personnel who would come over and bring some records, and then someone would cop something off a cousin or whatever, and it would take off. But we also started early here independent of them. So, the first-generation B-boys in Canberra actually cropped up at the same time as they did in Sydney and Melbourne.

We got it packaged as one thing – hip hop, breaking, graffiti, turntablism – it came as one culture. Even though in Canberra we were an isolated outpost with no real proper connections, we still had access to music. We had people here who got stuff directly imported to us. There was always a core little group of people in Canberra who were up on it, with the music, the breaking and the graffiti.

I was always looking for the next biggest thing, so I wanted to go to Sydney to do graffiti up there. I didn't go to join a crew. I just went up there, ran into writers and learned how to tag properly. Then they started coming down here and invading Canberra because the crew that I joined, KOA – that Hau and Daniel later became a part of – was pretty much a criminal crew, so they were coming here 'searching', to make money.

Searching was mainly raiding backrooms, taking cash bags and popping tills. Hence the runners, the shorts, the socks. Searchers had a uniform. A lot of the fashion that people wear today – kids call it 'eshay' stuff – that stuff was what people wore back then out of practicality, because you had to run if you got chased. It's like a competitive sport to search; people would compete for who got the biggest amount and which places they hit. There're legends in the searching scene who people still talk about. People would learn techniques, like how to hold the clamp that keeps the money in place in the till down so it didn't click when you pulled the bundle out, what type of key fits which till or cabinet, etc. They would pass it on like a skill or a trade. To me, it was a Sydney thing and it spread to other cities. I don't call myself a searcher – I'm a graffiti writer – but I was part of a crew that did a whole lot of other stuff.

When the Sydney lot were down here, we hooked up with them, and that's how it all started. People in Canberra were already doing grimey things, but we started learning from them, because in Sydney they were popping tills and doing breaks and robberies. That really wasn't happening here until the Sydney people brought it in late '88, '89. Well, it was happening a little, but with headbangers. Because, in Canberra, if you were a B-boy or into graffiti and hip hop you were looked at like a weirdo. It was a niche thing back then.

Because I was with a Sydney crew, whenever my crew mates would be down we'd fight locals. That's just how it was. Canberra's a small town, so there's a small-town mentality. If you're an out-of-towner, you can find yourself in trouble pretty quick. So Canberra was a pretty violent place. We'd fight with locals, but the problem was I lived here. My crew would go back to Sydney and leave me to deal with the repercussions. And there were always repercussions. So we had wars with certain sections of society, from full-blown adult gangsters way out of our league, to just other kids on the street. I'd have half the city turning up on my doorstep, cars full of guys looking for me. And so, what happened was, crews that were down here in Canberra would form alliances with any Sydney crew they could, bring them down here and get them to go against me.

One particular crew had linked up with some boys from Sydney, who were mainly Tongans, and they were causing some trouble down here. They were going round bashing people, robbing people for fun, and they put the word out that they were gonna kill me. They didn't even know me – it was the local boys who were fuelling them up.

But I was on my own. So I had to do it myself. When I heard they were after me, I said, 'Fuck that, I'll get them first.' So I did what any dumb kid with no regard for his own or anyone else's safety would do: I went looking for them. I heard they'd been hanging in an arcade, robbing people and stuff. There were a few Islanders there when I turned up, and I saw Hau. He looked like the guy I was looking for, but we hadn't met so I wasn't sure. I went straight up to him: 'Are you Siaosi?'

First of all, he didn't shit himself. He wasn't intimidated. I had this thing under my arm – it was basically an aluminium baseball bat wrapped up in one of those windshield reflectors. What I'd do was carry a bat and a ball or a glove, so if I got pulled over by the cops, I'd just say I was going to play baseball. But I was in a rush to go find those boys, so I just grabbed whatever was with me. Hau saw what I had but didn't show it, and he wasn't scared. Also, he thought that the crew were dickheads, so we instantly had something in common.

I worked out pretty quickly that Hau was an independent, doing his own thing. He knew everybody and got on with everybody, but he was his own man. So, after chatting with him for a few minutes, I left and went and found the guy. And, yeah . . . I put an end to it.

I started writing for BMA around '92, and Hau, Sione and Daniel released These Front Door Keys *in '93. I was so arrogant back then; I thought only me and my crew knew the go. Little did we know, this snotty-nosed kid out in Queanbeyan had already worked it out on his own. When I met him for the BMA interview, after that baseball bat silliness, we hit it off straightaway. I realised how smart he was. He knew the whole international scene; he knew who the best rappers were, the best releases; he knew his history, here and overseas; and he was just way more clued up than he should have been.*

And I was exceptionally strong on the whole accent thing, because I went to London in 1990 and London Posse, who were the first UK group to rap in an English accent, had a big influence on me. They were rapping about their own shit in their own tongue. I was eighteen at the time. I'd been into graffiti really hard for a couple of years, and I'd always wanted to go around the world. So I just took off and went to Thailand, London, Paris, Italy, all over Germany, New York, LA, Hawaii. When I went to London I hooked up with Drax, who's one of the kings, just by chance. I know this is meant to be about Hau, but trust me, the background is important.

I was racking paint and bombing lines by myself in an effort to run into the right people. One night, I got invited to the Wag, which was a big club at the time. It just happened that that night it was full of pretty much every graffiti writer in London. They sort of sussed out from what I was wearing that I was different. I had a mad Gucci watch on, a Valentino shirt with a Lacoste jacket and Trussardi jeans, so they were coming round, trying to herd me off into a corner to see if they could press me. They were trying to put it on me, but I was being smart back, and I also had a massive fucking knife in my pocket too that they didn't know about. I didn't have any brains back then, so I wasn't scared.

Drax saw this from the other side of the room and slid over and was like, 'How's it going, mate? Who are you? Where are you from?' I think he was just interested that I was this weird little kid on my own in this club, looking like a rooster surrounded by all of these guys who were trying to scope me out to rob me. He ended up taking me under his wing. We got on straightaway and started bombing together. After a while, he invited me to stay with him. We were into similar music, and he'd take me to illegal raves and Jamaican-only dancehall events. He was the one who introduced me to London Posse, Ragga Twins and that really early proto jungle sound. They were moving back towards the electronic stuff over in the UK hip hop scene, so I started to get into that shit, and I brought that stuff back here and introduced all of the boys to it.

I was still a kid but into all these different things that I'd brought back, from the fashion to the music. I came back with, like, sixty pairs of shoes. I bought two full crates of records and was walking around this town like some kind of freak. And Hau is one of the younger kids who it had an influence on.

So, you see, it does link back to the story!

THE TOOLSHED

It was the start of 1994 and I had just finished school. Daniel and I had a tape in record stores and were starting to get booked for the occasional live show around Canberra. Things were moving in the right direction. Still, we were hardly making any real money, and I knew if I was going to stay at home that I was going to need to get a job. Thankfully, Mum, as ever, was on hand with some good advice.

'Go on the dole,' she told me. 'This is what our taxes are for.'

We're proud people, Tongans, but we're not foolish. Mum had a point. So I paused my job search and claimed benefits. For a while it was a dream scenario. I'd half-arse fill out a few forms and get some money in my account a few weeks later. I was still getting free food and accommodation at home, so the amount was more than enough to live on. I could buy the records I wanted and have cash left over to go out with friends. After a while, I got cocky with it and started making up businesses owned by my mates, claiming I had applied for jobs there. Somehow, none of them ever materialised.

Since that party with Tunks, I was spending more and more time with him and his boys. On the one hand, there was his Sydney crew, led by two brothers from New Zealand: Metro and Mahem. These guys were graffiti artists who were gradually moving beyond street politics and into more serious shit. And they were always on point. Every time I saw them, either Metro or Mahem was rocking some European brand I'd never heard of. Tunks was the same. He introduced me to labels like Stone Island and C.P. Company – the sort of stuff no one in Canberra was wearing. I was always fresh, but they *really* inspired me to step my game up.

Then there were his Canberra mates, like Bain and Andrew. The two groups couldn't have been more different. Bain and Andrew didn't have a street bone in them but were some of the most genuine people I'd ever met. When the two worlds did occasionally collide, everyone got along fine. The fact Bain and Andrew got a pass around those guys showed their true nature. They never pretended to be anything but who they were. And who they were was a pair of goofy suburban nerds with a love for Rik Mayall comedy and an endless list of fart jokes. (I'm not gonna lie, this took a little getting used to. My family was always laughing and joking, but fart jokes were never part of our repertoire. I didn't take long to catch up.)

Bain was working in hospitality at the time so had most days free. He had a car with a mad sound system that looked like it had been taken straight out of *Back to the Future*, so he'd swing by, pick me up, and we'd cruise around listening to music. Bain must have been making some decent cash, because he was always copping new clothes. He wasn't Metro or Mahem, but he still had his style, more preppy than street, but it worked. *Most* of the time. On one trip he bought a Nautica jacket from David Jones for $500. At the time, that was like a month's wages! The jacket was fresh as hell, but somehow Bain didn't pull it off. He was a tall, skinny, lovable dork, and a new jacket wasn't gonna change that, no matter how much it cost. Tunks couldn't help but take the piss every time he wore it.

If we weren't at the mall or making trips to Sydney to buy new records, we'd chill at Bain's where he lived with his parents. The house was big and beautiful, but it would trip me out going there. First, the place was spotless. You got the impression that if a single picture frame was moved an inch out of place, you'd set off some secret alarm. This was a mile away from my household, which was hectic all the time with people coming and going. Then there was the food. The cupboards were full of chocolate bars and snacks that were half-eaten with the wrapper sealed back up.

Wow. People do that? If that was my home, that shit would have been long gone!

Bain and Tunks got me involved with one of their long-standing traditions: kung fu movie night. Tunks was obsessed with martial arts, and every Sunday the Centre Cinema in Canberra would show the latest kung fu movies direct from Hong Kong. It was real authentic, too. Most foreign films back then were dubbed, but Sundays at Centre Cinema were for the true fans. The theatre would be full of Chinese people, then in one corner, stoned off our arses, would be me, Tunks, Bain and the crew. They played films like *The Bodyguard from Beijing* and *Fong Sai-yuk*, introducing me to a world of martial arts beyond Bruce Lee and Jackie Chan. One night, I got so damn high I was convinced the characters were speaking English with an accent! Yeah, probably for the best I didn't smoke often.

It was an exciting time. To an outsider, we probably just looked like a group of late-teens cruising around the city not doing much. But between Tunks' gangster mates with their fresh outfits, and the Canberra boys with their practical jokes and esoteric movie nights, my world view was slowly but surely being cracked open.

After a while, my run on the dole came to an end. The idea of becoming a chef occurred to me one day while I was flicking through a newspaper. There was an advertisement for a course at

TAFE which, in just over a year, would make me qualified to work in a kitchen. The lifestyle was appealing. *It's a job that can take me all around the world*, I thought. Plus, the environment seemed exciting. Sure, I was hardly a whiz in the kitchen but I knew my way around a honey soy chicken, and I'd always been a quick learner. *How hard could it be?*

I was enrolled in TAFE but my focus was still music. Sione had left Australia to go back to Tonga and his mind was elsewhere, so Daniel and I were left on our own. We ditched Tribe Ledda L and for the moment were nameless. Since the success of *These Front Door Keys*, we were getting booked for more and more shows, making a rep for ourselves as the MC/DJ duo with a live band. People wanted to dance and we gave them that big band energy with a side of hip hop flavour. It was the early-mid '90s and live music was all about acid jazz – a hybrid of jazz and funk coming out of the UK. A lot of groups whose members had come up through the Sydney Conservatorium of Music were jumping on the bandwagon. They were technically brilliant, but something was missing. That *funk*. After all, there are some things you just can't teach, even if you pay thousands of dollars in tuition fees.

For a time, Daniel and I embraced it. It was me on the mic, Daniel DJ'ing and an accompanying band of a guitarist, bass player, saxophonist and drummer. We were playing shows with groups like Swoop and Skunkhour and getting a lot of love, too. But it didn't feel right. Our roots were straight-up hip hop, focussed more on sampling than live instrumentation. Like Run-DMC once proclaimed: 'two turntables and a microphone'. So, when we got offered our first contract by a label called Creative Vibes, and they wanted an acid jazz album out of us, Daniel and I were torn. Without a real job between us, most aspiring musicians would have been crazy to turn down a record deal before they were twenty. But it just wasn't us. If we were gonna make it, it was going to be from Daniel's beats and my rhymes. And if we were gonna fail, well, we'd fail on our own terms. We turned down the offer.

If anything, that only pushed us to step up our hustle. Away from the live shows, we got to work, experimenting with our sound, finding our own lane. At the time, there were so few actual hip hop artists in Australia; the blueprint was hardly set in stone. Locked away in Daniel's bedroom, we studied artists like Big Daddy Kane and LL Cool J while adding our own distinct Aussie flavour. Slowly but surely, we were finding our feet.

We got into a routine. Daniel was working during the day at Tandy Electronics and making beats by night. Wired from being up all night, he'd call me when he had something new and play part of the beat over the phone. I'd listen then make my trek over to his mum's place in Florey, a good 30–40kms from Queanbeyan. The journey involved three buses, which was a pain in the arse, but I used the time to write rhymes. By the time I turned up, I had something ready to go.

The set-up was hardly ideal. First, Daniel's mum's boyfriend had a real attitude and was always giving us the side eye for being at home. Mostly, we ignored him. Then there was the noise. Or lack of. His mum had just had a baby, so at odd times during the day we'd have to be deathly silent around the house. If it was nap time, you weren't even allowed to flush the toilet. Hardly the best environment for making music, but we made it work. That would become a habit for us: making the best out of a shit situation.

Entering Daniel's room, the first thing you'd notice was the huge Public Enemy wall-hanging. If I was a fan, Daniel was a fanatic.

Then, your eyes would take in the clutter. It was like the inside of a mad scientist's laboratory. You'd have to step around exposed wires, and there was recording equipment lying all over the place in various states of disrepair. We were broke teenagers, so buying some new fancy gear was out of the question. Instead, Daniel would visit Canberra's Trash & Treasure Market every Sunday to see what he could find. Being an insomniac, he'd stay up every Saturday night so he'd be the first one there on Sunday morning at 5 am. With the market to himself, he'd return with turntables, mics and other hidden gems that most people would have deemed broken beyond repair. But Daniel always knew how to salvage them. He would make pop filters out of pantyhose, and often I'd be halfway through recording a verse when the sound would cut off.

'Fuck's sake! Not again,' Daniel would groan before whipping out a soldering iron, and I'd sit back while he set about fixing the mic. I'd never seen anything like it. And he was incredibly particular when it came to his samples, insisting on only sampling records from the '70s.

The lengths we went just to record were ridiculous. One song would easily take a day to finish, after all the breaks to fix equipment or to accommodate the baby's nap time. But aside from the dodgy mics and inescapable mess was Daniel's computer: a brand-new, state-of-the art Amiga 500. This beast made up for everything. Opening up a whole new world of sounds and textures, the Amiga finally allowed me to hang up the torturous process of pause-stop recording that I'd been using. With that computer at Daniel's fingertips, we no longer felt like two kids with a dream. We were *musicians*!

Our next breakthrough came when an aunt of Daniel's visited the States. When she asked what he wanted as a gift, his message was simple: all the records you can carry. She did a hell of a job because she returned with a crate full of the hottest new records, one of which was a series of compilation albums called *Ultimate Beats and Breaks*. This was a game-changer. Since the birth of hip hop in the late '70s, DJs had been mining old funk and jazz records for their drum breaks. (For those who don't know, any drum break in a hip hop song, nine times out of ten, has been sampled.) And seeing as most of the big hip hop producers knew each other and moved in the same circles, they would end up sampling the same drum breaks. So this DJ from the Bronx, 'Breakbeat Lou', put together a series of compilations that included all the big tracks DJs were sampling. One song, 1973's 'Impeach the President' by the Honey Drippers must have been sampled over a hundred times, by everyone from MC Shan and NWA to Ice Cube and Bobby Brown.

Daniel and I sifted through that album like two kids in a candy store. *'Oh shit, that's the drum break from that Ice-T track!' 'Check this out, EPMD sampled it on "It's My Thing"!'* We were obsessed with finding our own unique samples that no one else was using, so it's not like we used the album to make our beats, but thanks to Breakbeat Lou we were able to discover the names of artists we'd been listening to for years. Growing up in Australia, we'd become hip hop heads on our own, consuming the culture but removed from it at the same time. Listening to *Ultimate Beats and Breaks* was like getting the blessing from New York – we realised we'd been listening to the same shit they had. The same artists, the same drum breaks, the same samples. For the first time, we felt connected to the source. Armed with Daniel's Amiga 500 and his newly acquired record collection, we got to work.

Sometimes it would just be Daniel and me obsessing over new tracks and putting together rough demos. Other times, we were joined by Tunks and the boys. Since we were all into hip hop, these sessions would quickly evolve into freestyle marathons. If we weren't rocking over roughly chopped and looped instrumentals of Chubb Rock, Grand Puba or Jeru the Damaja, Tunks would yell out, 'Aye, Daniel, make us a beat!'

Daniel would cook something up on the spot and the rest of us would kick dumb freestyles 'til our voices were coarse. It was me, Tunks, Bain and George, and we named ourselves the Toolshed, which, by the way, was completely unrelated to the famous gay S&M adult store in Sydney with the same name. We were hinting at the fact that we were just a bunch of idiots, i.e. tools, talking shit.

When it came to rhyming, there was only one rule in the Toolshed: it had to be funny. No one took it seriously, and if you did, the boys would bring you down to earth pretty quick. But what started out as a joke soon became a crucial part of my development as a rapper. Before those sessions, all my raps were about asserting myself as an MC and waxing lyrical on how my skills on the mic were better than anyone else's. In the Toolshed, we rapped about anything. And I mean *anything*. Shit got real dark, real quick. There were lines about digging up corpses, and the boys would come for me about my club foot. As long as it was funny, it was all fair game.

While we were passing around the mic and talking our shit, Daniel would have one tape deck playing the beat with another recording us. Afterwards, we would sit around for hours, listening back and cracking up. Yeah, I was the only serious rapper, but the others had skills too – it was just the wit that mattered. Bain was the comedian of the crew. In fact, his rhymes and his flow were too good for him *not* to be a rapper, but he always insisted that it wasn't for him.

While the others would be listening for the best punchlines, I was studying everything from my flow and cadence to rhyme patterns and delivery. It became a ritual – rap for hours then reflect on what I'd said. Rap. Reflect. Repeat. Not only did it help improve my technique, these recording sessions would become goldmines for later projects. A single phrase or idea would spark entire songs, and we even began sampling extracts and putting them on wax.

Looking back, it would be easy to dismiss the Toolshed as just some goofy fun among friends; a detour in my journey as an artist. It was anything but. It was my gladiator school. This was the era whereby, as an MC, if you couldn't kick a freestyle off the top of your head at any given moment, you were looked at like a fraud. Thanks to the Toolshed, I was always ready.

Though, if I ever go into politics, I pray no one ever sees those tapes! In fact, when I die, place them in my suit jacket pocket and cremate me with them.

THAT BEDROOM SHIT

During one of my trips to Sydney, I met a DJ called Dr Phibes, who owned the iconic Next Level Records. He was into hip hop and sounded serious about trying to grow the local scene. So I decided to give him a tape Daniel and I had made weeks earlier. It was barely a demo, just a random collection of recent songs we'd recorded, but it gave him a sense of what we were about. There was a song called 'Standards' on there, along with 'I Hate to Brag' and another named 'Koolism'. I handed it over and forgot all about it.

Meanwhile, Daniel and I were picking up steam. Groups like Def Wish Cast, AKA Brothers and Sound Unlimited Posse were laying the foundation, slowly starting to put Australian hip hop on the map. The industry was beginning to take note, and one of the early adopters was Mushroom Records. In late '94 they were putting together an album called *Home Brews Vol. 1* to showcase some of Australia's up-and-coming rap artists, and they wanted me and Daniel on there. Whatever hesitation we felt around the Creative Vibes deal was quickly put to rest. *This* was our moment.

When Mushroom Records reached out, they already knew what they wanted. They'd heard a song of ours called 'The Extra Ordinary' and wanted it for the compilation. The song title was a reference to Souls of Mischief's hit '93 'til Infinity'. As soon as I heard Opio introduce himself as 'the exxxx-traordinary dapper rapper' in that unmistakable high-pitched voice of his, I knew I wanted to flip it into a song. Daniel and I were thrilled: the music we had created in his mad lab of a bedroom was starting to get noticed.

Mushroom asked us to come to Sydney so we could re-record the song in a better studio environment. But before we did, we had to sign the paperwork, which was all well and good apart from one issue: since ditching Tribe Ledda L, we were technically nameless. For a while, we played around with the idea of calling ourselves Kahlua, after the drink, but thankfully decided against it. I can't remember if it was me or Daniel, but one of us had the idea to run with 'Koolism'. Because, ya know, we were the 'ism' of being cool. Or something like that. We signed on the dotted line and officially became Koolism.

When we got to Sydney, things didn't quite go as planned. Mushroom teamed us up with an in-house producer who was to work with Daniel on mixing the track. That was fine by us, but the producer didn't appear to have ever listened to hip hop a day in his life. Before we'd arrived, he'd cut nearly all Daniel's scratching and for some unexplainable reason added a tambourine. (I figured I must've missed all the Run-DMC and NWA songs that featured a tambourine solo.)

This sort of thing was really common back then. With the local hip hop scene still barely a scene, Australia's sound engineers and producers were used to the sounds of rock'n'roll. They didn't get that we preferred samples over live instruments and at every turn tried inserting them into our tracks. Sometimes it worked, at other times it changed the entire nature of the song, transforming a raw hip hop track into a commercialised entity that was neither real rap nor rock. After some back and forth with Mushroom we settled on a middleground we were all happy with.

If anything, the experience was a valuable one, teaching us how to reach a creative consensus without sacrificing our identity. Except, when the compilation album finally hit stores, Mushroom used the adapted version. The damn tambourine was back!

Man, Daniel was pissed. So was I, but it didn't take away the pride I felt. 'The Extra Ordinary' was the first song on the album, so it was like Koolism was introducing the world to Australian hip hop. We were alongside names like Rize and Tarkee, the Melbourne twins who had helped kick off rap in this country. Then there was Raph. Around my age, but from Melbourne, Raph was something of a phenom. Years earlier, I'd seen a photo of him as a thirteen-year-old with Aussie legend DJ Ransom, and word was he had mad skills as an MC. I hate to admit it but I was kinda jealous. In my head, he had become my nemesis. Now we were on the same album together! Needless to say, I deaded that secret rivalry and we went on to become good mates, even joining forces to release a song together.

Towards the end of '95, Daniel left Canberra and moved in with his dad in Sydney. He'd got into it with his mum's boyfriend and the situation at home became too much. He packed his bags one night and was gone. Fortunately, the distance barely slowed our roll. My cousin 'Uli had just moved to Sydney, and I was back and forth a lot by this point, so we carried on recording as if nothing had changed.

On one occasion, I was hitting a few record stores when some guy approached me.

'Hau! I heard that demo of yours,' he said. 'Love it, mate. When are we going to hear more?'

Uh? What demo? I was about to tell him he had the wrong guy when it hit me. The Dr Phibes tape! He must have dubbed it and passed it around.

'Appreciate it, mate,' I replied. 'We're actually working on a project now. Be ready soon.' This wasn't a complete lie. We were always working on material and had heaps of songs stashed away, though nothing that resembled a full album. But I wasn't about to miss an opportunity. This was the first time I was hearing that people outside Canberra were into the music. We had to feed the streets.

Fortunately, Daniel's stay in Sydney didn't last long and he was soon back in Canberra, this time staying with Tunks and another mate of his called Travis, a young graffiti writer who Tunks had taken under his wing. We nicknamed the house 'The Ice Box' because it was always freezing. It was out in Kambah, right on the edge of a valley, so it got all the cold wind hitting it, and the boys were too cheap for heating. But we didn't care, it was a place to make music.

Tunks ran a tight ship. He was a wild dude at times, but he also had the discipline of a Buddhist monk. There were parties every weekend but, regardless of what shit he'd been up to the night before, the next morning he'd be up and heading to work. The same couldn't be said for Daniel and Travis. One morning, Tunks came back from working a night shift to find Travis sitting at the kitchen table ripping bongs with some guy.

'Who the fuck is this?' Tunks demanded.

'This is Steve, we just met!' Travis responded cheerily. Turned out he was a cab driver. Tunks wasn't impressed.

'Steve, get the fuck out my house,' he said before walking upstairs to bed. This sort of shit was happening all the time, like two errant teenagers living with their stepdad. And with no parental supervision, Daniel's room was a tip. If things were disorganised before, now it was full-blown chaos. There was shit everywhere, and you could barely even make out a bed beneath all the clothes, records and food wrappers. Tunks had given him one rule when he'd moved in: make whatever mess you want, but it has to be *inside* your bedroom. I think Daniel took the instructions a little too literally.

With no one to tell him what to do, Daniel's sleeping habits got even worse. I walked in one morning to find him asleep in a laundry basket. Tunks found him another time asleep at his turntables – standing up! But, as usual, despite the mayhem and the mess, one thing Daniel never sacrificed was sound quality. The equipment was still pretty basic, but thanks to Daniel's ability to rejig things here and there, he was able to achieve incredible results. The man is a genius – not just smart, not just intelligent – a bona-fide genius.

Inside the Ice Box we got busy on our first official EP, *That Bedroom Shit*. Besides the mess, people were coming and going all the time due to a certain import–export business the boys had going on. But we thrived off the chaos. Toolshed sessions were continuing at full pace, so if the boys weren't at work – and I wasn't at TAFE – we were in Daniel's room cooking up new tracks. The environment set the tone for our future Koolism releases: these weren't just albums created by me and Daniel; these were family projects. Whether it was through ideas, providing good energy or rolling spliffs, everyone contributed.

The recording was done straight to tape deck, which meant everything was recorded in one take. If you listen carefully, you can pick up on small mistakes here and there, but we didn't care. It was authentic. It was raw. When we settled on the final songs, we got Tunks to design the cover art and George to make the layout. It was a proper team effort, and when it was finished the boys were just as excited as Daniel and me. While the project was complete, there was still one issue: we had no distribution partner, so selling the tape would be our responsibility. To be honest, we didn't even know what 'distribution' was; we just knew we had to get our music out there whatever way we could.

I went straight to Grace Bros, the department store in Queanbeyan. When the security guard wasn't looking, I slipped a dozen or so cassettes between my back and backpack and walked out. I then dubbed the tapes at home, added a photocopy of George's cover art and took the finished product to Next Level Records, who had agreed to sell them for us. We only had about ten copies for sale but fuck it – we had a full EP on shelves next to groups like Run-DMC and the Beastie Boys.

A few days later, Phibes called me. 'Hau, the tapes have all been sold. Can you get us some more?'

Holy shit! People are really checking us out.

'Yeah, course! Give me a few days.' Straightaway, I hit up Grace Bros again and repeated the routine maybe a half a dozen times: rack the tapes, photocopy the cover art, send to Next Level. Each time, Phibes would call me to ask for more.

Soon, we would have to figure out a new method of distribution.

KISS OUR ARSE!

In case you haven't already guessed, I didn't become a chef. It just wasn't for me. My initial impression of the kitchen as this cool, exciting place couldn't have been further from the truth. If anything, it was abusive. A lot of long days with even longer nights, and people screaming at you for minor mistakes. Fuck that. So I did my year and a bit and called it a day. The experience wasn't entirely wasted, though. I learned some skills, met some cool people, took one of the female classmates into the bathroom for a bit of extracurricular fun . . . *It was aiiight!*

Having left TAFE, I was back with a lot of free time on my hands. When I wasn't in the studio with Daniel, I was cruising around with Tunks and his crew. He'd been running with KOA since meeting Metro and Mahem back in the late '80s. If Tunks had a rep, Metro and Mahem had *legends*. These were real street guys. You had to be if you were deep in the graffiti scene back then – graffiti and violence went hand in hand. Metro and Mahem were great writers, but they were even better fighters. They were from West Ryde in Sydney but were hated – and feared – from Canberra all the way to Brisbane. Whenever they'd arrive in Canberra to go searching or whatever else they'd come to do, you'd hear the whispers: all-in brawls with guys pulling out meat cleavers, violent beefs with different graffiti crews in broad daylight. It was the stuff of fiction. A group of outlaws tearing up a city of rule-abiders.

The first times I met Metro and Mahem are still imprinted in my memory, like occasions that you instantly know will be memorable. I saw Metro sitting outside a cafe one day, before I was properly introduced. Just by laying eyes on him, I knew he was the guy I'd been hearing about. He had the aura of a hustler. Leaning back in his chair like Tony Montana in *Scarface*, Metro was wearing gold-rimmed sunglasses and was dressed so fresh he stood out like a sore thumb in Canberra. In a city without much style, Metro was an exception. He was neat. He had *taste*, like he had his own personal stylist shipping outfits from Europe. But Metro didn't need any help – he had his own means of acquiring stuff no one else had.

Mahem was the same. On one of our trips to Sydney, Bain took me to his house in West Ryde. Stepping inside his room was like entering one of those classic New York hip hop movies: the turntables, the record collection, the sneakers, the weed smoke. *This is a real hip hop kid*, I thought. Mahem had one of his mates, Julian, with him that day. When we pulled up, Julian was standing on the side of the road, wearing a full Ralph Lauren tracksuit and matching Ralph Lauren baseball cap with a pair of Nike Air Max on his feet – pretty standard these days, but no one was dressing like that back then. He looked like a million bucks!

It's hard to explain the significance these sorts of meetings had on me. Nowadays, a trend crops up, in Chicago or wherever, and within days – hours even – the whole world has access to it. Anyone can wear the right gear and act like they are part of the culture. Back then, you had to *be* about it. Meeting guys like Mahem, Metro and

Julian was like meeting mythical creatures. They not only knew all the right artists to listen to and the right brands to wear, they had them on deck. When I first laid eyes on Julian, I was trying to figure out how this street kid from Western Sydney could afford head-to-toe Ralph Lauren. But at the time, I didn't know the full extent of their searching capabilities.

Mahem had a cheeky, mischievous air to him. Immature in one way but also incredibly worldly, like he was never given the chance to grow up at his own pace. Their uncles were also heavy in the streets, so for Metro and Mahem it was normal. People like me and Tunks had the privilege to dip into their world then retire home to Canberra for the night. This was their life.

The closer I got with Metro, Mahem and the rest of KOA, the more I started to feel like I'd missed out not being around the crew when I was younger. I mentioned this to Tunks one day, and he looked at me sideways.

'No you don't, mate,' he told me. 'You were doing your own thing – music and footy.'

And he was right. That's what was so unique about those guys: it didn't matter what shit they were into, they never forced, or even encouraged, anyone else to get involved. That's not to say I wasn't getting involved of my own accord. Being around them on the daily meant it was impossible to hide from it. I'd join them on runs from Sydney to Canberra and back, picking things up and dropping them off. Sometimes I asked what was in the package. Other times I didn't. To be honest, I didn't care. I was twenty and not thinking about consequences. But on one particular trip, Tunks felt the need to offer a word of warning.

'Okay, you may see some things today,' he said. 'It's up to you if you want to take part. If anything happens, you stick with me.'

'Alright, cool,' I replied.

When we arrived in Sydney, we went straight to see Jo, a German mate of Tunks who was visiting. For the time being he was staying at a hotel opposite Hyde Park. Jo had a mate with him, and the four of us sat in his hotel room talking shit and having a few beers. I didn't drink at this point so was sticking to the waters. Nothing out of the ordinary so far. Then someone brought out the coke and Jo started cutting lines on a plate. As he passed the plate around the room I started thinking back to what Tunks had said in the car. I didn't feel pressured. More than anything, I was curious. *I may as well try it, right?*

I guess Tunks saw this coming because he'd given me a quick run-down on what to do before arriving. Roll the note nice and firm, block one nostril, one quick sniff. I took the plate as it was handed to me and dove in. *Wham.* That rush! Tunks had warned me about the numbness at the back of your throat, so I just sat there as I began to feel my body racing. A few lines of coke were nothing to the others, so I knew to not act out of pocket. I put the plate down and carried on listening to music.

About fifteen minutes went by. The excitement quickly turned to anxiety as I thought about my grandmother Fe'ao, who had died a few months earlier. My dad's parents had passed away before I really knew them, but we had always been close to my mum's side. They lived in between Tonga and Salt Lake City, Utah, for most of my life, but when we were able to see them it was always special. Fe'ao was a kind woman with a big smile and an even bigger heart. She also had a great sense of humour and could either be as soft as a goose-down puffer or as stern as a traffic cop. As I sat there staring at the wall, her voice spoke to me.

What are you doing, Hau? She shook her head, disappointed.

Fuck. I started spiralling. You see, coke wasn't what it is now, where anyone and everyone dabbles. You turn up to the pub on a

Tuesday and someone's offering you a cheeky line. Back then, you really had to know someone. It was a sign you were either a junkie or into some street shit. I asked myself, *Which one am I?*

By this point, I was blocking out all sound from Tunks and the others. It was just me, my grandmother and my shame. *What have I done?* As the coke continued to make its way round my body, I reflected on the world I was entering. Sure, being around weed and booze was normal, but anything harder was new to me. *Is this really you?*

Then something snatched me out of my thoughts. Jo went into his bag and took out a gun, carrying on the conversation like it was nothing. He mentioned to us that he was prepping it to be sold. As with all Germans, Jo had served a few years in the military, so he knew how to handle a pistol. Like a scene out of a movie, he swiftly got to work taking it apart to clean. I watched in silence as he pieced the gun back together, all in a matter of minutes. When he was finished, he left it on the table next to the coke.

I don't know if it was the coke or just my curiosity, but I couldn't help but pick it up. Looking down the barrel, I pointed it at the mirror and pulled the trigger. *Click.* It felt satisfying, so I did it again. And again. Until Jo told me to quit it.

'Firing a gun with an empty chamber will fuck up the mechanism,' he told me. The scene reminded me of the outro to Mobb Deep's 'Man Down', where one of their boys is playing with a pistol and someone has to tell him to 'stop fuckin' around'. Yup, that was me.

'Besides, it's time to go,' Jo added. We were meeting a few of the others at a bar in the city.

Jo quickly readied another plate of lines and started handing it around. Tunks gave me a look that said, *One's enough.*

Yeah, good call.

***

In late '96 I was officially put down with KOA. It's not like those LA gangs in the movies; I didn't have to fight anyone. It was after a gig in Sydney, and Metro and Tunks, who by this point was one of the more senior members, pulled me aside. Metro put his arm around me and, in his jittery manner, told me I was part of the family. It was an emotional moment. I'd been with them for a couple years, but not everyone was invited to join. You had to fit the profile.

By the mid '90s, the crew was in a transitional phase. The wild on-sight beefs earlier in the decade were largely behind them, and the focus now was getting money and spreading the crew's name via other means.

That's where Daniel and I came in. We were like the new arm of KOA, growing the rep through the music. We started dropping the name in songs, and I think it took a lot of people by surprise. I was the big, friendly Islander of Australian hip hop; at gigs I made a point of talking to everyone and always showing love. I figured it was the least I could do if people had taken the time out to come see me perform. Then when people saw me with KOA, the most hated crew in Australia, they didn't know what to make of it. *Ha!* The looks I'd get when I'd turn up to a show flanked by Metro and Mahem. It was like these rappers had seen a ghost!

Apart from no snitching, which was a given, there was only one unwritten rule in KOA: if shit popped off, you had to stand and fight. No questions asked. You back your boys no matter what.

Daniel was invited to play a DJ set at Club Mombasa, one of the few bars in Canberra to play live hip hop. He and another DJ had a friendly clash, trading records back and forth. I joined them on stage for a bit, but I mainly left Daniel to it and watched the set with a mate of mine called Hasim, who I'd been introduced to via Tunks.

Hasim is the best and worst person to have around when there's drama. He's always ready to fight, then again he's *always* ready to fight.

We'd wind him up about his short fuse all the time. I'd clocked one of the other Canberra crews inside the venue but didn't pay them much mind. I knew Tunks had had his issues with them but it wasn't that deep. The funny thing was, these guys actually looked up to Tunks. It was the same with most of the crews we beefed with. They copied his style, but rather than taking it as paying homage, he took it as disrespect. And if one of us had problems with a crew, we all did.

When they started looking in our direction, I couldn't help but poke Hasim a few times.

'I reckon he said something about you, mate,' I told him with a grin, motioning at one of the fellas closest to us. *Dumb move.*

Hasim took a look over, got out his seat and walked to where he was standing. 'What are you looking at?'

Before the guy had a chance to respond, Hasim decked him. In the middle of the club. With everyone watching. It was on. As their crew began piling on, I ran over and grabbed one of them by the neck as he went for Hasim. Pulling him back, I got off two punches to the face before throwing him to the side while Hasim carried on swinging at anyone who came close.

After a few minutes, the owner (who we were mad cool with) de-escalated the situation, and for the moment things were calm. Seeing as it was only Hasim and me – Daniel wasn't much of a fighter – I was keen to leave it there. But when their entire crew followed us downstairs, I knew that wasn't about to happen. One of them yelled at Hasim, calling him a pussy. Again, *dumb move.* It was back on – except this time it must have been six or seven of them versus me and Hasim. I took a boot in the eye that knocked off my Kangol.

Hasim, meanwhile, was getting the brunt of it. As I was punching on with one of them, I saw a guy come up behind Hasim and crack the back of his head with a beer bottle. Instead of smashing, the bottle just bounced off his skull. Stunned for a moment, Hasim looked at the guy before smacking him up.

One of their crew had brought a lamp from upstairs, and bottles and chairs were flying everywhere. It was complete fucking mayhem. As the fight spilled onto the road, I looked for Hasim. *The cops are gonna be here any minute now*, I thought. Glancing up the street I saw him running towards us. *Oh fuck.* He had gone to his car and brought out a nine-section whip, the kind you see in Jet Li movies. Running down the middle of the street, with cars honking and people staring on in disbelief, Hasim was slashing people's chests open with a fucking whip! It was like a scene from our kung fu movie nights, only this time the shit was real. Before driving off, Hasim tried running a few of them over in his car, narrowly missing some passers-by.

When Tunks heard about the brawl the following day, he called one of the olders of the other crew and told him that he and the others would have to apologise or there would be consequences. Before we bumped into them again, we started hearing that the guy who knocked my hat off was going round acting tough, saying he'd stolen it. When I saw him, his energy changed real quick.

'I've still got your hat, mate,' he told me. 'I'll give it back next time I see you.'

'Nah, fuck that!' I told him. 'You need to buy me a new one.'

So he did. A month or so later, I ran into him in a mall and he had a brand-new hat with him. He handed it over quietly before slumping off. I was shocked. *Has he been carrying this around the whole time on the off chance he sees me?*

∗∗∗

I've thought back on that night with Hasim more than a few times. It could have gone a lot differently. Hasim and I could've caught a punch, a bottle or worse, that would've put us in intensive care. And what about the other way around? What if Hasim *had* hit one of them with his car? Would I be here writing this, or sitting inside a prison cell as an accessory to murder?

We were one of the lucky ones. Unfortunately, not everyone we were with back then can say the same.

KOA SOUND SYSTEM

But before we go on, my name is Hau not Ren
It's me again, the one that got it locked and
rock fans head bang with there long hair in head bands
got skaters to players in the Raiders who play this
like Alligators in 2005 or we cater for crews
with a crystal "clear fuck off" for the hater in you
swingin like monkeys from trees for your junkie disease
Koolism hip hop in your veins make ya nod
to the rhythm embeded in your blood,
(I dont know if) I've said it enough, need to get it repetitious stuff
and not forget it bro we're second to none
grab mics to wreck it for fun and thats what I have
flows like peanut butter slats, another jab
from the Koolism repetoire step in a state of mind
where eyes dialate beyond comprehension
rhymes suspensful on all terrain suspension
prevention against sucker mc's buckle their knees
they fall in a heap, girls pulsate and talk in their sleep   LATER
wake up refreshsed & walk to the beat
of the capital, finger tap it all day
lyrical pornos set emotion in motion
ocean to ocean host with the most infect
none comes in close contact w the bro's got flows on top
grab, schemer
the big kahuna from the islands gotch smilin

TUNKS

KOA stands for Kiss Our Arse. Metro is the one who came up with the name. I joined in '89, so I'm not a founder but a first-generation member. And then later I became co-president.

There's a very rigid and traditional sort of structure and set of laws in graffiti, which is funny – it's like an outlaw pastime and it's supposed to be countercultural, but it's actually quite controlled, 'cause we copped the law handed down from New York. So you have mentors and you have apprentices, and then you have to be put down in a crew. There's a process to go through; it's not easy. You're breaking laws doing graffiti, so you need to trust the people in your crew.

A lot of what Australia learned about graffiti culture came from Style Wars *and* Beat Street *–'80s movies like that – and the rest of it from* Subway Art, *which is a book from New York. It's the most stolen book in the world, apparently. Kids would sit there and pore over those pictures. There was stuff in there about the structure of crews. Even the terminology was copied straight from New York.*

Without trying to make out that they're gangs, the structure of graffiti crews is pretty similar. There's usually a president, and that's usually the person who founded the crew, the person who normally gets to say who's in and who's out. Some crews are much more relaxed and, you know, anyone can put anybody in. But our crew was very strict. The membership was small, and it was hard to get into.

I'm a traditionalist, and by tradition, graffiti writers have to steal their paint. That's kind of gone out the window now because people can buy it. I wasn't a criminal, but I was a graffiti writer, and I wanted to do graffiti properly. So I racked paint. You know, it's kind of a gateway thing – first you start racking paint, then you start doing breaks for paint, and then you're robbing and stealing just to get money so you can travel to write.

And then you start to justify it. 'Oh, I'm doing this because I'm a writer and I need to do graffiti and it's part of the culture.' The next thing you know, you're doing full-blown crime. I'm not saying I was any kind of criminal, but I understand how people moved on to those things. And then heroin hit and maybe eighty per cent of the searching and graffiti community were hooked.

There's also a lot of flash in graffiti and searching. A lot of the kids who were involved in the scene just wanted to be something, ya know. And this was their way to be something. Some people just wanted to be classy and look fresh. With our crew, we were big into the fashion – the music and the style. We were known for that. Everyone had to dress proper. Everything had to be fresh. Anything that everybody was into – what all the scum crews were wearing – we wouldn't wear any of it. We'd have none of it. As soon as a lot of people started getting on something, we'd drop it. Our crew would be walking around in designer European brands, luxury Swiss watches, high-end sneakers, loafers, Timberland boots, Ralph Lauren and stuff like that in the early '90s.

We were always trying to get stuff that no one else had. And we were hip hop heads, too. So we learned a lot from record covers. In those days there was no internet, so you'd flip over the copy of, say,

Eric B. & Rakim's album cover, and check every single tracksuit, the shoes, the jewellery. We'd be going in close-up on photographs of people, you know, stuff that we had seen in London or whatever. Some of the crew would occasionally get European fashion magazines. Things like that. We were always looking out for stuff to make us stand out from other crews.

LIFT YA GAME

My twenty-first birthday arrived in January 1997. In Tongan culture, your first and twenty-first birthdays are the big milestones. Sabne turned twenty-one in 1990 and damn near half of Tonga showed up. Her birthday is in February, but we ended up celebrating it midway through the year just to accommodate everyone. We even built an extension on the house to fit all the family who were visiting! But this was because she was *fahu*. Because of her status, everyone wanted to show their respect.

I wanted mine to be more low key. Just a barbecue with family, both of them: KOA and kin. All my uncles were there, and during the afternoon we headed over to the oval behind my house to play touch footy. After the game, everyone had worked up a thirst, but I still wasn't a drinker. I can't really explain why, other than to say that it's what everyone did. And when everyone goes one way, I tend to go the other. I didn't judge; it just wasn't my thing. I felt like I didn't need it.

However, sitting around the garden that day, sweaty from the game and surrounded by my loved ones, I figured I'd made my point. As everyone tucked into their beers I got someone to make me a vodka orange juice. I was a twenty-one-year-old enjoying his first proper drink.

1997 turned into a transformative year in more ways than one. As I was shaping my sound with Daniel and getting into shit with KOA, my rugby was stepping up, too. I was playing for the Canberra Kookaburras and starting to understand something my uncles had said about me years earlier. I must have been around twelve at the time when I overheard one of them – I think it was Mum's brother Sione – mention that I was a promising player.

'He's got a real shot at playing for the Wallabies one day,' he said, 'but he needs to find his animal instinct.'

I had no idea what he meant, but the comment stuck with me. By the time I was playing for the Kookaburras, I realised what he was talking about: being a contact sport, to really stand out you have to play with such ferocity you're willing to die on that pitch. Throughout school, I'd been a strong player, but when I joined the Kookaburras I was an animal!

Saturday morning games had been a ritual since before I could remember. Those early starts during the winter were brutal. Before the game, we'd put our jersey on the radiator to warm us up – anything to stop the shivers. Dad would be on the sideline every week, come rain or shine, waiting patiently until the ride home to give his thoughts on my performance. He wouldn't say much, but I'd listen as he shared a few pointers. He'd always tell me to 'look for the ball', reminding me to hit the ball at speed whenever I'm running onto it. When I played badly, there was silence; those car rides were the worst.

Mum rarely came to matches. She saw me get into a fight one game and from then on preferred to stay home. In a maul, I was trying to grab the ball when I felt someone bite me. *What the fuck!* I pulled my arm back and began whaling on the guy, catching him with a few uppercuts before the ref pulled us apart. Mum was mortified, but like I said, the prick bit me! What was I supposed to do?

I was in love with the sport, but as soon as the final whistle was blown, I was outta there. I didn't join the boys in the clubhouse and didn't get involved in their drinking sessions on the bus home from away games. I sat in the back with my headphones on, listening to music and chilling. I wasn't isolating myself – I'd stay part of the banter – but I wasn't trying to neck eight beers on a bus full of other dudes. Nor was I into the casual nakedness. What the fuck is with footy heads and wanting to get naked in front of each other? The team was split between the private school boys, who were mainly idiots, and the country boys. I always got on better with the country boys. They were more down-to-earth – and more inclined to keep their clothes on.

Playing for Canberra was a big opportunity. The competition was fierce, and more than a few players had gone on to represent Australia over the years. When I got the call-up, Dad was over the moon. Coming from a working-class family, footy offered a way out. His brothers Talia'Uli and 'Uaisele had played for Tonga, and one of my cousins had even played in a few World Cups. He was supportive of my music, but I knew that deep down Dad was hoping I'd go on to rep the green and gold. In a way, so was I (though I was always more interested in playing for Tonga, if I'm honest.) But music and footy never seemed mutually exclusive to me – until I was forced to make a choice.

One of the biggest names in hip hop, DJ Q-Bert, was coming to Sydney. If guys like Jam Master Jay and DJ Cash Money had originated the whole turntable scene, Q-Bert was taking it to a new level. This was the late '90s, when DJ'ing was still a big – if not *the* biggest – part of hip hop. Q-Bert and others would sell out venues on their own, with no MC, and shut the place down. His shows were legendary, and I couldn't be sure he would ever come back to Australia. I had to get a ticket – except, the concert was at the same time as a Kookaburras game.

I went back and forth on the decision for a week or so. On the one hand, the Q-Bert show would be epic and I may never see him again. On the other, playing for the Kookaburras is something that a lot of kids would kill for. And I knew it wasn't just about me – my dad hadn't come to Australia and worked his arse off to have me waste opportunities like this one. But my mind was made up: if I didn't attend the Q-Bert gig I would live to regret it.

My parents had always taught me to be respectful. If someone helps you, you show your appreciation. If you stay at someone's house and they aren't there when you go, you leave a note and say thank you. So, after everything my dad had done for me – all the games he had watched and all the advice he had shared – I wasn't about to take this decision lightly. The night before the concert, I took out the pad I used to jot down my rhymes and wrote him a letter:

'Dear Dad, I know you're disappointed but please understand how important this is to me . . . '

I put it on the kitchen table as I left for the gig that night. We never spoke about the letter, but I heard from Mum that he took it well.

'He gets his way with words from you,' he told her.

After that night, I carried on playing like nothing had happened. I loved the game too much to stop completely. But I knew something in me had changed. There was no mistaking it: rugby was my first love, but hip hop was my calling. It had been going that way for years, even before the Q-Bert gig. I was always a little detached from the culture of footy, with the private school cliques and sloppy piss-ups, but it was more than that. I loved game days, but training? Not so much. I was never into the fitness side of things. For the most part I got away with it, relying on my strength and natural talent, but that lack of work ethic is always going to get found out sooner or later. I had teammates who would live for that shit. Training would finish and they'd start their own session, working drills to improve their weaknesses. Not me. But when it came to the music, that was a different story.

It wasn't like I was thinking far ahead or planning a career, I just knew I had found my *thing*. That thing that keeps you up at night, that thing gives you purpose. Training on the footy field was brutal and at times boring, but working on rhymes or perfecting songs with Daniel never felt like work at all.

By 1998, Daniel had moved again. Tunks moved in with his girl so Daniel found a place in Phillip, in south-west Canberra. He gave me a set of keys so that when he was at work I could go and play around on the computer, messing with beats or writing rhymes. We were loosely working on our next project, the follow-up to *That Bedroom Shit*, but mainly we were just having fun. I was listening to a lot of Hieroglyphics, the Oakland collective made up of rappers Del the Funky Homosapien, Casual, Pep Love and Souls of Mischief. My style was inspired by Tribe Called Quest and De La Soul, but lyrically I was all about the complexity of Hieroglyphics.

Their production had that rawness of the East Coast sound, with those crisp boom bap drums, but what they were into most was their lyricism. The wordplay was sophisticated and the flow effortless;

no one else sounded like them. Oakland in the '90s was rough, and you could tell they all had a bit of street in them, but they largely left that side out of their music. That always appealed to me. If you are really from that life, you don't need to be shouting it from the rooftops for everyone to hear. You just carry yourself a certain way. Sometimes it's what you *don't* say.

My focus was always authenticity. Being unique. I thought of myself as a rapper's rapper, tackling subjects others wouldn't touch, dropping references to the sorts of things I was seeing in my day-to-day. You listen to someone like Nas and you feel like you know the Queensbridge Houses in Queens where he grew up. The same thing with NWA and Compton. Their music was atmospheric; they'd drop lines about their favourite places to eat, their sports teams, the types of drugs they were dealing. They were painting a picture, and I wanted to do the same, only mine would be Australian.

Yeah, I was sometimes hanging around with Metro and Mahem on their runs, but I always felt that was their story to tell, not mine. I wanted to rap about the life I was leading, centred around footy and family, dropping references to the slang we were using. Like a lot of Aussies, I said 'cunt' a lot, both affectionately and aggressively, so I used it in my songs. A lot. We all used to call each other 'big fella', so I had a song called 'Big Fella'. It might sound obvious now, but no one was doing this at the time. They were looking to America and asking, *How can I sound like them?* I wanted Australians to hear our shit and feel proud, or at the very least recognise it as home.

My wordplay was getting more and more creative, lines like, 'Fuckin' oaf, practice makes perfect / You need to heed that cos you need that, your tape's worthless,' from the song 'The Naked Truth'. But there was no real structure to the album. We were still playing around with form, so when Daniel and I had enough songs that we were happy with, we pieced it together without too much thought.

If anything, we approached it like a DJ set: start off by building some energy before a small dip, then a big crescendo to finish.

Tunks was the one who came up with the name: *Lift Ya Game*. It fit the bill perfectly, touching on the rugby metaphors I was using while sending a subtle message: these other rappers better get their shit together, because Koolism is coming.

After *That Bedroom Shit*, Phibes and his mate Blaze, who worked with him at Next Level Records, asked us to officially release *Lift Ya Game* through his new record label, Parallax View, one of the only labels pushing hip hop in Australia. It wasn't a huge operation – they basically just funded the manufacturing of the vinyl – but it helped us reach a wider audience. With such little support and infrastructure around us, Daniel and I had got used to doing things ourselves. The formation of Parallax was one of those lesser-known landmark moments in Aussie music, adding one of the first bricks in the house of Australian hip hop.

Phibes offered to let us record the album at their studio beneath Next Level Records. Daniel's home set-up was fine for playing around and crafting the beats, but when it came to recording, we needed bigger, better equipment. We only had one session to get it done, on 16 June 1998. This just so happened to be the same day Run-DMC would be in Sydney. It was the tour where they teamed up with house DJ Jason Nevins for the remix of 'It's Like That'. Daniel fucking hated the Nevins stuff, but Run-DMC was in his blood, and mine too, so we bought tickets anyway. The plan was to nail the recording then celebrate at the concert at the nearby Metro Theatre in Sydney.

We loaded the beats onto CD and drove to Next Level Records on Liverpool Street. You had to walk up a few flights of stairs before you hit the record store. There was graffiti lining the stairwell walls from

CLOSE KNIT...

Tougher than mell or a ruck, bond with family cos its all-in-the-blood
My Tongan family brand me...
The Kings helper, Langomi-E-Hau brings-wealth-fa
You mind, Me & my cousins recline & design
Family reunions, (plug?) & tune in the PlayStation
the Jonah Lomu rugby game is always placed in ...
the system, twist' em controls like steering wheels
Im feeling girls in S.P., cos my guess-be....
We head-swayin' to reggae in the club
brown sugar baby bub want coconut love
Me & my cuz chuckle, cos we all fired up
fools retired but we stay, for sambucca replays
cos these-days I drink a little
we link a little handshake for love cos were strong as straight rum
We relate one..on one cos we're close knit
We toast it ... a toast to that "One Love Bro" shit!

           Family & friend ...near & far
           You know who you are!

floor to ceiling, and as we walked up, Daniel and I spotted pieces by the artist Mister E and a couple by Sereck of Def Wish Cast. The studio was on the first floor, directly beneath the store on level two. Although, to call it a studio was a stretch. Let's be honest, it was a storeroom. Phibes had cleared most of the shit out of the way, but there were still records everywhere and the equipment, although better than ours, was hardly ideal. We spent the first fifteen minutes figuring out how the hell we were going to dub the lyrics over the beats. But, thankfully, we were used to working in chaos.

The vibe more than made up for the dingy studio. Sleeping Monk, Mr Clean and Apex, who were part of a collective called Easy Bass and some of the first rappers we connected with in Sydney, were milling around, so they sat in with us and chopped it up for a bit. Meanwhile, Phibes, who was an obsessive documenter, was taking photos and videos of the session. It felt like we were making history. Remember, we had no real hip hop institutions in Canberra. Sure, there was Happy Days and Firehouse, and Impact Records and even Central Station had a spot there for a while. But there was nothing like a Next Level Records that could act as a hub for the culture. We were more DIY with it back home. But in Sydney, it felt like we were part of something. Surrounded by walls full of graffiti, with the street noise simmering below us and the thought of Run-DMC going through sound check just a few blocks away, we closed the door and pressed record.

There were a dozen songs to get through. At this point, all the music was made, so it was largely down to me nailing my verses. Daniel would loop up the beat and I would get to work. I'm usually quick with it, but my verses for Lift Ya Game were technically complex, so it took a few runs to get it right. It would take me a few years to realise that sometimes less is more with lyrics. Cramming in complex metaphors and similes can dilute their impact.

Daniel and I had an unwritten language when it came to the music. When we were recording, we'd communicate through grunts, nods and murmurs of approval. On stage, we didn't even need that. One of us would take the lead and the other would follow, riffing off one another 'til we found our rhythm. We literally never rehearsed before a show. Not once. This wasn't about being lazy; we just didn't need to. We were both musically inclined and could count bars, so everything felt natural. There was no need to force it; we were in sync. Besides, the impromptu nature of it all made the shows seem raw and unpredictable.

In the zone, Daniel and I started getting through the track-list. I was focussing on my lyrics while Daniel had that zoned-in look of his, staring intently at his computer screen, obsessing over some minor detail or sound. As Run-DMC's set approached, I saw him check his watch a couple times, but for the most part we were locked in.

Several hours passed like this until we were happy with what we had. *Lift Ya Game*, our third official project, was officially complete. As Daniel put the final touches on the recording, we called a mate who confirmed what we already knew: the Run-DMC gig was over.

All good – we had done what we came to do.

HIP HOP AND WHOREHOUSES

Since leaving TAFE, I'd been jumping around a few different casual jobs – some cash-in-hand construction work here and there, and my mate Hasim owned a cleaning business, so occasionally I'd join him for a job or two. Between that and show money, I was sweet. Then Alvin hooked me up with a job at the casino soon after my twenty-first. He'd gone back to Tasmania with his dad after leaving school and started working at some dive bar frequented by ex-cons. There were fights more or less every evening until, finally, Alvin decided he'd had enough. One night, with bottles flying past his head, he picked up the phone and rang a number he saw in the paper for a job in the Canberra casino. He got the gig right then and there and was on the next flight home. I joined him a few months later when another opening came up.

It was easy money. We worked the keno tables, which is basically a type of bingo where you match the numbers on the card with those called out. Alvin and I were in charge of punching tickets and calling numbers. Towards the end of the night, we'd start messing around, using funny voices and accents when we announced the numbers to see if people would notice. Occasionally we'd get a laugh, but mostly people were too engrossed in their gambling or their booze to care. It was a grim place, to be fair, but the job was convenient. If we had an away rugby game on Saturday, I'd crash at Alvin's around the corner after my shift so I could get picked up by the team bus on the way to Sydney.

For the rest of the week, I was with the boys. There was a German dude named Ivo who we were becoming tight with. KOA had international connections all over the place from various crew members living overseas and hooking up with other crews. We had ties in New Zealand, Asia and Europe. Ivo had visited Australia a few years prior to coming to live in Canberra for a stretch. He was a funny guy, really into hiking and all that outdoor stuff. He was also a street dude and kept a knife on him wherever he went.

Ivo was always telling us we needed to visit Germany. He was a DJ and part of a hip hop crew in Heidelberg called Advanced Chemistry, so he told us he'd be able to hook us up wherever we went. The offer sounded tempting, and after a while Daniel and I decided to take him up on it. *Lift Ya Game* had been delivered to Phibes, so we had some time on our hands. Along with Alvin, we packed our bags and set off for Europe, my first time leaving the Southern Hemisphere.

When I told my parents I was going to Germany they were a little confused. 'Why would you want to do that?' they asked. This was before the 1999 Rugby World Cup, which triggered a bunch of Polynesian footy players moving to the English or French leagues. Before then, it was rare for an Islander to visit Europe, let alone Germany, but we didn't care – the stories Ivo told us had Daniel, Alvin and me excited. According to him, Germans really fucked with hip hop, so we were keen to see that for ourselves.

We flew into Frankfurt and were met by Ivo's buddies, Torch and Boulevard Bou, at the airport. Torch was tall and broad-shouldered with dark facial features that stemmed from his Haitian side. Bou, on the other hand, was a Turkish brother, shorter, with a smile as broad as Torch's shoulders and a contagious energy. Both were super nice and welcoming, which is what we wanted after a long-arse flight. (In fact, they were so buzzing, I don't think they'd been to bed from the night before.) They greeted us with '*Alles klar?*', a German phrase we were going to hear a lot and one we began using ourselves. Technically, it means 'Everything is clear', but it's used more like, 'How are you doing?' or 'You all good?' With Torch and Bou cracking jokes, we jumped in the car and set off for Heidelberg.

When he hit the highway we got our first taste of German efficiency. With rain coming down and Torch behind the wheel, we started picking up speed. Then a little more. And then some more. I glanced at the dial, trying to act like everything was cool: 170km/h. In the pouring rain! *Bloody hell!* But the craziest thing was the cars cruising by us like we were in the slow lane. *Man, I thought only Tunks was this reckless behind the wheel.* But I had no idea then just how safe those German autobahns are.

My knowledge of Germany was patchy at best. To be honest, everything I knew came from studying Nazi Germany at school. So when we got to Heidelberg I was expecting a sea of blond-haired, blue-eyed white people staring back at me. Man, how wrong I was. There were different skin colours everywhere. Torch took us to see his crew, and it was full of different races and ethnicities: African, Middle Eastern, Turkish. I was pleasantly surprised.

After passing through a bunch of quaint cobblestone streets, we pulled up to their studio. Advanced Chemistry were huge at the time. They were affiliated to the Universal Zulu Nation, one of the original hip hop collectives in New York led by Afrika Bambaataa. Needless to say, they were official. Thankfully, their English was also perfect – while my German sucked – so we drank and hung out for a few hours before someone pulled out a few mattresses for us to crash on.

It was a really generous move, especially since we had nowhere lined up to stay that night, but when Torch and his boys left I was sceptical. We'd all heard the stories of the 'Zulu Sandwich', where two guys and one groupie would . . . Well, you get the picture. God knows what Torch and his boys had been up to in that studio where we were about to lay our heads. Alvin was cracking up about it. 'Don't touch that!' he'd shout whenever Daniel or I sat down. But we'd just flown halfway across the world, so I was exhausted. I wrapped myself up tightly in my sleeping bag and crashed out.

Despite Ivo's warnings, nothing prepared me for how much Germany was in love with hip hop. We all knew the mecca was New York, and it was huge in LA and the entire West Coast. There was a strong scene in London, and we'd even seen a few pictures of rap concerts in Japan that looked wild. But . . . *Germany?* And they weren't just into their hip hop – it was the whole culture behind it. The States were moving away from breakdancing and the whole B-boy thing, but in Germany that stuff was very much alive and kicking.

Ivo was true to his word. Torch and his boy DJ Rick Ski were like local celebrities out there, so we cruised round with them, visiting all the different record stores during the day and the clubs at night. We did a lot of crate digging, which for the uninitiated is when you dig through old crates of records in the hopes of finding something to use in a song – whether it's some horns, a drum break, an instrumental to loop or even just a unique sound. I loved the process of it all. We would spend a few hours visiting the stores then rush back with our records like kids waiting to open their presents on Christmas Day. We'd put the needle on the record and sit there brimming with anticipation at the thought of finding some hidden gem no one else had sampled. There's a lot of skill to crate digging, learning not only where to look but *how* to look. Obviously, you start with the classics – James Brown, Parliament-Funkadelic, etc. – and branch out from there. First, you study the cover; sometimes if it looked cool that was enough. Usually, though, we'd flip the record over and dig a little deeper. We would learn the band members' names and the individual producers who worked on certain projects so we could spot them when they showed up on other things. Then we'd look for the record label. Even if we hadn't heard of an artist, if they were signed to a label we knew, we'd have a rough idea of the vibe and whether or not we'd be into it. Then we'd look at the year of recording. By this point, Daniel had moved on from only sampling '70s records and was open to anything. His taste was broad and eclectic, which I reckon was a result of crate digging itself. He'd buy records to sample then end up getting super into whatever type of music it was. We'd know by the year what the record would sound like. If it was made in the late '60s or '70s, it would have that raw funk sound. It was also sonically unique, as it would be recorded on cassette. If you moved into the '80s, the quality had improved and the sound had moved towards R&B and soul. It was the Prince era, and they were using a lot of slap bass and drum loops. Daniel could go even further than that, distinguishing between recordings just a couple years apart. It's like birdwatching or coin collecting for hardcore hip hop heads. Daniel could easily spend an entire day in a record store, eyes narrowed, flicking through record after record after record. I didn't quite have his stamina, plus the German women were baaaaad, so I was a little distracted. Thanks for taking one for the team there, Daniel.

After hanging with Torch for a few days he asked me to jump on an upcoming compilation album he was creating called *50 MC's, Vol 2*. Torch told me to pick a beat to rhyme over and I chose the Beatnuts' 'Are You Ready'. With that nasty bassline, man, I haaad to!

Torch looped it up and I went in like an open door. It was a crazy experience; hearing my voice rap alongside different languages made me realise how big hip hop was becoming. When I was growing up, it was considered a fad, an American pastime that would go out of fashion in a few years. And yet, fewer than ten years later, all the way in Heidelberg, Germany, there was already a whole industry behind it. *Maybe the same will happen in Australia*, I thought.

Torch lined me and Daniel up with a small concert at a club one night. I don't think anyone in the crowd could understand what I was saying, but they seemed to get the vibe. Although, I was too busy checking out the women to care. When we were leaving, Alvin told me about a conversation he'd had with Torch about an Ice Cube concert at that club a few years prior. Advanced Chemistry were opening for him and they had a habit at the time of starting shows with the instrumental from 'The Message' by Grandmaster Flash and the Furious Five (feat. Melle Mel and Duke Bootee). You know the one: 'It's like a jungle sometimes, it makes me wonder / How I keep from going under.' It's classic shit – one of the first officially recorded hip hop songs ever. Torch and his boys would freestyle over it to get the crowd jumping. When Cube saw this, he was into it. 'I like how you guys do that,' he apparently told Torch after the show.

A few months later, Ice Cube released his hit song 'Check Yo Self' (feat. Das EFX). The beat he was rapping over was none other than 'The Message'.

We had other places to visit besides Germany, so after a week or so we moved on from Frankfurt. But not before Torch took me to a few of his favourite spots around the city. First stop: the brothel. The Advanced Chemistry boys had a favourite one located inside this huge building several stories high. Alvin had left by this point to do some travelling around Europe, and Daniel was off doing something with Rick Ski. I'd never been to a brothel before, but, ya know, when in Rome! Or Frankfurt, in this case.

After a few drinks, we drove to the spot. As we entered, we were asked to take a tour up the levels, with each one dedicated to a specific region. That was a trip. The first one was African, then German, before we landed on South America. They had the Latin music jumping and the women looked incredible. 'This is me!' I said, jumping out the elevator like a kid into a theme park. A true host, Torch got out and joined me.

We left Germany a few days later, travelling from Italy to Switzerland before heading back to Frankfurt for our return flight. We got dropped off at the airport, passed through security, and boarding was about to start when Daniel started freaking out.

'I can't find my ticket anywhere!'

'Just double-check your bags, mate,' I told him. 'Didn't you just have it?'

I wasn't tripping. Daniel did this sort of thing all the time. He began frantically unpacking his shit, trying to find his ticket, while I watched on, semi-amused. A couple minutes went by, still nothing. Getting nervous, Daniel went and spoke to security, explaining that his ticket had been stolen. They told him to speak to the police, who in turn just shrugged. Okay, now I was starting to get a little worried.

He made calls around, first to see if he could get his travel insurance to pay for another ticket, then to Rick Ski to see if he had left it in his car. Nothing. The intercom announced final boarding for our flight. *Shiiiiiit. Am I going to have to leave Daniel here?* As he ran up and down the gate panicking, I sat down and prayed. Speaking to my grandmother Fe'ao, I asked for God's help in finding the ticket.

Please, God. Daniel is about to be stranded with no money . . .

DANIEL

Man, it was Biblical!

I'm there at Frankfurt International, trying to tell these German cops I'd lost my ticket, and they just didn't give a fuck. It was a really slow process to try and make a police report, and I was hoping something might come through for me. At that last minute, as I'm sitting there with the police, Hau runs in and he's like, 'Man, you're not gonna believe this! I prayed to God to find your ticket and something told me to check your record box. I lifted the lid, and no shit, the records parted, and right in the middle was your ticket!'

Hau was very religious then, and we used to argue about it a bit. I was staunchly atheist. I'd be like, 'Fucking God believers, man.' We wouldn't have heated arguments or anything, but we'd have annoying back and forths where I'd try and rationalise with him and convince him it didn't make any sense.

In many ways, Hau and I were like boyfriend and girlfriend back then. The relationship between him and me was like any romantic relationship I've ever had, except obviously we weren't having sex. We would bicker just like a couple. Not often – generally we were on the same page, having fun – but there were a few times when we would argue about things like religion. I was trying to get him to give up on that stuff, but it was still such a big part of his life.

NO TIME FOR A PLAN B

Lift Ya Game came out soon after we got back to Canberra. What a moment – our first release on vinyl. When I got hold of a copy, seeing our music etched onto it, I remember thinking, *This is real now. Super real.* There's a series of landmarks for an artist: making your first recording, your first live show, your first pay cheque through music, and so on. For me, hearing my voice on wax was what I had always wanted. I fell in love with hip hop listening to old vinyl – placing the needle on the record, the moment of static noise before hearing the music play. I'd waited nearly twenty years to hear my own voice boom through the speakers, and now it was finally happening.

The album sold okay, but we were still so underground we weren't really expecting much from the sales. Although, we were getting a lot of props from those who had heard it. Respect from peers was everything. That, to me, was a sign of success. I remember having a conversation with MC Hunter about it. (RIP, big fella.) Hunter was like the Perth hip hop connect. If anything was happening out west, he'd be there, showing love or pulling strings behind the scenes. After he heard *Lift Ya Game*, he told me he was inspired to use the word 'cunt' in his raps.

'That's our word,' he told me. 'A name we call ourselves *and* our loved ones. Just like Americans use the n-word, we can use "cunt"!'

I laughed, not entirely sure if that was a good or bad thing. The record also meant we started getting booked for more gigs. On 30 October 1998, we performed our first show in Adelaide. The promoter said they'd pay our flights, accommodation and $500 for the show. It might not seem much now but that was mind-blowing at the time. *We're being paid to get on a plane to go rap?* Daniel and I couldn't believe it.

As the plane sat on the tarmac, waiting to take off, I turned to Daniel excitedly. 'Can you believe this, man? This is actually happening!' What a crazy feeling. The gig itself was small, maybe fifty people or so. That was standard for most Australian rap shows in the late '90s; the crowd would largely be other artists and people connected to the music. Because there were so few hip hop events, whenever anything was happening, everyone would show up. And when it came to Australian rap back then, 'everyone' was not a lot of people.

This was when rap was very regionalised. Before the internet made everything accessible, each city would have its own distinct vibe. Melbourne rap was dark and gritty, closely connected to the graffiti scene there, which was always big. Guys like Brad Strut of Lyrical Commission epitomised Melbourne rap in a nutshell. They had a real 'fuck everyone' attitude. I never understood why it was all so dark until I actually visited Melbourne and saw how cold and grim the place can be.

Sydney, on the other hand, was very divided. You had groups like Easy Bass in the City of Sydney, which our mate Sleeping Monk was a part of. (RIP, Illpickl.) Easy Bass were like Koolism, except we were a little more up-tempo. Like us, they were lyrical and they were also crate diggers, so their songs would be full of unique samples. The music out west was a different story. Reflecting the environment,

Western Sydney hip hop was tough and grimey, with Def Wish Cast still setting the standard out those ways.

Adelaide had its own thing going but it borrowed heavily from Melbourne. There was one group in particular, Hilltop Hoods, who were starting to get popular. Made up of local MCs Suffa and Pressure, and DJ Debris, they had just dropped their debut EP *A Matter of Time*. The cover art was an illustration, so we had no idea what they looked like 'til they introduced themselves after the show. Super nice guys, but I wasn't a huge fan of the music. They could rap, there was no denying that, but it just wasn't fully connecting for me – yet.

It would be a few years 'til they blew up and changed the face of local rap forever.

I used to love Saturday mornings at home. Each week, I'd wake to the sound of Tongan music with the faint hum of the vacuum cleaner floating somewhere in the background. There was always such a beautiful energy. Mum and Dad would be chatting away, preparing breakfast and doing chores, a house full of love, music and laughter. Hearing traditional Tongan music takes me back home – more of a spiritual home than a literal one, like my heart feels at ease. There's a dreamy feel to it, full of acoustic guitar, keyboard, banjo, pre-programmed drums and hymn-like harmonies. It's why a lot of Tongans love country music; they have a similar sound. Dad would always have the car tuned to QBN FM, listening to some American country crooner as he drove me to rugby games.

I was in no rush to move out. I toyed with the idea a few times, once considering getting a flat with Hasim. When I mentioned the idea to Mum, she was like, 'Why would you want to do that? You have everything you need here.' And she was right. Mum and Dad enjoyed having me around as much as I enjoyed being there. The only times we disagreed were when we discussed my career. They were supportive of my music, but they always said I needed a back-up plan.

'You have to have a Plan B,' Mum would say. She encouraged me to think about going back to school or getting into hospitality. Neither idea appealed to me. I thought having a back-up plan was a bad idea, as if the comfort would somehow reduce my drive. *If you're going to chase something*, I'd tell myself, *you have to be all in*. Part confidence, part naivety.

Still, I understood where Mum was coming from. Her dad was a school principal, so education had a huge importance for her family. Dad, coming from a working-class background, was more relaxed about things like that. But he came with his own suggestions.

'You need to get a good job because you're not good with your hands,' he'd tell me. *Haha*, he had a point! I was not built for the tradie life, that's for sure. Largely, though, my parents left me to it. They could see I was focussed. Had I been cruising around not doing anything productive, their approach would have been a lot different, but I was always working towards something, whether it was a specific album or Daniel and me just perfecting our sound. I was self-motivated, and my parents trusted me to do my thing.

Grandpa Ma'ilei came to stay with us in 1999. He lived between Tonga and Utah, but since Fe'ao died, he'd been moving around a little more, spending stretches with different family members. To be honest, I was a bit jealous of my cousins in the States for having spent so much time with him. Yeah, we saw him at family gatherings in Tonga, but that wasn't the same. When he lived with us, we were able to enjoy the small things.

He would always carry three things: a Bible, a pocket radio and a torch. (It gets real dark in Tonga without much light pollution.)

He didn't have any of his Tongan stations, so he left the pocket radio behind, but the Bible and torch went with him everywhere. I didn't say this but I'm pretty sure streetlights in Queanbeyan would have done the trick. He enjoyed soft food, so I'd prepare him things that reminded him of home, like fish and mashed sweet potato. Porridge was another favourite. He'd have it simple – just with milk and a little brown sugar – and Mum would make him a small fruit salad on the side.

I never understood it when I heard mates say how it was such a punish having family come to stay. Man, I loved it. Then again, maybe their grandparents weren't as funny as mine. With that cheeky smile of his, Ma'ilei would quiz me about whether I had a girl or not. I'd shy away from those conversations because it felt a little awkward talking about relationships with a grandparent. Having a couple of kids myself now, I can see the kind of connection Grandpa was trying to build.

I used to love coming home to him each day. Everything Ma'ilei said was considered and thoughtful. Mum would often talk about their conversations – the love, the knowledge, the respect. He was always well put together whenever it was time to step out; his dress sense was as sharp as his wit. Maybe that was from being a principal? You always gotta look the part. Come to think about it, maybe that's where I get my dress sense from?

He was slowing down physically but still as mentally alert as ever. I looked forward to talking with him, discussing things back in Tonga or how my music was going. Just like Mum and Dad, Grandpa was behind me a hundred per cent. Even so, I was nervous as hell when he came to see me and Daniel perform. *How is he gonna feel about my swearing?* I wondered.

We had a show at a museum in Canberra, playing songs off *Lift Ya Game* as well as a few new ones. Mum took him, finding a quiet

Grandpa,

Here are the lyrics to my song. It maybe a bit hard to follow, but here it is anyway. I hope you enjoy it.

BLUE NOTES

[VERSE 1]

Its funny how God teaches lessons, sending your loved ones back to this so called "essence", I count my blessings...

I guess since the days of a youngen, raised as a Tongan

strong in the mind, while belonging to times...

I remember well, family gatherings would be packed

On special days, through rain or sun rays, how could you lack...

happiness, for sure God had me blessed with love,

With uncles and aunties who were obsessed with hugs

Half of the relatives were in Tonga to take care of kids...

and live the island lifestyle, while...

Every second year or so, we would go

I remember my cousin Pou' would work so he could go

Cos bro' if you felt how the wind blows

Between palm trees off the south seas, you'd know...

that, Tonga is gracefully, the place to be

Its been great for me since '85

But '88 was my favourite year

Cos of our re-union tears of happiness cos we all made it here,

I thought this made it clear, we'd be here forever

Out last the rainy season, over come the stormy weather

But as you know, the Lord works in mysterious ways

Taking their lives, putting you through some delirious days

many weeks, many months and for me even years

Grieving tears, were leaving memories and leaving tears...

place in the back for his wheelchair. I shouted him out during the set, so people were coming up to say hello and shake his hand. They left early, but judging by the huge grin on his face, I figured he'd enjoyed himself. It wasn't until I got home that I was able to find out from Mum how he really felt.

'I can see Hau is bringing happiness to people,' he told her. 'I'm glad God has given him this platform.'

That floored me. Having our music on vinyl was one thing, but hearing those words from Grandpa was a different story altogether. More than anything, I was just thrilled to see how proud Mum was from his reaction. She had left Tonga decades before, sacrificing a lot along the way. And now, she was able to show her father the new life she had built and the type of children she had raised. I was glad I was able to give her that.

THE VERSACE-WEARING TONGAN

Since high school I'd had a steady run of girlfriends, but nothing ever felt serious. I'd been seeing a girl for a bit when I was at TAFE, but to be honest the situation became kinda annoying. I mean, look . . . she was an awesome person with an awesome family, but she decided she wanted to be a rapper too, and I just didn't know how I felt about that. It started to create tension, as if we were competing against each other. Teniela was different. We met in one of the chat rooms I visited to talk hip hop or meet other Tongans. She lived in Auckland but we quickly realised we had a lot in common. My mum knew her dad from back in Tonga, and her cousin in Australia had married my cousin's cousin. It's always like that with Tongans – if you look hard enough, there's a connection there somewhere. We sent a few messages back and forth online, mainly talking about family and the music I was making. After a couple of weeks we worked up to a phone call.

This went on for around six months until Teniela visited Sydney to see family. We met on the steps of Town Hall and wandered around the city for a few hours. She had her cousin with her and I brought 'Uli along, so it's not like we had any privacy, but it was still fun. Just holding her hand felt exciting. She stayed for a few weeks and I crashed at one of my cousins' places out west so we could hang out during the day.

Next, it was my turn to visit Auckland. I had my cousins there too, so I saw them first then stayed with Teniela – in different rooms, of course. It's the Tongan way. To be honest, I was a little surprised I was allowed to stay at hers at all. But like mine, Teniela's parents were pretty relaxed. Her dad was Tongan and reminded me of my own: quiet, kind and supportive. He was a teacher at Wesley College as well as a rugby coach and had coached the great All Black Jonah Lomu. Her mum was Māori and staunch as. Loving, but staunch as. She held her tongue for no one and had no qualms screaming at her kids in front of me. Not like she was mean or anything, but you did not wanna cross her.

Teniela had a job at the local supermarket on the deli counter, so when she was working I was either networking with other artists or hitting up the local mall. Security was so light I couldn't help but rack a few items. There was this one Versace shirt that I slipped under my hoodie. Man, it was so fresh. It was a lot of money but I could have afforded it. I wasn't doing it because I needed to; I was doing it because I could.

Hip hop in New Zealand was more advanced at the time, so I reached out to a few artists before going over and we arranged to hook up. The first group I met was Urban Disturbance, a trio made up of rapper Ollie Green, DJ/producer Rob Salmon and a guy called Zane Lowe, who did a bit of both. Metro and Mahem knew them from their time in New Zealand, so as soon as I said I was KOA, they were keen to link up. Urban Disturbance were way ahead of their time. I was a big fan of Zane in particular, but he'd just been picked up by MTV Europe for a presenting gig so was no longer in Auckland. Ollie and I chopped it up one day while Teniela worked.

This was an amazing era for hip hop in Aotearoa. Aside from Urban Disturbance there was this independent label called Dawn Raid that was on the rise. It was run by Brotha D, a giant Samoan who had rapped with the group Lost Tribe, and his partner, a white guy called Andy. These guys were doing it big. They were from South Auckland and had that hustler mentality. If you were from that part of New Zealand you were either tough or at the very least resilient. Brotha D and Andy were both. Instead of going the traditional route, they had got their big break running market stalls, selling T-shirts aimed at the Pacific Island community with a very 'for us, by us' attitude. Their shirts were basically playful rip-offs of famous brands, with slogans like Cocoland instead of Timberland. People went mad for them. We're talking millions of dollars generated. Brotha D and Andy had met at marketing school, so they were into the business side of things. Before the music came, they were building an empire. Along-side the market stalls they had a barbershop, and all the branding was super slick. There was nothing like that in Australia at the time. I was just a kid soaking everything up and learning what I could.

They were a lot further along than we were back home, but I still knew that I wanted to do things differently. For one, I never under-stood why they rapped in an American accent. These were proud people who repped their neighbourhoods and Islands of origin every chance they got, but when they rapped, they sounded American. And it wasn't just the music. Their whole style – flat-brimmed hats with baggy shorts and oversized white tees – was straight out of New York. Even their gangs – the Bloods and Crips – were ripped from LA. I didn't get it. Then again, they didn't get us either. They thought we were bogans; we thought they were wannabes. But, shit, you couldn't help but give them their props.

On her next visit to Sydney, Teniela was allowed to stay at our place. She was in the house while I slept in the garage, which had just been converted into an office. When everyone was asleep, I snuck her into the garage and we started mucking around. After a few minutes she stopped me.

'I'm saving myself for marriage, Hau,' she told me. 'It's a gift for my dad.'

Not having sex before marriage I understood, but a gift to your dad? That was a bit weird. Besides, I never got the impression he was even like that. But, I didn't say any of this. If that's what she wanted, then cool.

The artists signed to Dawn Raid were starting to do their thing. The Deceptikonz – the Four Horsemen, as they were known – outta South Aux broke through the underground and made a huge splash. One of the members, Savage, went on to do some pretty incredible things, of course. But there was someone else I was dying to meet: King Kapisi. The name said it all – Kapisi was rap royalty. He was born in Wellington but his family were Samoan, and he put on for his Pasifika brothers and sisters every time he picked up the mic. He was blending breakbeats and bars with Island music, rapping over guitar instrumentals and stuff like that. He was authentic through and through. If anything, some people found him a little *too* real. In his music, Kapisi was critical of religion, and religion is one thing you don't play with in Polynesian culture.

In his song 'Fix Amnesia', he's got the line, 'Religious idols play cool games, mind roulette. (Someone constantly watching over you) it's just religious bullshit.' This type of honesty fucked people up. He got a lot of pushback from other Islanders saying he was being disrespect-ful. There was this one rapper in particular, another Samoan New Zealander called Ermehn, who stepped to Kapisi about it. Even for me, it was pretty out there. I was never as hardcore with the faith as my parents, but I was still a believer. Daniel and I had just released an EP called *Blue Notes*, and in the liner notes I made my feelings pretty clear: 'First and foremost: God. *Mālō 'aupito* for the endless guidance and blessings.' This was standard. If you questioned Christianity you probably did so in private. But King Kapisi didn't give a fuck.

I didn't really expect him to reply when I reached out, but when he did, he not only invited me to come stay, he said he'd pick me up from Teniela's house in Pukekohe, which was a good hour or more from where he lived. Just like Urban Disturbance, my crew had a history with Kaps (or, as he was known back then, Bran Muffin). Kaps is a mountain of a man who wouldn't look out of place in the First XV for the All Blacks or Manu Samoa. For his stature, you wouldn't think he would be as soft spoken as he is, especially when he screams down the mic with command and passion. But in that gentle tone, Kaps said, 'Yeah, *sole*. I'll swing by and pick you up. No problem.' What a bloke.

He lived west of Auckland in a little spot called Piha. It was beautiful, with stunning coastlines. A bunch of New Zealand stars, like Crowded House's Neil Finn, lived nearby. Kaps had his crib right by the water and, man, it flipped me out. *All this is from music? From hip hop?* It was my first time seeing something like this. Daniel and I were on a mission, but we were mainly just interested in doing something different and finding our voice. The thought we'd make a full career out of it, with money, houses and all the rest, didn't really occur to us. And here was this rapper, who looked like me, making music like me, and he was killing it! That was inspiring.

Then there was his wife, Teremoana Rapley, the unofficial Queen of New Zealand hip hop. She was the singer of Upper Hutt Posse, who were super popular in the early '90s, making a fusion of rap and reggae, and she was stunning. Kapisi had it made. We spent the night smoking weed and recording. I crashed out on the floor of his home studio, among his collection of Star Wars figurines, and went back to Teniela the following morning.

Today was a good day.

Back in Australia, Daniel and I got booked for our first gig in Melbourne. For the occasion, it seemed only right to don the Versace. I completed the outfit with some fitted Hugo Boss dark-blue denim jeans and black leather Diesel loafers. No one was wearing this sort of thing at the time. Sure, I looked more European holiday-maker than an MC out of Queanbeyan, but hey . . . I had to step out stylin'. Other rappers would play shows dressed in an old T-shirt and a pair of daggy shorts. To me, they looked like they'd just rolled out of bed. I was already thinking differently. Every time I got on stage – shit, every time I left the house – I was fresh. I'd plan my 'fits in advance and would mix luxury labels – most of which I'd racked – with Tongan shirts and beads. I was a showman, giving the people something to look at. It's probably why people thought I was trying to dress up. I wore an Armani Exchange bucket hat to one gig, and it got a few comments.

'What the fuck is that?' someone asked. I just laughed. My man DJ Flagrant replied, 'Only Hau could wear that and get away with it.' The day after the gig, Flagrant wrote a review in the local street press, with the title, 'The Versace-Wearing Tongan'. Glad to see someone was taking note.

THE SEASON

My boy Bain loved his helicopters. No idea why, but the man was fascinated by them. In his twenties, he turned his fascination into a career and got himself a pilot's licence. Bain's dad was a geologist and got him a job as a camp hand at survey sites around Australia. After a few years cooking and cleaning around the camp, he'd saved up enough money to put himself through flying school. Soon, he was working all around the world – the NT, Alaska, Canada – and enjoying every minute of it. Just like me, he had found something he loved.

On 30 June 2000, he was ferrying workers to and from remote locations in the gas fields of Canada. I remember the date because it was a few days after Tunks' wedding, which Bain missed to take the job. He was flying back to base camp when a tiny screw in the fuel control unit came loose, causing the engine to leak and eventually cut out. Desperately trying to land the helicopter, it looked like he had achieved the impossible when, metres from the ground, the tail rotor hit a fence. The helicopter exploded, killing Bain instantly. He was twenty-nine.

His death fucked us all up. It was brutal for Tunks, who had just got back to Australia after spending the week in the Cook Islands

Two of the most beautiful people I know: Dad and Mum.

Ya boy with the Tongan Elvis!
Haha . . . Love ya, Dad.

With the fur trim looking slim! Kambah BBQs were the best. Here with my uncle Talia'uli and my cousin Mamapu. Both have sadly passed away.

Up the Mighty Whites! The photo was taken on the same field where the front cover was shot: Taylor Park, Campese Oval.

I got sick one year in Tonga and my aunty Vaiola (RIP) performed some traditional methods of healing to get me right as rain again. My cousin Aneti, looking on with delight . . .

Uncle Maile dropping me off on my first day of school.

I was very fortunate to travel to many places with my family. Here we are in Tonga with Dad, Mum and my sister, Sabne. I'm rocking my Mambo kit and fake Converse.

What a photo – I love this one, taken in Tonga, my family working the fields, as usual. *Left to right*: Uncle Soni, Uncle Sele (RIP), my cousin Patala, Uncle Sione (RIP), my cousin Siua (RIP) and Dad.

A day I will never forget. The funeral for Uncle Maile, my first uncle to pass away. *Left to right*: Uncle Sione (RIP), my cousin Lotte, Uncle Sele (RIP), Uncle Soni (RIP), Uncle Talia'uli (RIP), Uncle Tevita (RIP) and Dad.

Top: Stylin' in South Auckland – loved visiting my fams there. Here I am, rocking a CD necklace and Chuck D pout, with my Uncle Tonga (*right*).

Left: Chillin' at my bro Alvin's house. How about those posters? So dope.

Middle right: The first press photo of Koolism – Daniel and me on top of Mount Ainslie Lookout, about to embark on one hell of a journey.

Top left: Seth One has painted many classic characters over the years, but this is my favourite. Murder Mouse. 1991 rude boy shit. Big fella was in a different league.

Top right: Diggin' in the crates with Daniel at the iconic institution, Impact Records.

Dan's Dojo in Watson. In this magical, messy spot, many a record was made and many a story was told. If you're thinking to yourself, *Where does he sleep?*, I'm sitting on it. *Haha . . .*

Top Left: Day trading or music making? Daniel and me in deep concentration.

Top right: Finding my mojo in the Dojo.

In Italy with (*left to right*) Essa, Albin, Torch, DJ Skizo and Daniel.
Big up the Euro crew. They showed us a lot of love.

Probably the only time I've ever actually
dressed up for a fancy-dress party. Went as a
footy player. Didn't really have to do much.
Haha . . .

Koolism super stylin', courtesy of 55DSL.

Many a discussion was had in this exact type of scenario:
Tunks holding court while Daniel, Axe and myself listen.

Top left: Seeing there's a bright future ahead. How about that Cocoland tee. Big up Dawn Raid all day.

Top right: One of my fav nights performing with King Kapisi (*middle right*) and DJ Raw (*left*) at a club in Manuka, Canberra.

Below: Classic material. A day I never thought would happen – recording with the Don, Rodney P (*left*). Tunks and DJ Skitz were in the session as well.

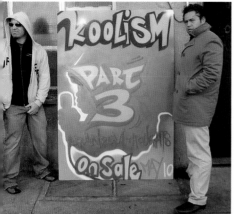

Top left: With my man Axe and some promo art from Seth One. This photo was taken behind Landspeed Records, another iconic music store. Big up Blake, Byron and the crew.

Top right: Taking press photos for *New Old Ground*. This one was taken at a spot called Revolve, a knick-knack store that was right next to the rubbish tip.

Left: Performing at ANU, Canberra, when we supported the Black Eyed Peas in 2002.

The infamous Boom Boom Room. A common sight: Daniel on the decks, me on the mic and much debauchery going on.

I mean, DJ Koo fkn Herc in Queanbeyan. *Haha* . . . That shit is too absurd.

At New York's infamous SOB's with a distracted Ghostface Killah after he snarled at me for asking him an innocent question. What a crack-up.

The GOAT and reggae royalty – Nas and Damian Marley – backstage on the Perth leg of the 2011 Good Vibrations tour

The Abstract Poetic, Q-Tip, with me and hani. New York fkn City.

Up in the Bronx with the legend Kurtis Blow. Big fella was our guide on a hip hop tour of NYC. Very surreal.

No trip to New York is complete if you don't go check out the graffiti. Big up the Tats Cru – some of the best to ever do it.

right: Celebrating Aki's first [bir]thday back in the 2620. Sitting on [Pap]a's lap as the big fella cooks a pig [on] a spit – or, as they call it in Tonga, [t]u puaka.

[mi]ddle right: Dad and me at the [blow]wholes in Tonga. One of my most [liked] photos ever.

[bot]tom: Aki and me recreating the [sho]t, but at Good Samaritan Beach [in] Kolovai.

[op]posite top: One of the best days of [my] life, getting married to my homie [bet]ter friend under the Sydney Harbour [Bri]dge and celebrating the occasion [wit]h close family and friends.

[op]posite bottom left: Skin-to-skin [tim]e with our firstborn, Aki. [A s]uper-emotional time.

[op]posite bottom right: Grabbing a few [Zs] with our daughter, Maila, just after [mo]ving into our new crib.

Top left: 'Uli and me rocking the new Koolism merch made by Article Don. The photo was taken on a Gold Coast bender for my mate's debaucherous bucks' night. *Haha . . .* (For the record, 'Uli was sober.)

Top right: The birth of Forever Ever Records. Grateful to the team at Sony both past and present for giving ya boy a crack.

Below: Representing on the red carpet at the 2018 ARIA Awards with my boys Briggs and Nooky. When I posted this to Instagram, the caption read, 'When I said we're shifting the culture, I meant we're shifting all the culture.'

Top left: With the god, Che Fu. Recording with the man is a definite highlight of my career. Super talented, super humble.

Top right: Working on my solo album, *The No End Theory*, with the masterminds, Sensible J & Dutch, in the House of Beige. One of the greatest times of my recording life. (Photo by Michelle Grace Hunder)

Above right: First session with ONEFOUR. It was exciting, it was uncertain, it was energetic. Who knew where this session was going to take us? *Left to right*: T, J Emz, YP and Marlay. (Photo by Jimmy Nice)

Below: The Golden Era, in the triple j studio with the Hoods, Briggs and many others.

My inspiration, my everything.
(Photo by Christopher Riggert)

with his wife, Cammui, for their honeymoon. He was out of reception the entire time, so when he landed and turned his phone back on there were a few dozen messages telling him to get in touch urgently. I got the news from Andrew before calling Daniel, who in turn didn't seem to comprehend what was happening. 'What do you mean he's dead?' he asked me.

'He died in a helicopter accident, bro,' I explained, the tears evident in my voice. Silence.

'I don't . . .' Daniel managed to utter. 'I don't understand.' I hated having to make that call. I knew how it felt to receive them, and I fucking hated them both equally. Later Daniel would tell me he knew something was wrong as soon as he answered the phone.

Daniel hadn't been through a death like this before, so the whole experience hit him like a ton of bricks. I had. I'd lost family members – either through death or deportation – but never a mate, and definitely not one who hadn't yet hit thirty. After hanging up the phone, I felt the energy seep out of my body. Numb, I lay down on my bed and went to sleep.

We had the funeral a few weeks later at the Norwood Park Crematorium in Canberra. It went about as good as we could have hoped. The first thing you noticed about Bain was his sense of humour. Whether he was cracking jokes in the car as we cruised around Canberra in his DeLorean-looking arse whip or coming up with ridiculous punchlines in our Toolshed sessions, laughter followed Bain everywhere. It's part of what made him so much fun to be around. That's what Tunks focussed on for his eulogy: Bain the court jester who lit up every room he entered. Man, he was such a sweet soul.

Seeing his coffin wasn't easy. Bain was a big guy, 6' 4" at least, but the coffin was more like five. No one spoke about it, but we all knew what that meant: Bain wasn't in there, at least not all of him. The service went on for about an hour before we went back to Bain's for a few quiet drinks and small talk. His parents, John and Peta, as well as his brother, Tim, kept it together really well. They were happy to see us all and better understood what Bain meant to us. At first they thought we were a bunch of ruffians who were pushing Bain onto the wrong side of the tracks. Less so with me – I was always minding my p's and q's – but they definitely didn't trust Tunks. Bain had told us that after meeting Tunks for the first time in school, his parents were afraid he was going to go back to their place and rob the house! But that afternoon they could see the crew for who we really were and how much we cared about Bain and each other.

We should have called it there, but we decided to go back and kick on, raising a few drinks to our boy Bain. The energy started off okay, then a few of the lads got too fucked up and started making it about them. I kept it together; after all, this was far from my first wake. I could tell some of the others hadn't been through anything like this. It's partly because of how I grew up. Not only did we have a big family, we were part of the close-knit Tongan community in and around Canberra, so there was always more chance of knowing someone who had died. Then there's the underlying health issues. Whether it was through obesity, high blood pressure or diabetes, a lot of my uncles had died younger than they should have. Other communities didn't seem to have this problem. Of course, there's a flip side to this. Having a big family may have meant we experienced a disproportionate share of death and tragedy, but there was always joy in equal measure. There were a lot of reasons to mourn but also a lot of cause for celebration. That's often the side of the story that doesn't get told.

***

SCOTT BAIN

In loving memory of my bro' Scott Bain, we set it off
like the choppers that he loved so much, we ~~hold it down~~ *the crowd touch down*
for the sounds that we got sewed up
dedicated to the one Rainmen
the mysterious figure in the trench coat
off the work bench float rhymes like a maniac
classic like Michael Jordan fadin back
we got him living through our music everytime we use it
also thru our thoughts & prayers, everytime we blare
our beats thru the speaker, we speak o' the devil
feel his spirit flow thru the words I blow
and grew like a settlement, Koolism never hesitant to
show emo'...shuns
we honor Scott Bain with a 21 gun salute & shoot
for the celebration from the root to the fruit
remember when I come to devour ye crew
I come thru *& spit* with the power of two

A few months after the funeral we were getting ready to make our first music video. Continuing with the footy and family vibes of *Lift Ya Game*, we wanted to give our fans something they could recognise as their own. The song was 'The Season', and I was rapping about the stuff we'd do during the summer: big family barbies, touch footy with the boys and all the rest.

> We rise like cholesterol and rock our summer gear,
> I show no fear in a game of touch football,
> Swimming at Pine Island, smiling 'cause it's all good, y'all.

It was like an Australian version of DJ Jazzy Jeff and the Fresh Prince's 'Summertime'. We hired Daniel's mate Rob as our videographer and got the whole crew together on a huge reserve in the southside of Canberra. Our instructions were simple: let's just do what we do and film it.

Everyone was there. Mum, Dad, Teniela, my cousins 'Uli and Maile, and obviously Tunks and all the boys, minus Bain whose presence was sorely missed. The video opens with my dad marinating some prawns, getting them ready for the barbecue, and my little niece, Sabrina, is by my side throughout. We're eating, drinking, playing footy and dancing. Just a day in the life.

The video had a big impact for Islanders in Australia. I had guys coming up to me saying they were seeing themselves on screen for the first time. That was huge for me. But when I showed it to Teniela, she could only focus on one thing: 'Why is Shani in it so much?'

What? Is that all you have to say?

I was pissed. I'd grown up with Shani – her dad knew my parents from back in Tonga, and she'd been around since we were kids. Plus, she was close mates with Sabne – of course she was there. She was part of the family. *Was Teniela jealous?* I tried not to dwell on it, but her reaction bummed me out.

'ULI

Hau was the trendsetter of our family. When he started really getting into hip hop in his high school years, he was wearing the medallions of Africa around his neck, and I'd go into his room and there'd be posters of artists I had never heard of. He introduced me to this whole culture, people like Public Enemy and Big Daddy Kane – names you wouldn't have heard of in the schoolyard in Australia. Not in the '90s.

My dad passed away in 1989, when I was about five years old. From then onwards Hau became a big brother to me. He guided me a lot. I spent a lot of time at his rugby games, and he'd come to my school plays. Our family was like that. We all grew up like brothers and sisters. It was a really close, tight-knit family. I suppose, because my dad had passed away not many years prior, I was always really happy to see my big brother.

I used to see him get dressed up in Hammer pants and stuff like that. I'd be like, 'Where are you going?' 'Oh, I'm just going to this hip hop club,' he'd tell me. There used to be a place called Firehouse, where he'd go do dance battles. It was such an exciting thing for me to see my cousin in these dance competitions, and being involved with this culture that I was unaware of, because everyone else was into

Def Leppard – that was my school environment. And then my cousin was into this type of music that involved guys of a similar skin tone to us, speaking on things that were really attractive to me. Then I tried to stick up a poster of Public Enemy on my wall, and my mum pretty swiftly took that down.

I looked up to Hau a lot. He even encouraged me to write my own rhymes. It was just something that I caught off him. Like I said, he was a trendsetter in a lot of ways for our family, with clothing as well. He had this bright yellow Nautica jacket. I remember as a teenager thinking, Damn that's cool!

And then Hau found pockets, like with Tunks and other guys, who became family. Tunks became my big brother, too. I can't tell you how much of an influence they had on me from such a young age. Like when I moved to Sydney at twelve, that was a real tough transition for me. They knew that. And so they would bring me in, encourage me and make sure I was okay.

They just kind of formed this underground group that was into stuff I'd never heard of – and that a lot of people in Australia had never heard of. They used to get together at Dan's place, and I'd go along every school holiday. I'd listen to hours and hours of samples from Dan. Sometimes Hau would get me to record something. I've actually been on a few of Koolism's albums over the years. He'd always help me with my own rhymes. 'You could do this with your tone here' or 'You should try and give more energy to that.' When I did music for high school, I would write songs and he would come and critique them and give me guidance. Kids in my class would ask, 'Where'd you get the music for this?' And I'd be like, 'Ah, you know, my connections!'

The more I think about it, it was such a cool time, watching these guys create stuff from very little. Hau used to have libraries of scrapbooks, where he would write rhymes and doodle. I would watch and observe him. And then when his albums started coming out, I was so proud. Like, 'This is my cousin!' I was so proud of him and proud to be related to him. And when I was living in Sydney and Hau would come up to do shows and I'd see Koolism posters around, I'd be like, 'That's my cousin! He's in a hip hop group!'

But I do have to say he was into Def Leppard and Poison before hip hop. There are some photos of him rocking the bandana, if you can source them. Ya know, just to prove that point.

CROSSROADS

Things with Teniela were good for about a year or so. There was even one point where we discussed who would make the move so we could be together. But, if I'm honest, I never really considered leaving Queanbeyan. I should have ended things then and there, before they got complicated, but it was easier to just ignore it. I'm not trying to make excuses – it was partly the distance, partly the ecstasy – but I did something I'd never done before. I cheated.

Hasim was my right-hand man at the time. We did everything together: drugs, girls, fights, the lot. He was dealing a little, so if nothing was happening the two of us would take a pill and just hang out, listening to music and talking shit. We called them Two Man Parties. (Tunks knows those real well.) One night, there was a girl there, and one thing led to another. It just happened.

The next morning, after she'd left, Hasim and I were chilling when Teniela called me.

'I had such a weird dream last night,' she said.

'Oh yeah?'

'I dreamed you cheated on me, Hau.'

I looked at Hasim. *What the fuck!* I laughed nervously. 'Man, that's crazy! You know I wouldn't do that.'

We'd been drifting apart for months. At first it seemed like we had heaps in common: hip hop, family, Tonga. But in reality we were different people, and it wasn't long before I was hiding things from her. When Teniela came to visit Sydney and I'd take her out for a night with friends, if I took a pill or whatever, I wouldn't tell her. It's not like I was ashamed or anything; I couldn't be arsed to have the conversation. She'd see my pupils were dilated like crazy but had no idea what it meant. And I wasn't about to tell her.

After that night at Hasim's, I should have ended things with Teniela. But I took the easy route, and after I cheated once, I couldn't stop. Soon, Tunks pulled me aside.

'Bro, you can't keep doing this. You're either with her or you're not. Choose.'

'Yeah, yeah. I'm gonna end things,' I told him. 'Soon.'

Before long, I had other things on my mind. Daniel and I were now being managed by a guy called Blake, who ran Landspeed Records – the iconic record store in Canberra. In March, 2002, he got a call from Resin Dogs, who had just released a new EP and wanted us to join them on tour later that year. *Our first national tour!*

This was huge. After releasing their debut album, *Grand Theft Audio,* Resin Dogs had blown up. They were a mixture of big beat and hip hop and broke down a lot of barriers in Australia. They were one of the first to get the backing of triple j and started getting booked for festival slots, way before other hip hop acts. The group had a long list of rotating members but it was led by Dave Atkins aka Dave Dog, the drummer and musical director, and DJ Katch, who handled the production. Dave and Katch were around during that first wave of acts coming up in the early '90s alongside Sound Unlimited, Def Wish Cast and AKA Brothers. They formed Resin Dogs a few years later. Groups like 1200 Techniques and The Avalanches followed them. Four or five years older than us, Katch and Dave looked at Daniel and me like the new kids on the block. We couldn't wait to go on tour with them.

In the midst of all the excitement I got another call from Teniela. This time, it took me a few minutes to fully process what she was saying.

'Some guy tried to kiss me,' she told me. Before I could say anything, she added, 'But I told him I'm pregnant.'

'Who's the guy?' I demanded.

'Hau, did you hear what I said?'

'Yeah, I heard. I said, who's the fucking guy?' I still don't know what was going through my head. Maybe it was a coping mechanism, maybe I was just trying to pretend it wasn't real. It took a few more minutes before the news sank in. We chatted for a bit, then I told Teniela I needed to get off the phone to digest the news.

I was going to be a dad.

Mum was the first person I told. She was over the moon. My sister had just had her first child, so the thought of having another grandkid brought her to tears. But she also realised the implications. Mum had spent a bunch of time working at Bega Flats, a notorious housing commission in Canberra, so she had seen first-hand the effect of unplanned pregnancies. She was traditional, raised on good Christian morals and a sense of responsibility, but she was also pragmatic. She understood there were other options. She trusted me to make the call that may not have been necessarily right for the situation but the one that would sit right for me.

I was stuck in two minds. Things with Koolism were really beginning to pick up momentum, and if I stopped now, that would be it. But I always wanted to be a dad. *What if this is my only opportunity?* The next person I told was Tunks. It was the night before the tour started and he was helping me pack up our merch – a line of hoodies with 'Koolism' printed in the 'College' font on the front. I told him I was considering moving to New Zealand to be with Teniela.

'How's that gonna work?' he asked me. 'What you gonna do, work in a factory?'

I didn't answer. *How the fuck was I supposed to know?*

'Mate, it's your decision but, if you want my opinion, you can't do this. Not now.'

We packed up the rest of the hoodies in silence. But after Tunks left, my mind was made up. I knew it would be difficult, but I kept thinking, *Maybe I can do this.* Like Furious said, anyone with a dick can make a baby, it takes a man to raise one. My mind was made up: I was all-in.

But first, I had a tour to do.

I decided not to tell Daniel about the pregnancy. It was such a big moment for us; I didn't want to tell him that this would be not only our first tour, but also our last. I pushed the thought to the back of my mind and tried to enjoy myself. For the most part, it wasn't that hard. Everything was so new; I barely had time to think. Being around Dave and Katch every day made a big difference.

Concerts can often turn into big, raucous parties backstage, but Resin Dogs were smokers, not drinkers, so the vibe was more relaxed. Plus, they were true professionals. The way everyone was in control of their part to play, on stage and off, was impressive stuff. They were a well-oiled machine. Daniel and I just watched and learned.

Dave and Katch were running the show, but they still had a whole band behind them. There were keys, percussion, guitars, bass, horns – a whole spectacle. When they hit the stage each night you could *feel* it. Daniel and I had moved away from the big-band sound we were playing with after *These Front Door Keys*, and were listening to a lot of jungle, experimenting more with electronic sounds. Still, we knew we needed to capture some of the presence that Resin Dogs had. It was just the two of us on stage, so we had less to work with, but with Daniel's MPC player we were able to mess around with samples and effects.

Watching them smoke was almost as impressive as watching them play. One night, after our set, I watched Dave punch three cones back to back before walking right on stage to perform. He sat down at his drum kit . . . *One, two, three, four.* Without missing a beat, the show began. For an hour, Dave was locked in the zone, playing drums and coordinating the entire band. A true master at work. I stood on the side of the stage thinking, *How the fuck does this guy operate?* Half a cone and I'd be passed out.

There was another rapper on the tour, Abstract Rude, a heavily revered MC from the heavily revered crew Project Blowed. He was from LA and had a song with Resin Dogs that was popping, so he joined them on stage and did a bit of his own set. Super nice guy – loved his weed and loved his women – but there was a definite cultural disconnect. Americans often don't get my dry, sarcastic sense of humour at first. I'd be winding Rude up and he would just look at me like he wanted to deck me.

'*Nah, just messing with you, bro! Haha.*' The relief on his face when he realised I was joking!

I got a call from Teniela before one of the shows. I forget which one. To be honest, the whole conversation is a blur now. I can't remember specifically what she said, but I do know she told me she had decided not to have the baby. This time I had nothing to say.

It's a strange feeling to describe. I was relieved, but I was also incredibly sad. In the end, I just felt numb. I carried on with the rest of the tour on autopilot, speaking with Teniela on the phone every now and again.

Yeah, I had said all the right things – it's your body, your choice; I'm with you whatever you want to do – but she could tell my heart wasn't in it. She was a motherly person, always babysitting other people's kids. My reaction was far from perfect, and she clearly resented me for it. I could hardly blame her.

LILO AND STITCH

Okay, maybe Teniela had a point about Shani. When she got jealous about Shani being at the video shoot for 'The Season', there was nothing there – we were just friends – but truth be told, I had started to see her differently. Shani and I had known each other since we were kids, but mostly she was just another face I'd see at family barbecues. After leaving school, she and Sabne became close friends, and they were at ours a lot. Shani was becoming a woman, and a beautiful one at that.

In 2002, Shani moved to Sydney. She didn't know anyone, so whenever Daniel and I would get booked for a gig in the city, she would come along. After one of the shows, she invited me back to her place in Chippendale. We slept together that night, and I could tell immediately that something was there beyond the physical attraction. I did my best to ignore this – I was too focussed on my music, not to mention the fact that I still had a girlfriend.

I called Teniela from Shani's apartment the following morning. I felt like a dick telling her I loved her while Shani was in the room, but I didn't know what else to do. The relationship had clearly come to an end, but since the pregnancy I felt like I wanted, in some way, to support her. Plus, I didn't want to give Shani the impression it was anything other than physical. Until I had my shit together, the last thing I wanted to do was lead her on.

Admittedly, I may have taken this a bit far. A few months later, we were in Sydney after another show, and this time we were staying at Metro's place. He had a pad in Bondi and was hardly ever there, so he'd let us use it if we needed a place to crash. Shani and I were in bed when, caught in the moment, she whispered those three fateful words: 'I love you.'

I damn near jumped off the bed!

'What did you say?'

Seeing my face, Shani tried brushing it off.

'You know, I love you like a mate,' she said. 'Like I love Tunks and the others.'

Riiiight. Evidently my plan wasn't working.

That's enough about my love life for a second. Let's talk bars. If I was on stage right now I'd quote the great KRS-One: 'Lyrics? Somebody want lyrics? From the lyrical terrorist?' Well, let's get to it.

With each release throughout the '90s, Daniel and I were becoming more and more confident in our craft. The show started in '93 with *These Front Door Keys* before the accidental Phibes demo spread like wildfire through the underground rap community. In '96 came *That Bedroom Shit*, which bottled up all the cheeky playfulness of the Toolshed years. *Lift Ya Game* in '98 was when I really stepped into my own, using lyrics to reflect my everyday life and my community, before the EPs *Blue Notes* and *The Season* allowed us to continue to cement that identity.

It wasn't just my subject matter that was becoming more advanced – my whole style was maturing. Since school, I kept my pad on me everywhere I went. Any spare minutes would be filled

writing bars and thinking up ideas for songs. When I had something I was happy with, I'd take it to Daniel and we'd find a beat that
matched. This worked fine up to a point, but the music ran the risk
of sounding a little disjointed. It wasn't until I began writing to a
beat, matching my cadence with the rhythm and tempo of the music,
that I found my pocket. My second realisation came when I began
writing in the studio instead of at home. Writing on my own always
helped me perfect my bars and make them technically faultless. But
rap isn't about being perfect; it's about being funky. I found that if
I wrote in the studio, with my boys cracking jokes and that contagious energy flowing around, my bars would become punchier, less
rehearsed and more intuitive, tapping into a real moment in time.
From then on, Daniel and I were in harmony.

In 2002 it was time to put our learnings to the test and drop our
first full-length studio album, aptly named *Part 1*. Unlike nowadays,
where releasing music is a very singles-driven operation, back then
albums were what artists wanted to make and what fans wanted to
buy. You got a sense of who the artist *really* was and the type of music
they *truly* wanted to make. I mean, albums only came around every
two to three years, but that was fine because you got to live with
those albums. Take in every song, absorb the craftsmanship of the
lyricism and production. That's what we wanted to do. Craft a body
of work that told our story up to this point.

We decided to combine the two EPs – *Blue Notes* and *The Season* –
plus add a couple of new joints to freshen up the tracklist. One of the
new ones was the intro to the album, 'Fakataputapu', words said by
Grandpa Ma'ilei when he was living with us. I sat him down in front
of a tape player and, using the in-built mic, I let him speak his heart
about the family. It was almost like a Welcome to Country, acknowledging the land, our family and where we're from. It was a perfect
way to start the album.

Seeing as I can't play it for you, I'm gonna run you through some of my favourite lyrics. Let's start serious. With the first song on the album, 'Blue Notes', I wanted to talk about the passing of loved ones and the fine balance between mourning their loss and appreciating life.

It's funny how God teaches lessons
Sending your loved ones back to the so-called essence
I count my blessings I guess since the days of a youngan, raised
as a Tongan . . .

There's a very fine line between sounding sincere and sounding corny when writing about something like this. I knew that in order to not sound corny, I had to set the tone correctly with the first few lines. I felt like I did that.

With the song 'Bell 47', I discussed losing Bain, the title a reference to the type of helicopter he flew. This tune was hard to write, but I knew it had to be done. And it had to be perfect.

In the memory of my bro, Scott Bain, we set it off
Like the choppers that he loved so much
We touch down for the sounds that we've got sewed up . . .

Much like 'Blue Notes', I had to set the tone off strongly and keep away from being clichéd. And if you do get to hear this song, you'll hear a chopper sound that Daniel made by cutting a record back and forth. To wrap it all up, we had one of the boys offer a prayer in the middle to really send the message home. The song contains a lot of hurt, but also a lot of heart. I remember playing it for Tunks when we first recorded it. The three of us sat in silence as the song played, and before it was finished I got a text message. It was Tunks from the other side of the room, too choked up to talk and not wanting to speak over the song. *This is really good, bro*, he told me. *Proud of ya.* That was all I needed to hear.

Now, from the serious to the profane. Daniel and I were getting heavily into old reggae, dancehall and ragga around this time, which was really obvious in a lot of the samples we chose. Tunks was the man with the tunes and the knowledge; he schooled us on the early stuff, then Daniel and I took it from there. The song 'Run the Place Hot' is a good example. 'I grew up with respect so to Dad I give thanks / Have a quick wank, listen to Cutty Ranks.' This is a reworking of Phife Dawg's line in 'Jazz (We've Got)' by A Tribe Called Quest. The Five-Foot Assassin says, 'I grew up as a Christian so to Jah I give thanks / Collect my bank, listen to Shabba Ranks . . .' I wanted to tip my hat to Quest and get cheeky with it, replacing Shabba with Cutty, another legendary Jamaican dancehall DJ. (RIP, Phife Dawg.)

Let me hit you with one more. And this one is vintage Hau, if I do say so myself. Man, I was such a smart arse on and off the mic (still am), and this side of me was always creeping into my lyrics. On the song 'Phenomenomenonone', I rap, 'They call me Tip Top cos I'm good on ya mum . . .' That's me flipping the meaning of a jingle for the bread company Tip Top. The line goes, 'Good on ya, mum. Tip Top's the one. Good on ya, mum!'. *Haha* – people loved that one.

Okay, class dismissed.

In September 2002 I was in Sydney, spending time with my niece, when Shani and I took her to see the animated film *Lilo & Stitch* at the Hoyts Cinema on George Street. As we were picking up the tickets, I realised I needed to call Teniela.

'I'll meet you in there,' I told Shani, who just gave me a look in return. She knew exactly what I was about to do.

I called Teniela from the payphone outside. We must have talked for over an hour. Like always, the conversation was going round in circles: me trying to comfort her but getting annoyed; her trying to explain to me how she felt but resenting me for not understanding. We were talking in two different languages. Meanwhile, Shani was inside taking care of my niece. When I managed to take my seat for the second half of the film, I could see she was pissed. I didn't take this too well, if I'm honest.

Why is she annoyed with me? I thought. *We're not even official.*

Looking back, it's painfully obvious. I was trying to please everyone but, really, I just ended up hurting them both. I never did have the heart to end things properly with Teniela. I retreated further and further until she got sick of trying to contact me. Then we stopped talking. And we haven't spoken since.

SECOND TO MUSIC

Whatever shit the boys were into, I tended to leave them to it. But after things ended with Teniela, there were a few instances where I decided to get involved. No one forced me; I chose to do what I did. There was one time when an acquaintance approached Hasim about a woman who was being harassed by some guy – an ex-boyfriend, I think.

'We want it to stop,' he told Hasim.

The woman's friend was the one who had reached out. The job seemed simple enough: rough the guy up a bit to scare him into leaving her alone, then get a little sum of money in return. Hasim said yes and asked me to drive. *Sure, why not?* To be honest, I didn't have the heart to do things like that for no reason. If the guy owed some money or something like that, I wasn't down. But if I heard he deserved it, then I could talk myself into it.

The others knew the guy's routine. They told us to go first thing in the morning and we'd find him leaving for work. We got there a few minutes early and waited. Sure enough, he came out of the house on time and headed for his car. Hasim got out and asked the guy for directions. Getting close to him, he held out a piece of paper, as if to demonstrate where he wanted to go.

As soon as the dude stooped his head to take a look, Hasim dropped him. *Crack!* The guy hit the floor. I started the car as Hasim legged it back and we got the hell out of there. We heard a few days later he got the message. Mission accomplished.

The next time, we were a bit bolder. The guy in question was also in the wrong, so I felt okay doing what we did. On this occasion, Hasim and I staked out the place together, waiting outside where he worked then following him back to his place. The first night he wasn't there, but we returned on the second to find him at home. Rather than wait for him to come out, Hasim knocked on the door and chased him through the house. A few minutes later, Hasim sprinted out of the still-open front door before jumping into the car.

'*Drive!*'

I dropped Hasim off at home and we both laid low for a couple days.

There's no doubting these were dumb things to do. We could have easily been caught or picked on the wrong guy, but it never seemed that deep at the time. I know it sounds convenient to say this now, but I always felt in control. This is probably because I didn't have a *need* to do some of the things I did. I guess I just did them because they seemed fun and exciting at the time.

Most people who get involved in street stuff do so because of one or both of the following: there's something missing at home – money, love, etc. – or because that's what everyone around them is doing and they don't see another route. Neither applied to me. My parents couldn't have been more loving, and they always put food on the table. To be honest, it's partly *because* they were so loving that I had the luxury to do some of the shit I did. It wasn't like my home life was falling apart and I was forced to become a criminal.

My parents got on my back about finding a 'proper career' every now and again, but the home they created was safe and supportive. I could dip in and out as I chose, knowing when to not take part in anything *too* serious.

A big part of that was the company I kept. Tunks, Metro and the rest of them might have *looked* like tough cunts, but they were also genuinely good people. They wanted to see me do my music, not get wrapped up in what they had going on. Whenever any of the KOA boys visited my home, it was nothing but respect. They'd take their shoes off, say hello to my mum, shake my dad's hand. My parents loved my friends and vice versa – Tunks especially. Because he grew up with Tongans, he automatically knew the importance I placed on family, and he never tried to sway me from that.

That's the thing about choosing the street path: you better be built for it. I wasn't. I was built to be an MC. If being a criminal is what you want to do, you better be prepared for the consequences. Luckily, I was able to avoid them – though there was one time when I thought for a second it was all over.

I was with Hasim, heading back to Canberra after visiting Sydney to pick 'something' up. The drive home was dark, and we started to feel tired, so I suggested we take a pill, half-expecting it to keep us going. (Really, I just wanted to take a pill.)

'Yeah, fuck it. They're in the back,' Hasim said.

With Hasim driving, I reached into the back seat and took two pills from where he was keeping the stash. It wasn't long before they started to take effect. We were laughing and listening to music, and soon we were approaching Lake George, a huge body of water that signals you're not far from Canberra.

As we neared the lake, there was a truck a hundred or so metres ahead. Hasim was picking up speed and we were getting closer and closer to the truck. A hundred metres turned to fifty. Then twenty.

OK, I guess he's going to overtake. Then ten metres. I turned to Hasim and the fucking guy was fast asleep!

'Hasim!'

As I screamed, he jolted awake and tightened his grip on the wheel, swerving to avoid the truck. On the way past we clipped its back wheel and went flying into a guard rail. We didn't total the car or anything, but it was pretty beat up. As we got out, checking ourselves for injuries, the driver of the truck came running towards us.

'You boys okay?' he shouted.

'Yeah, yeah, all good, bro!' we told him. We were trying to act casual but the adrenalin combined with the ecstasy had us rushing hard. The last thing we needed was cops arriving. The driver stopped as he got close, probably seeing us chewing our faces off, and hesitated for a second before getting back in his truck and driving off. *Thank fuck.*

Then the paranoia started to set in. *What if he did call the cops?* He clearly saw we were off our faces. *Shit.* I started to panic. Turning around, I found Hasim hiding behind the car with his pants down. 'Bro, what the *fuck* are you doing?' He had taken the little bag with the rocks of coke inside and was stuffing it up his arse.

'In case the cops come,' he said. 'Quick, let's get out of here.'

We drove the last thirty kilometres or so in stunned silence. All I kept thinking was, *We could have died.* Hasim, meanwhile, kept shifting around in his seat – clearly those rocks weren't sitting too comfortably. When we finally arrived back in Queanbeyan, the fear had subsided, replaced by relief.

'Man, that was a close one,' I said, turning to face Hasim for the first time.

'Yeah man, that was fucked.'

'I'm still buzzing. What you wanna do?'

'Casino?'

'Sure.'

We went to the casino and spent the rest of the night drinking and reliving our near-death experience. The next day we knew we had to tell Tunks – after all, he was big bro, and he'd find out some way or another. But Hasim wasn't about to cop the blame.

'It was a fox,' he said. 'The little cunt just ran in front of us!'

'Oh yeah?' Tunks just shook his head, half-amused, half-disappointed. From then on, the 'ghost fox' became a running joke – whenever someone would get into trouble, they had an excuse at the ready.

Must have been the fox!

I was back home in Queanbeyan when Shani called, setting an ultimatum. 'I can't keep up like this,' she told me. 'I want to be with you, Hau. Either we're doing this or we're not.' It took me off guard, but I knew she was right: I had to choose. The thought of having something – or someone – distract me from my music didn't sit well. I told Shani I needed time to think.

I called Hasim. My right-hand man. 'Bro, Shani wants to make it official.'

'Yeah?' He didn't sound enthused. 'You want to do this now? You really want to get tied down, just as stuff's going well with your music?' I wasn't sure. Then he started hitting me with the hypotheticals. 'Say you're at a gig and some chick comes up to you after the show. She's bad as fuck and she's all over you. You telling me you're going home to Shani?'

He was trying to talk me out of it, afraid to lose his partner in crime, but Hasim's words had the opposite effect. *Yeah*, I thought, *going home to Shani is exactly what I'd do. These other women don't compare.* Because, really, it had *always* been about Shani. I tried to tell myself it was just physical, pushing my feelings to the side so rap would remain my number one priority. *It has to be,* I'd told myself. Just like I didn't need a Plan B, I didn't need a relationship slowing me down.

But that was then. I told Hasim I was gonna take a few minutes to think, but I knew I was ready to call Shani back with an answer. I was twenty-six. The past several years had been a wild ride. I'd released six official projects with Daniel, each one getting better and better. I'd joined a crew and lost a close mate. I'd travelled to Europe and recorded with some of my idols in New Zealand. There'd been fights, fall-outs and I'd nearly died – or got arrested – more than once. And then there was the pregnancy. A day didn't go by when I didn't think of how things could have ended so differently with Teniela. *Man, you could be in New Zealand right now*, I told myself, *working a dead-end job and raising a child with a woman you don't love.*

Throughout your life, you are met with a series of intersections – like sliding doors. Opportunities present themselves, and in those moments you either go one way or you go the other. Red pill; blue pill. Sometimes you don't get a choice. Bain didn't have a choice. But I did. Choose Shani, an amazing, beautiful, talented woman who's clearly crazy about me. Who *understands* me. Or what, choose a bunch of hypothetical one-night stands? Fuck that. *Get out of your own way, man. You're ready for your next chapter.*

But there was still one thing I had to say. I called Shani back.

'You're right, Shani,' I told her. 'Let's do this. I want to be with you. But I need you to know one thing.'

'Yeah, what is it, Hau?'

'I need you to know you will always be second to music.'

PART 3
EARN
2003–2011

I'm fresh off the iron horse, of course
I'm found at the train station
Exactly where? Man, I don't know
I'm somewhere lost in translation
Searching for higher ground –
Chinatown, London, Spokane, Tokyo
On award tour with Dan my man and an open road
(so it goes)
A little something like this . . .

– 'Movin', Koolism, 2010

EVOLUTION AND EGOS

The end of 2003 was a major turning point. Hilltop Hoods' third studio album, *The Calling*, became an overnight success, and from that point forward Australian hip hop was changed forever. In fact, it's when Australian hip hop became *Aussie* hip hop, but we'll get into that in a bit.

I was pleased for the Hoods. Since we'd met them after our gig in Adelaide, they'd been putting in work. They had the talent and were pulling in bigger crowds than most acts, even before *The Calling* dropped. If one of us was to blow, it made sense it was the Hoods. Plus, they were – and still are – super-nice guys, so everyone was stoked with their success. It's to their credit that after several number-one albums and all the accolades that go with it, they've never switched up. Real down-to-earth dudes.

Of course, *The Calling* wasn't the first milestone in Australian rap. Sound Unlimited deserve their props for being the first to do it, and then Resin Dogs took it to the next level after they started getting booked at festivals. I remember seeing them interviewed on Channel V after playing Big Day Out in 2001. International stars like Nirvana had played that stage, and then a local hip hop group was on the same bill. That was a big moment. 1200 Techniques were the next to carry the ball further up field. In 2002, their track 'Karma' blew up, winning them two ARIAs and getting them triple j and commercial radio spins, which at the time was unheard of. Another moment.

But Resin Dogs and 1200 Techniques always carried the stigma of not being 'real rap'. Resin Dogs had that big-band energy while 1200 Techniques had a guitarist, so their music was always heavily rock influenced. Whatever you wanted to call it, it was still hip hop, but some in the underground didn't mess with it. Coming out of Perth, Downsyde looked to be the ones who were going to take the scene even bigger. There was no denying Downsyde was straight-up hip hop, and they had a song 'El Questro' that started to be heavily rotated on radio. With its catchy sample full of Latin horns, it was fun and therefore more palatable than a lot of Australian rap at the time, which tended to be darker and grittier. It was one of the first local hip hop songs to be recognised by the mainstream, but that was a few months before *The Calling* engulfed all the attention.

Before this point, Australian hip hop was best characterised as an underground community; for the most part, everyone knew and supported one another. If there was a gig in your city, you turned up and showed support because you knew they would do the same when you toured their city. It was a beautiful time; a lot of lifelong friendships were forged since we were all in it together. Because rap wasn't yet mainstream, we all had a part to play in building the culture. But when *The Calling* started going crazy on triple j and commercial radio, the landscape changed entirely.

The first to come were the egos. Some artists no longer had the time of day for their fans and other aspiring artists. It was like they replaced humility with arrogance overnight. Before, gigs would be like a community gathering where artists and fans would mingle with no real hierarchy. Then some acts went all Hollywood, acting like they were too big of a deal to associate with fans or artists who were on the come up. The funny thing was, this wasn't coming from the Hoods themselves – it was everyone else, as if *they* had somehow blown up by association. I won't name names; I feel kinda bad even talking about it now, since no one ever said anything slick to me. I think because of the way I carried myself and the work I'd already put in, people treated me with respect. But whether it was aimed at me or anyone else, it wasn't a good look.

The next shift was a more gradual, sonic one. It was evident that triple j throwing their support behind the Hoods was a big factor in helping them blow. So younger artists coming up started looking at it like a science: *If I sound like the Hoods then maybe I'll get the triple j co-sign, too?* They started mimicking the sort of songs that were getting a lot of attention – that up-tempo beat with a singalong chorus and festival vibes. It was fun, like the sort of music you'd belt out during a road trip. And then there were the flute samples. 'The Nosebleed Section' was the song to really take off from *The Calling*; it had a flute sample throughout, so people looked at that like a cheat code.

While triple j had been slow in getting involved in hip hop, that's not to say they weren't supporting Black music in general. A few R&B acts, like Perth's Selwyn and Jeremy Gregory from Sydney, who were both signed to major labels, were getting a decent amount of airplay. But this was when R&B was its own distinct thing, far removed from hip hop. Because of what I'd listened to growing up, I always had time for some R&B, but most of the hip hop scene saw it as soft and a bit corny. Until triple j joined the party, real hip hop had been reserved for community radio stations like Sydney's 2SER or Canberra's 2XX. They played a wide range of rap music and, more importantly, they really repped the culture, hosting cyphers, rap battles and things like that.

Regardless of the egos, the weird flute samples and the power of the triple j machine, after *The Calling* there was more attention on Australian rap than ever before. And that was a good thing: the more people listening to hip hop the better; it meant new potential listeners for everyone else. Except that wasn't exactly the case. I remember talking to a few fans who told me, 'We don't like hip hop, but we love Hilltop Hoods.'

Sorry, what? You mean Rakim, Big Daddy Kane and LL Cool J don't do it for you, but the Hoods you like? That was unbelievable to me at first, but then a part of me understood. I guess it's about representation, right? The majority of listeners in Australia are suburban white kids, and they didn't see themselves in a lot of the '90s hip hop. Groups like NWA were a long way from their everyday reality. The same with Australian acts; back then it was a colourful scene, far more so than the country was in general. Because hip hop has its roots in the working class, immigrant and more marginalised communities gravitated towards it early. In Australia, that meant Islanders, Aboriginals, Europeans and other people of colour. That's in part why I felt groups like 1200 Techniques were never fully accepted. It wasn't just that they weren't 'real rap', they weren't 'real white' either. Their vocalist, my bro N'fa Jones, was a tall, handsome, proud Black man with dreadlocks. Not exactly the picture mainstream Australia was used to supporting. The same went for Downsyde, who had one member of Indigenous-Pakistani heritage and another Malaysian-Burmese. In Hilltop Hoods, on the other hand, white kids had found their saviour.

That part I understood; it's the fact that this support came with a side of nationalistic pride bordering on racism that bothered me. As crazy as this sounds, a decent part of the Hoods fanbase were of the opinion that the birthplace of hip hop was the Adelaide Hills. Now, I'm not saying everyone needed to know their BDP from their

MOP like I did, but to not understand – and respect – that hip hop is a Black art form was troubling. All the artists and fans coming up on Australian hip hop in the '90s had the same cultural reference points: we had grown up listening to the same artists and had the same knowledge of the genre's history. The new fans didn't know and, more to the point, many didn't seem to care.

And so 'Aussie hip hop' was born. Gigs went from a supportive, diverse place to a hostile one, with guys turning up draped in the Australian flag and stuff like that. It's not like the Hoods were to blame; if anything they actively tried to move their fans in the other direction, even releasing statements that told fans if they wanted to be racist then they didn't want their support. I felt kinda bad for them – after all, you can't choose your fans.

But not everyone followed suit. Bliss n Eso were the next ones to blow, and you got the impression they were okay with the new legions of fans they were receiving. They released a line of merch with the Australian coat of arms, and a few years later they made the song 'Coastal Kids', supposedly based on Australian culture. It's all about dirt bike riding and surfing, and unsurprisingly it's full of white faces. They knew who their fans were. Watching that I was like, *Wow, you guys are really embracing this.* I don't know if that was their intention, but that's definitely how many of us felt.

This started to alienate a lot of people, especially those of colour. I'd talk to the next generation of listeners and artists, who told me they either didn't like what the Hoods and others were doing, or they did but didn't feel welcome at their shows. They were looked at like outsiders. I hated hearing that. Hip hop was supposed to bring people together, not divide them. Though, there were at least some silver linings to come from all this. As Aussie hip hop became whiter and more exclusive, little pockets of creativity began to open up, as those who felt excluded began doing their own thing. Artists like

Mr Zux and the group K-1 began to pop up, full of kids with African heritage out in Western Sydney. They rapped in accents that reflected their heritage, and even though their fashion was still ripped from the US, they had fresh perspectives, telling unique stories about their countries of origin. They were told they didn't have a place in the new scene, so they carved their own. That was beautiful to see; *that* was hip hop.

Meanwhile, Daniel and I continued in our own lane. While a lot of local artists started trying to replicate the Hoods' formula, I was always more interested in repping *me* and *my* point of difference: being both Tongan and Australian. Besides, we'd never been into copying trends; we wanted to do the opposite of the crowd, not follow them. And it was working for us. We had respect from our peers and the critics were into what we were doing, too. After *Part 1* dropped, an article in the *New York Times* described Koolism as the 'standard-bearer in Australian hip hop'. That was cool to see, but respect can only take you so far. I'd be lying if I said I didn't go through a little self-doubt during this period. I loved watching the Hoods succeed, seeing them secure massive national tours and sell out venues that were typically reserved for international artists, and I was happy with what Daniel and I were doing, but there was a part of me that asked, *When are we gonna break through?* I think every artist goes through these moments. I was usually able to push these feelings aside by asking myself what the alternative was. *Make music that doesn't move or inspire you, in order to get validation?* Hell nah.

With *Part 1* on shelves, we were busy on our follow-up. We had it all mapped out: just as *The Season* and *Blue Notes* came together to form *Part 1,* we were working on the two following EPs, *The Butcher Shop* and *The Epic*, which would form the lead-up to our next full project. We were going to bring it all together with the cover art: in the middle was a Koolism illustration drawn by Tunks, then in each of the four corners was a collage of different images relating to the themes of the different projects. George cut the layout design four ways for each of the four covers. When you brought the EPs together, they would form the complete image.

Most of the music for *The Butcher Shop* was already finished. In keeping with the title, it was us on our gangster shit – Daniel's super-hard, grimey beats and me rapping my arse off – but it was proving difficult getting Daniel motivated to actually complete the project. His attention span was fleeting, so if he moved on to something else it was almost impossible to get his focus back. It started driving me fucking crazy. We'd finish a song during a session then I'd return the next day and it would be different.

'What happened here?'

'Oh, I'm just playing around with a few things,' he'd tell me. And then the song would sit there unfinished while he shifted to something different.

And there was nothing I could do. As Daniel was the man with the technical skills, I was essentially at his mercy. I had to wait until he'd worked his magic before anything could be released. It was starting to cause an issue but, if I'm honest, it was usually worth it. Daniel's quirks were all in pursuit of better quality music. He was always striving for perfection, even if it meant things didn't get finished. It was the same for our live shows. In the lead-up I'd be doing the rounds of the venue, chopping it up with fans and other artists, while Daniel would be working right up to the point we went on stage. It didn't matter if we had done the exact same set the night before – he'd be busy tweaking something that, to him, didn't sound right. Even if no one else would notice. His records would be strewn across the floor, the show minutes away from starting, and he'd be scrambling around like a mad professor mixing potions in his lab. The same qualities that made him a nightmare at times were the exact things that made Daniel great.

Queanbeyan has always been a safe place for me. It's home. There may not be much going on but it's got my family, and more often than not that's all I need. And since Sabne had moved home with her daughter, Sabrina, the house was buzzing with life again. On the days Sabne worked, I got to take care of my niece, taking her to and from school – just the two of us. It was always something I looked forward to. Things with Teniela may have gone left, but I was still ready for my role as the cool uncle.

In late 2003, I started to feel a shift in myself. Small moments, like dropping Sabrina off at the school gates or helping my dad out round the house, usually filled me with joy. And even though Daniel was making me tear my hair out, we were still sitting on good material. But something was missing, and I couldn't figure out what. I was getting irritable; I struggled to get out of bed some mornings. It was a feeling I'd never experienced before, and haven't since. Looking back, it's a classic case of depression, but I didn't know that at the time.

It came to a head one morning during the school run with Sabrina. I dropped her off, and instead of driving home, I just sat there staring out the window. It was like all the energy and motivation had been sucked out of me. Previously, I was unshakeable in my belief in what Daniel and I were doing, but my routine had become stale and uninspiring. I was watching other artists we'd come up with take off, and here I was in Queanbeyan, staying still.

I needed to switch things up. Maybe moving to Sydney was the answer?

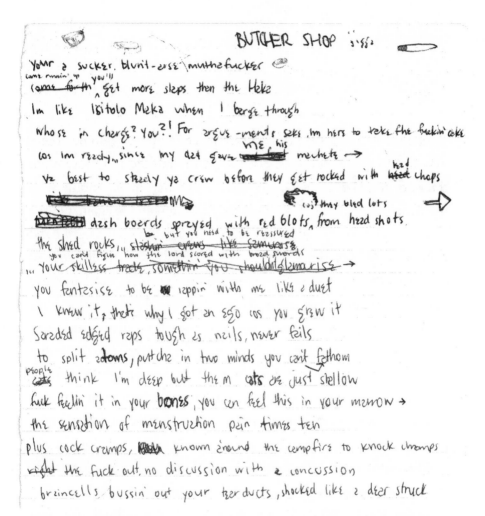

BUTCHER SHOP

Your a sucker, blunt-arse muthefucker
come runnin' up you'll
come forth get more slaps then the Heke
Im like Isitolo Meka when I berge through
whose in charge? You?! For argu-ments seks, im hers to take the fuckin cake
me his
cos im ready, since my dad gave ~~it~~ machete →
yr best to steady ya crew before they get rocked with ~~head~~ head chaps
cos they bled lots →
dash boards sprayed with red blots, from head shots,
but you need to be reassured
the shed rocks, slashin crews like samurse
you cant figur how the lord scored with broad swords
... your skilless tracts, somethin you shouldnt glamarise →
you fantasise to be rappin with me like a duet
I knew it, thats why I got an ego cos you grew it
Serated edged raps tough as nails, never fails
to split ~~atoms~~, puttchs in two minds you cant fathom
people
~~cats~~ think I'm deep but them cats ae just shallow
fuck feelin it in your bones, you can feel this in your marrow →
the sensation of menstruation pain times ten
plus cock cramps, known around the campfire to knock champs
~~right~~ the fuck out, no discussion with a concussion
braincells bussin out your tearducts, shocked like a deer struck

WATSON

Koolism was never just me and Daniel. It was a family affair, with Tunks, George, Travis, Alvin, 'Uli, Mai and all the rest of the guys contributing in some shape or form, every step of the way. That's why you've heard from a few of them throughout this journey – there's no way I would be here if it wasn't for them. We may have been a chaotic family, but we were a family nonetheless, and in 2004 we gained a new member.

Real name Dave Atkins, Axe was a professional footy player who got his nickname because he would treat his opponents' necks like chopping blocks. When he played for the Canberra Raiders, he was teammates with a bunch of the Queanbeyan boys I grew up with. One of them mentioned he was a fan of our music and would blast out Koolism in the Raiders dressing room before games. After hearing that, I gave him a subtle shout-out on 'X10' off *Part 1*.

But before we go on, my name's Hau not Ren
It's me again, coming out the lock and . . .
rock fans head bang, with their long hair in head bands
got skaters to players in the Raiders who play this . . .

We eventually hooked up at one of our gigs. The Raiders had just played the Broncos, and after the game when everyone else went to get pissed, Axe rocked up to the show still wearing his Raiders track-suit. He told me that night he'd been a fan ever since I dropped a line off *That Bedroom Shit* about 'kicking goals like David Furner', who he played with at the Raiders.

He may have earned his money on the footy field, but at heart Axe was a rapper. We hit it off straightaway, and he quickly became a part of the crew, contributing to song ideas and jumping on stage with us at many shows. Younger than us by a few years and ambitious, he brought great energy to the studio, which was now at Daniel's new pad in Watson. Compared to his place with Tunks and Travis, the new apartment was tiny, which made the mess even more noticeable. There wasn't even enough space for his records, let alone a bed and several human beings, so he maintained his vampire ways and would sleep sitting up on the couch. And to make matters just that little more interesting, he'd adopted himself a cat. Delightful.

With Axe and everyone else coming through on their days off, the Watson home studio was gross and overcrowded, but musically we were entering the best period of our career. On every project throughout the '90s it felt like we were experimenting, but in Watson we not only had a clearer idea of what we wanted to do, we were more skilled at doing it.

Everyone had a part to play and was playing it well. Tunks, who used to be a little abrasive in his feedback, had learned the art of tact, which helped his message get across. Even Daniel and I were getting better with our critiques. Previously, he was the producer and I was the MC; we would leave one another to do their job. But after *Part 1* we became more confident; Daniel would suggest I redo a line here or offer more emphasis there. It became a proper collaborative environment. That's where the magic happens.

It was during a studio session in Watson when I decided I wanted to stop swearing in my raps. Maybe it was adolescence or maybe it was spending so much time with Tunks, who swore every second word, but it had become second nature for me. I wanted to get out of the habit. For one, it meant my niece Sabrina would be able to listen to my music. I'd also begun to think it was just lazy. Swearing so often meant I wasn't flexing my vocabulary, which for an MC like me is where I draw my strength. And it wasn't just in my lyrics; I wanted to cut it in conversation, too. This way, if I did decide to swear, it would have a much bigger impact. Tunks and Daniel would press me about it, claiming I was self-censoring. I didn't understand that. Self-censoring is when you're not doing or saying something you normally would in your everyday life. This was me trying to grow, to change my behaviour on and off the mic for the better. Once I explained myself, they dropped it.

I was listening to a lot of Jay-Z at this point. It was handy because I could get inspired by Hov and very few people could tell, because not many of us in Australia were really into him at the time. Well, the underground heads weren't, anyway. We were all about Nas. Jay was the slick rapper, talking about money and fame, which was less relatable to Australians. If anything, he was considered corny. Give him a few years and he'd be on everyone's top-five list. Lil Wayne's group The Hot Boys was another influence during the Watson sessions. Travis was always playing them, but at first I didn't get it. Then I heard the song 'Bling Bling' and all the dots connected. Like the Hot Boys, Southern hip hop is all about the energy and that bounce. Listening to them, I learned to rein in the lyricism at times and focus more on the feel of the song.

As our confidence grew, Daniel and I became more creative and playful with our ideas, like making our own sound effects and ad-libs to build a sense of atmosphere. It was something we picked up from De La Soul and Public Enemy and a way to include the wider crew in the album-making process. For a song we had planned for *The Butcher Shop*, I had a line about chopping something, so we had Tunks re-create a knife hitting a chopping board. Not one to cut corners, he went and got himself a massive meat cleaver, which cut straight through the board, nearly slicing his hand off in the process. There was another line about making a toast to Daniel, so we all got drinks and re-created the clinking of glasses. This one proved more problematic than I'd imagined. Daniel's girlfriend at the time was in the studio that day, and she was a mad weed smoker. When we asked her to join us for the toast, she told us she didn't drink.

'Yeah, that's cool,' I explained. 'It's just a sound effect – you don't actually have to drink anything.'

'Yeah, no . . . I know. But I don't drink.'

'You don't have . . . Never mind.'

One of my favourite songs from this era is 'Adrenalin'. Daniel killed it on the production. Just listen to the percussion, the sample (no finding this one on Whosampled.com!), the synths, the bassline . . . amazing. Whenever he brought his A game like that, it inspired me to be on point with my pen.

Siana, it's all mana, when we step inna de place
chase the dream like a lemon after a shot of tequila
the venomous talk, taught to be all I can be and ah . . .
what I can be is one killer MC . . .

'*Siana*' is a Tongan word for something like 'man' and 'mana' and is a pretty universal Pasifika word for 'pride'. Don't tell me that wordplay isn't hard. Your favourite rapper could never.

But there's no magic without a bit of tension. It was steadily becoming more challenging handling Daniel's moods. He could be on top form one day, full of ideas and motivation, and then the next he might not say a word. He was the definition of a chaotic, cantankerous genius. This is where Axe really stepped up. Daniel and I had been in each other's pockets for a decade by this point, so having Axe as a third wheel helped defuse a bit of tension. Daniel was more likely to open up to Axe if something was wrong, so it helped him get things off his chest without creating arguments. It was a roundabout way of doing things but it worked. Sometimes, if Daniel was in a funk and we had songs to finish, I'd just send Axe to the studio to save any dramas occurring. We both had a running joke: before studio sessions we'd go to the servo across the road for supplies to help manage Daniel's mood. We'd buy three things: a Cherry Ripe, a can of Coke and garlic bread. You never knew what vibe he'd be on, but this would always sweeten the deal.

Cracks were appearing in our relationship, and Axe was helping us paper over them with service station snacks.

Our first international feature was recorded in Watson. Our manager, Blake, was one of the first promoters to bring rap artists from overseas to Australia and had booked Rodney P of London Posse, along with his mate DJ Skitz, to play a run of shows across the country. I'd been a fan of London Posse for years, even before Tunks came back from his trip to Europe with his bags stuffed full of records. Their debut album *Gangster Chronicle* is a straight-up classic.

Blake told Rodney about us and he agreed to come through the studio. Thankfully, Daniel cleaned up a bit and stole a few milk crates from the local shops for seats. I was rocking my Evisu jeans and an Armani cap when he showed up.

'I see you stylin', bro!' Rodney said when he saw me.

What's the saying: real recognise real? Yeah, something like that. He was dressed sharp and simple: fitted jeans, a tracksuit top with the Jamaica colours and a pair of Stan Smiths. A real London geezer, he was exactly as I'd hoped and imagined: super friendly, cool and laid back. He just seemed happy to be there.

KOA had a connection with London Posse after Tunks had hooked up with some of their wider crew – Drax and King Robbo (RIP) – while he was living in London. You've probably heard of Robbo. He was the one who allegedly slapped Banksy back in the day. The story goes they were both at a bar in London, and apparently Banksy was acting like a jerk. Robbo asked Banksy if he knew who he was, to which Banksy replied, 'No.' Which was a lie – a big deal in the graffiti world, everyone knew King Robbo. Robbo took one look at him and slapped him across the face, telling Banksy, 'Well, you'll never forget me now.'

After discussing our mutual friends, we got down to business. Daniel pulled up the beat and we asked Rodney if he was keen to lay a verse. He said he was.

'Sweet!' I replied. 'What do we pay you, bro?'

'Get me a bag of weed, a bottle of Jack Daniel's, a box of KFC and let's work.'

Now *that* was some gangster shit! The song was called 'Warm and Easy', and after eating, Rodney wrote and recorded his verse in less than an hour. His superpower was his charisma and simplicity on the mic – it was all in his delivery – so a couple takes was all he needed. I decided to just take in the experience – one of the hip hop originators on the same track with us! – and write my verse later. And we didn't have much time, anyway. Rodney and Skitz had a show that night in Canberra, so we had to get moving.

I drove with Rodney and Skitz, and on the way to the venue they were telling me how excited they were to see a kangaroo while they were in Australia. I'm not sure they were prepared for it when they did.

'Look, there's one there!' I said, pointing out the car window.

'Where?' Excited, Rodney and Skitz were searching the horizon for this mythical creature they'd heard so much about.

'On the side of the road, mate.'

Apparently roadkill wasn't what they had in mind. I had to explain that, yes, kangaroos are beautiful creatures but in Canberra, where there's so many of them, they can become pests. Then I told them we even eat them, and it was like telling a kid Santa Claus doesn't exist. I changed the subject.

The gig was at Club Mombasa, the same spot where we'd had the massive brawl that ended with Hasim bringing out a nine-section whip. (Somehow, we hadn't been barred.) The place was packed when we arrived. A rival crew was in the building, but the beef wasn't that deep so we ignored them. After a quick drink Rodney kicked things off, mainly playing old London Posse tunes as well as a bunch of freestyles and a few solo joints. Skitz and Rodney had that same natural energy on stage that Daniel and I had; they didn't have to force anything. A lot of what they did was inspired by the Live PA style of music, like you see at Caribbean raves: the DJ plays the beat with the MC 'toasting' over the top, which is like rapping but more free form. All charisma, Rodney could switch between London cockney slang and Jamaican patois within the space of a few bars, without missing a beat. Incredible. After a few songs, he shouted me and Daniel out and brought me up on stage. We had nothing rehearsed but you know I was ready with a couple freestyles. Those Toolshed years had paid off.

Approaching me after the show, Tunks was buzzing. 'Those dickheads came to see Rodney P and you're on stage with him,' he said laughing. 'They must have been spewing!'

We joined Rodney and Skitz for their Melbourne show a few days later. This time, there were a bunch of local acts on the bill;

us and the Hoods were the main support, while a few others including Mnemonic Ascent and Lyrical Commission also played a set. It was a big showcase of Australian hip hop alongside one of the UK's greats. But the afterparty was even more memorable than the show. A few of us went back to the promoter's house to kick on, and after a couple drinks someone pulled out the E, offering me and Rodney a pill.

'Ah man, I may go a little crazy on a whole one,' said Rodney.

'Wanna split one?' I offered.

Rodney P verse 2

(for real) deal riddim killers - stealin' the show
murderers - killin' the beats, killin' the flow
Glo-bal rude boy shit, spit it with ease
the get away car driver with a trick up his sleeve
believe we, home boy, we came to mesh it
as if you didn't know, between the K and A is the 'Oh!'
my gosh, watchovas off we go
dying to get out like a costrophobe
(ya lost the road now you wanna get back on the right path)
(watch me get loose on that tight ass)
Danielson puntur lungs spin the dub
you know where we'll fuckin' be - you can find me in da club
bottle full of bub'. look brother I swing it if you wanna snug up
on the rug.
its lights out!

AXE

It was back in 1997 when a mate of mine took me to Next Level Records in Sydney and provided me with the first opportunity to own a piece of Koolism history. I'd heard about Koolism, but at the time I actually knew more about Tribe Ledda L and the KOA crew. To be honest, my key mission was to hunt down these Toolshed tapes, which were proving more elusive than capturing compelling evidence of Sasquatch (probably for good reason too!). I saw a Koolism cassette on the countertop and asked the fella working there, 'Are these lads good?' He was like, 'Hell yeah, they're dope!' So I purchased it; the beats were dope and the MC was talking about footy, Canterbury leisure gear and being an all-round sick cunt. I really dug it and still feel it holds up today.

A year later, I was playing professional footy for the Canberra Raiders and I lived in an apartment close to the city centre. One day, I saw a flyer for a Koolism gig and that's the first time I met Hau. Soon after, I bumped into Hau and Tunks at Landspeed Records while I was there digging for records. The three of us had a yarn, and that's when things really started. Shortly after, I went to England for a few years to play in the Super League for the Huddersfield Giants.

We had formed a bit of a friendship and would text rap battles back and forth. We were just connecting, ya know. On return from England I re-signed with the Raiders and snapped both the ligaments in my right knee. After that, I was ready to call it a day in regards to playing footy and focus on what I was always more passionate about, which was music. I started going to more gigs, and Hau and Daniel would do this thing at their shows when they'd invite a few of the local MCs on stage. There was one gig where Hau got me up to do an actual verse with him. I was probably meant to hop off stage after, but I stayed up there and just did back-ups for the track 'Adrenalin'. After that, Hau asked if I wanted to come on tour and be his hype man. I was like, 'Yeah cool – sounds fun!'

By then I was already building a good relationship with Hau and Daniel, and I was gravitating towards them as people. And I had friendships with both of them, but the relationships were very different. You know, Hau's the extrovert – he's that cool dude who everyone loves. And then Daniel is this mad, big-hearted introvert. In many ways I became this sort of unofficial third member of the group.

I was in Watson for a lot of the making, mixing and mastering of their next album. I was there a lot of nights just chilling with Daniel while he worked on the tracks. It took him two to three weeks just to mix a single song at times. He took his time perfecting it. I was probably there, like, four nights a week, and Daniel was so engrossed in the album he was living on crumbs. Daniel would have this joke that he'd do anything for a bag of chips and a bottle of Coke, 'cause that's just how he was living.

There was definitely tension between the two of them. They are just very different people. And I'm sure Hau worked very hard on his lyrics, but Daniel is like a genius and a perfectionist. So for him to do things to the level that he wanted, it was an incredibly long journey. And there would be some frustrations. Hau would often say, 'Mad, this sounds great.' And Daniel would be like, 'No it doesn't!' Because I got on so well with both of them I became this independent body that they could come to, talk to and confide in, knowing that I wouldn't relay it to the other person. Because, you know, sometimes people need to get things off their chest. It doesn't necessarily mean that you're attacking the other person; sometimes you just need to get it out. Then everyone feels better. I became like a buffer, someone who they could talk to and say how they were feeling. It's more about saying it than acting on it.

Then with the shows, I think I added my own element. I brought my own style to it, and naturally we just vibed. If Hau was having a night where he couldn't remember lyrics or something, he would throw to me so he didn't have to carry all that weight. And if Daniel was stressing out about something, there's someone else there who can say, 'Hey, I get it, man. I understand – it's fucked.' Daniel would always just say, 'That's enough, all I needed was for someone to validate how I feel.'

Later, when that stuff happened with the records, that brought a lot of stress on the group. Daniel and I spoke about it for years after, so I know it impacted him heavily. And for Hau. I think because they didn't have that awareness of the stress that it placed on each other, it was just a trigger moment for both of them.

THE GAELIC CLUB

By the end of April 2004, Daniel and I were sitting on a ton of new material. *The Butcher Shop* and *The Epic* were nearly ready to go, as well as a bunch of new stuff, but we began to have our doubts organising the release of our next project. We had decided on our plan for the EPs years ago, but when it came time to actually release *The Butcher Shop*, the first of the final two EPs of the series, the music felt dated. We were more excited to release all the new joints we'd cooked up in Watson.

So we parked the EPs to one side and put the new shit forward for our next full studio album. It just made more sense. Had we released the EPs, we would have to wait a year or two to drop the new stuff, by which point it might no longer have its appeal. We would be stuck in a loop playing catch-up. Daniel and I decided that, if we wanted, we could always come back and revisit *The Butcher Shop* and *The Epic* if and when it felt appropriate. This probably seems funny now. *Why don't you just drop the EPs as free mixtapes on streaming services a few months before the album?* In 2004, it wasn't that simple. The cost and time involved in producing and recording all that music would have broken us.

We thought up a funny marketing ploy to explain ourselves. Rather than calling the next album *Part 2*, which would have been the logical follow-up to *Part 1*, we skipped straight ahead to *Part 3*. So when anyone would ask what happened to Part 2, we'd just say we'd advanced beyond it. We then added the 'Random Thoughts' to the title, as it summarised the feel of the album, which flowed together like a stream of consciousness – or random thoughts.

So, *Part 3: Random Thoughts* was released on 10 May 2004, via Invada Records – an indie label run by my guy Katalyst – and distributed by Inertia, who had a big part to play in building Australian hip hop culture. Since the Hoods blew, more eyes and ears than ever were on local rap, but Inertia had been investing in the culture for years. They were pushing electronic music and hip hop way before it became a trend.

When the album was out I knew we had made the right decision; this was our best work to date, there was no denying that. It felt like our arrival. You often hear artists, especially rappers, talk about the importance of their debut album. You get to distil all your life experiences up until that point into one body of work that will be your introduction to the world. It's a high some artists never reach again. With us, it felt like we'd been building towards this moment. *This* was the project that would define us.

I was growing as an MC. I'd never shied away from difficult subject matter, but now that I was no longer overworking tracks with too many lyrics, I was able to actually capture what I felt. It was the first time I was getting really intimate and personal on the mic – not just reflecting what's going on around me, in my community, but trying to come to terms with whatever *I* was feeling. The song 'Self Portrait' is probably the most personal I ever got:

Back in the day, I'm not as young, I'm not a kid anymore, but
    some days I sit and wish I was a kid again

A 27-year-old citizen of life, no kids, no wife, I'm quite happy
    with how things are going knowing I've got a loving fam'
    and supportive friends
So I know I've got a roof over my head and never short of
    ends . . .

This is why Daniel and I were such a good duo. This song isn't just about my lyrics; I was inspired to go there because of Daniel's production. In Watson, he bought a piano and an electric guitar and was experimenting more with live instrumentation. With this song he was really in his bag. Watching him work like that pushed me to go places I hadn't been on the mic; I even discussed my leg for the first time:

Had to prove to myself,
    that even with my leg I didn't need help,
See, as a baby I had an operation on my right calf
    that cast a complex on my arse.
Even though I had less power,
    I'd still tower and devour competition like . . .

When Tunks heard those lines he knew straightaway their significance. For a rapper, like any artist, the more honest you are with yourself, the better you are at your craft. As a teenager I never really talked about my leg, but it still lingered in the back of my mind. Acknowledging its impact in a song was me being totally honest, with my listeners and myself. It was a stepping stone in my development.

The cover art reflected the intensely personal feel of the album. The photo is in Tonga, of me and my dad when I was younger. It's an image that represents family and a lot of love. The way we're sitting, as if looking out on an ocean, encapsulates the sense of reflecting on the past while also looking to the future. Daniel designed the actual layout. He was into a lot of Japanese art at the time, and you can see that in the rising sun imagery. He would make the layout by literally cutting things up, pasting them back together and then photographing the final product. Not only did it always create something unique, it mirrored the DIY nature of our music.

People seemed to be feeling the album, but it was always hard to get a read on how well it was doing in general. Remember, this was before the internet really took off, so word of mouth still had a big part to play. You had to go out into the world and see it for yourself. With our first national tour booked to start in June, that was exactly what we were going to do. Fourteen dates, starting in Melbourne, passing through Brisbane, Sydney, Adelaide, Perth and finishing in Jindabyne. No longer the supporting act, this was *our* tour, *our* moment.

Since the album dropped, our profile was growing. The first time I knew we were onto something was when I saw someone other than a mate rocking a Koolism T-shirt. Then, I started getting recognised on the street, which at first was a little odd. Considering our history with KOA, I often mistook the attention for someone wanting to start something.

The *Random Thoughts* tour began in Melbourne, but it wasn't until we passed through Sydney that the show really started. The gig was at the Gaelic Club in Surry Hills, which in itself proved how far we'd come. We were used to playing the iconic hip hop venues like Oxford Street's Goodbar and Blue Room, but the Gaelic Club represented the next level up. It had a capacity of around 800, so when you started getting booked to play there, you knew you were on the right track. Until that point, I'd only ever been as a fan. The whole night felt surreal. It was Daniel's birthday. Mahem did an opening

DJ set, which was super rare, and the place was packed. Daniel and I killed it.

The next night we played Katoomba in the Blue Mountains. The gig was another success, but it was what happened after that mattered. The moment that changed everything.

Daniel was visiting his grandad in the Blue Mountains after the show, so Shani and I packed the gear and drove back that night in her little Mazda Eunos. We should have just got a hotel, but Shani had work the next day so we stayed at her place, arriving home around two or three in the morning.

We parked the car in the private lot under Shani's building and went to bed. I woke the next morning to Shani calling in tears.

'It's gone!' she screamed down the phone. 'They've stolen it!'

'Stolen what?'

I couldn't understand what she was saying through her sobs, but I could tell she was still downstairs. I went to see what was going on. Scrambling to get changed, I ran to the parking lot to find Shani standing in front of her car with glass by her feet. The windows had been smashed.

Oh fuck . . . our gear!

During the night, someone had broken into the backseat of Shani's car and stolen our equipment from the show. I stood there panicking – everything we had was in that car: Daniel's records for our live shows, zip discs with all our unreleased material . . . everything.

I felt like I could kill someone. With Shani in shock, I checked the boot of the car where we'd left Daniel's DJ hardware – thankfully, it was still there. That meant it was just an opportunistic smash-and-grab; everything they'd taken would have had little to no value to anyone but us.

When I called Daniel he was surprisingly chill about it. Or, more likely, he was also in shock. We were halfway through our tour and our entire set was now missing; the hidden treasures of records that Daniel had picked up crate digging, all gone. For a DJ, your records are what make or break you. Daniel had built up an extensive and rare collection, and it was through all those unique sounds and samples that he'd become the DJ and producer he was. Now, he was going to have to start from scratch.

After Shani went to work, I spent the rest of the day searching through bins in the local area. Whoever had taken our shit would have realised soon after that it was worthless to them. Surely, they would have just dumped it? Like a maniac, I went from Chippendale to Redfern, looking through back alleys and digging in the bottom of bins. Nothing.

Our next tour date was in Wollongong in six days' time, and we had an entire set to rebuild.

Fuck.

DANIEL

Yeah, it's still one of the most pivotal turning points in my life. It still hurts, but not the loss of the stuff itself, just, like, the ramifications of it . . .

There was so much that went into it. I mean, it just burned me out because, leading up to that tour, I went through a process of quitting all my jobs. Before that, I was DJ'ing, of course, but I also worked two full-time jobs at once, in the same building, for two different businesses. So I practically lived there. When I think back, I don't know how we managed to still do shows and make our music and all the stuff that we were doing at the time. If it wasn't for the way I was living, we probably would have been way more prolific.

I never slept. I lived on caffeine and sugar. I don't know how I got through it, but there were a few times where I went three or four days without sleeping, which is crazy and definitely had an effect on my health and my brain. But anyways, at some point it just clicked in my head and I realised, I can't keep living like this. Like, if I wanted to do any of these things, I needed to focus on one thing.

And it felt like we were going somewhere. When Hau and I had only just got together and were promoting our first tape, we did an interview on the local Channel Seven news with Jessica Rowe. And in that interview she asked us what our long-term plan was; for how long would we do this? We had already talked about it and agreed we'd do it until we were about twenty-one. If we weren't getting somewhere by then we'd move on. And here we were nearly ten years later, and finally we were really getting somewhere.

So I leaned into it, quit all my jobs and bought a pair of speakers for about four grand – which was a major investment for me – as well as a new computer. I borrowed some instruments and an old Wurlitzer electric piano and just went to town. For the next six months to a year, all I did was make music. I tried so hard to take it to the next level, and that's all I did. I barely slept, I didn't even have a bed, actually.

I did that pretty much until the Random Thoughts *tour. I remember almost passing out from exhaustion when I handed in the album. But I didn't stop, because I felt like I was hanging my whole life on this. I didn't want to go back to IT or anything like that. I wanted to make it with music.*

When the tour started, the show at the Gaelic Club went off! All those years of doing those routines on stage amounted to this moment in time. It's hard to describe, but there was a lot of energy in that year around local hip hop. And Sydney was our hometown in terms of music. Canberra was, really, but it's such a small place. Sydney considered us to be their group and we had a huge following there already. The whole hip hop scene turned out for our show that night. Def Wish Cast were there; everybody who was anybody in Sydney was there, and everybody loved it. Hau and I felt like we absolutely ripped it up. It was probably the best show that we ever did.

So the next night the plan was that my girlfriend at the time and I would go straight to the Blue Mountains, and Hau and Shani would take the gear, which we never did – I always packed up and lugged the gear myself, because it was my stuff and I was precious about it all and a bit of a control freak. So this was just an unusual night.

When it happened, I went into problem-solving mode and kept the show on the road, but at the end of the tour, or, well, during the tour – and this kills me now to remember it – I was just really angry about it all. So I wasn't really talking to Hau. I was just keeping to myself. It was a bad, bad vibe.

That was kind of the beginning of the end. I've never had family family, but I can say that Hau and I were like brothers, or what I imagined brothers to be. Maybe even better than that. We never argued or anything, we were a unit – you know what I mean? And then that just kind of ruined me emotionally. Because of everything that led up to it, I felt like we'd finally cracked it. All the hard work was starting to pay off. And then it felt like this massive setback.

Yeah, it still hurts.

'AMERICAN WANNABE TRASH'

Despite the loss, we managed to finish the rest of the tour. Daniel used the week break between shows to build a new set, buying whatever records he could through eBay and scrambling together the rest. It wasn't the same but we did it, often explaining to crowds that we'd had all our gear stolen so we were doing the best we could. I think they appreciated the effort and the fact they were getting a one-off performance, but still, it was disappointing.

I never did find out who the thief was. We suspected one of the locals; they seemed kinda shifty and were always turning up in different cars. One day, convinced they were the culprits, I showed up at their place to confront them.

'Oi . . . open up!' I screamed through the screen door.

The front door was closed but I could hear someone inside. Banging on the door, I kept shouting at them to come outside but no one did. After a few minutes I just left it. It was probably for the best; I'm not sure what I would have done if I found out it really was them.

We laboured away at remaking the music that was lost, but we could never recapture the magic. Those studio sessions at Watson were so vibrant. Even if the music seemed nearly identical, every-thing came out as a try-hard remake. After a while, we gave up.

Then we took a break. Things between us were still a little tense since the incident, so Daniel and I took some time off after the tour. Even if it wasn't for the loss, we both needed time apart – from music, from each other. I spent most of my time with Shani in Sydney; Daniel stayed in Canberra with his girlfriend.

The break gave us both an opportunity to reflect on the album. We may have lost all record of *The Butcher Shop* and *The Epic*, but *Part 3: Random Thoughts* was really beginning to pick up steam. The reviews were coming in and they were all really good. The *Sydney Morning Herald* gave it three and a half stars:

> Hau's mellifluous tones and Tongan heritage play an integral part in Koolism's sound. He reaches into a seemingly bottom-less well of personal experience, penning some intriguing rhymes about everything from the attitudes of rock'n'roll sound engineers at live gigs to free-flowing reverie about public transport.

The publications with bigger ties to the underground were even more enthusiastic. *Inthemix* (now *Junkee*) called it a 'great fucking album':

> All in all [it's] a refreshingly different approach to Aussie Hip Hop that people who appreciate good music regard-less of their genre will really get into. Like the Hoods and Hyjack, Bonez & Torcha, they are experimenting musically and pushing some boundaries which in turn is making our home grown scene healthier and stronger. Beg, borrow or steal this album.

All the complimentary words were great to hear, but it was the fact people were understanding and appreciating what we were doing that I found so encouraging. Matt Levinson of *Cyclic Defrost* wrote:

The production and rhymes are killer, but the best thing about *Part 3* is just how much fun it is. It sounds like a band messing around and having fun in the studio, and the fact that it's come through on the record is just as exciting as the wildly original music and lyrics.

'Having fun in the studio' was exactly what we'd done, so it was cool to hear that that was evident to the listeners as well. But what really took me by surprise was when people – mainly DJs – started telling me they had picked *Part 3* on the ARIA preselection nominations list. This was a first for many reasons. Before 2004, the ARIAs barely even acknowledged that hip hop existed. 1200 Techniques had won in 2002 for their song 'Karma', but they were shoehorned into the Independent category. Finally, after the success of *The Calling* had taken local hip hop mainstream, we were finally given a category of our own, the oddly named 'Best Urban Release'.

To hear we were even in the conversation was cool, but I didn't expect anything to come of it. Then, in September, the nominations were released and Koolism was on the list! Our first-ever award nomination. A few of the names alongside us showed how far the ARIAs had to go in their hip hop education. For some reason The Cat Empire and Daniel Merriweather were considered 'urban'. 1200 Techniques and J-Wess, a US-born Melbourne-based producer who was enjoying some commercial success, rounded off the list.

Shani, who had a journo mate who gave her the news early, called me immediately. I'm not sure if it was a spur-of-the-moment thing or if I was subconsciously channelling Rodney P, but I told her I was going to celebrate with one of my old favourites: a box of KFC.

Still, we didn't plan to go. The nomination was validating, there's no doubt about it, but the ARIAs were never on our radar. In the underground hip hop scene, our attitude was simple: they don't care about us, so we don't care about them. It's not like in the States where any up-and-coming artist dreams of winning big at the Grammys one day. Plus, there was the fact our chances of winning were slim to none. *There's got to be at least a few acts with a better shot than us,* we figured. And considering the ARIA board was charging $300 a ticket, Daniel and I weren't sold on the idea of paying that sort of money to show up and lose.

We soon changed our minds. The thought that we might not make it here again made me and Daniel want to go along and see what the fuss was about. So Inertia paid for our tickets, and I bought one for Shani, and the three of us went along to the Sydney Superdome on 17 October. Hosted by Rove McManus, this was the year of Jet, Eskimo Joe and John Butler Trio, who each had seven nominations.

I couldn't control if we won anything, but with the awards broadcast to more than a million Australians, I knew I was going to have to look fresh. For the occasion, my aunty Lesieli, 'Uli's mum, made me a *kahoa*, a Tongan tradition similar to a reef of flowers worn around your neck at special occasions. When I went to her house to pick it up, aunty asked if I had my speech ready.

'I don't have a speech!' I laughed. 'Aunty, there's no chance we're going to win, so I'm not going to bother with all that.'

Made of gardenia flowers, the *kahoa* was stunning. Gardenias hold great significance in Tonga, where they are called *siale*. There are songs written about their beauty and unique scent, and Mum told me that as a young student they would wear them whenever there was a special occasion. My aunty was so keen to make the piece for me that she asked her neighbour to spare some flowers. She told me she murdered the poor plant, she used so much of it.

I felt proud to wear something that was so significant to me and my family on such a big stage, but the thing weighed a ton. It was like carrying a fifty-pound chain around my neck! When it got to the night, I decided to leave it behind. I just didn't fancy lugging it around the whole time and risk losing it. Looking back, that is the first of several regrets of the evening.

When we rocked up to the Superdome, we could tell no one knew who we were, but we didn't give a shit. I wasn't wearing my *kahoa* but you know I was still styyyyyylin'. I had on a pair of fly khaki combat pants and a turquoise shirt, both from 55DSL, a fresh pair of Uptowns, before rounding off the 'fit with my signature Kangol flat cap in all white. Shani was wearing a silky, flowing green dress while Daniel stepped out in a more classic hip hop style – baggy pants, tracksuit top and black baseball cap.

Making our way down the red carpet, we were pointing out all the local stars to one another. 'There's Delta Goodrem,' Shani whispered. 'And Marcia Hines.' Meanwhile, I'd spotted someone else, but I couldn't be certain it was who I thought. *Naaah*, I told myself. *There's no way he's here.* Among the sea of white faces, and us, was a towering Black man, his long, slightly greying dreadlocks hanging loosely by his side. *Wait, it is him!* Excited, I turned to Daniel.

'Yo, it's Kool Herc!'

Standing before us was the man who literally *started* hip hop. He originated the very thing that I had dedicated the past fifteen years of my life to. Let me paint a picture: 1973 was the year, and Herc's little sister was trying to raise money for her back-to-school supplies, so she asked her older brother Herc, who was eighteen at the time, to host a party in their building. On 11 August at 1520 Sedgwick Avenue in the Bronx, Herc threw the now-famous 'Back-to-School Jam' where the very first sounds of hip hop were heard. Playing all the classic funk joints – James Brown and the like – Herc would isolate the instrumental part of the record to focus on the drumbeat, known as the 'break'. By playing two copies of the same record side by side, he was able to stretch out the break, allowing dancers, known as B-boys and B-girls, to do their thing on the dance floor. Over the top, Herc would shout out instructions to the crowd in a rhythmic tone that led to what we now know as rapping.

In other words, the man was a bloody living legend! A true trailblazer, he never quite got the credit he deserved. Others like Afrika Bambaataa and Grandmaster Flash adopted his style and made it commercial, turning it into actual records. Around the time of the ARIAs – thirty years after Herc's famous block party – there was a movement to get him the recognition, and money, he deserved. But all that was going on back in America. In Australia, he was our guest of honour and being treated like the King he was.

We introduced ourselves to Herc and his crew – trying our best not to fan out – before taking our seats. On our table was country singer Adam Brand and a few other people I didn't know. These nights run like a wedding, where you make small talk with those on your table as you wait for the speeches to arrive. Thankfully, our category was during the early part of the evening, with the Black Eyed Peas presenting the award. I was a big fan of the group back in the '90s when they were like an LA version of Tribe and De La. But then they added Fergie to the mix and became super poppy, at which point I lost interest. As Rove introduced the Black Eyed Peas, I noticed a cameraman approach our table, his camera line planted firmly on me and Daniel.

That's a bit weird, I thought. *Do they really have to show our faces when we lose?* Jokingly, I turned to Shani and Daniel and came up with a skit for when we lost. I didn't want to look like those nominees who respond with a fake smile and clapping hands; I wanted to have fun with it. I decided I was going to grab my phone as if Mum was calling, breaking the news that we didn't win.

Then will.i.am and Fergie started announcing the nominations. When they got to us and played the video clip to 'Adrenalin' on the big screen, that's when the whole occasion dawned on me. It was overwhelming to have our creation on display for so many people to see. A lot of hard work and sacrifice had gone into us making it this far.

'And the winner goes to . . . Koolism for *Part 3: Random Thoughts.*'

Wait, what? What did they just say? Koolism? We won?

We won! I couldn't believe it. My attitude wasn't some fake humility – I genuinely didn't think we had a shot at winning. If you watch the video clip, you can see our faces in complete shock, with Daniel just saying, '*What?*' over and over. In the madness of it all, I forgot to give Shani a kiss before I went on stage. Regret number two.

Daniel and I shook hands with the members of the Peas before being given the award by Apl.de.ap. It was at this point I remembered I had no speech. Daniel took the mic first and shouted out the boys.

'Thanks to the KOA crew,' he said. 'Tunksy back home, Blake, Landspeed, all our friends.'

I went next and for a few seconds was lost for words.

'We would like to accept this on behalf of the whole Australian hip hop community,' I said after I'd gathered myself. Then Daniel jumped in.

'To Mnemonic Ascent and all the Australians that keep it real, for want of a better phrase. Be yourselves,' he told the crowd before adding those now-infamous words. 'Enough of that American wannabe trash.'

The crowd went nuts, well aware of the irony of talking about 'American trash' while standing in front of an American group. Noticing this, Daniel quickly clarified his comments.

'No, these guys are all good,' he said, pointing to the Peas. 'But I'm talking about the Australians that wanna be something they're not. That sucks!'

I didn't think much of the comments. After all, it was exactly how we – and a lot of people within the scene – felt. But making our way off stage, I realised a different error: *I forgot to thank Kool Herc for creating the culture we now call home.* You gotta realise, we were in the presence of greatness. How many times – if any – would you have the creator of an entire genre of music alive and in the house. *Damn!* Regret number three.

The afterparty was a lot of fun. Daniel, Shani and I danced for most of the night, buzzed from our win – and a couple of Eric Wrights, our nickname for ecstasy. (Why? Because people used to call them E's for short, which we renamed Eazy-E's after the NWA frontman, and Eric Wright is Eazy's real name. Simple.)

It was crazy to think just a few months before we were close to rock bottom, our records and unreleased material stolen, and our relationships put to the test. Now here we were, ARIA award-winners.

Regardless of our attitude towards the board and their treatment of hip hop, it was still Australian music's night of nights, and to come away as winners was surreal. But it was bigger than me and Daniel. Although the feeling was amazing, the award meant more as a cultural statement. We were the definition of underdogs: just two kids making music in a bedroom, not affiliated with any major labels. Our win was a win for the scene and a win for the kids of colour.

Years later, the Australian singer Adrian Eagle – who has Maltese and Fijian-Indian ancestry – came up to me after a gig and told me how much it meant to see us win. 'When I was a kid, it inspired me so much,' he told me. 'Because I saw myself on that stage.' That meant more than any trophy ever could.

A few days later, we bumped into the Black Eyed Peas and Kool Herc at a club on Oxford Street. Someone grabbed will.i.am and brought him over to where we were sitting.

'You know Hau,' they said. 'You presented him with the hip hop award at the ARIAs.'

will.i.am looked at me without the slightest bit of recognition, and I certainly wasn't about to clamour for his attention. Herc was a completely different story. The man was all smiles and just happy to be there. We started chatting and I told him to put his wallet away; the drinks were on me.

'You sure, man?' he asked in that deep, booming New York drawl of his.

'Bro, it's the least I can do!'

At the end of the night, I went to Herc with a proposition that Daniel had thought of. He was touring Australia, playing a run of DJ shows across the country, and in talking to him I found out he had a short break over the next few days.

'Do you want to come to Queanbeyan?' I asked, to which he obviously replied, 'Where the hell is Queanbeyan?'

'It's only a couple hours south-west of Sydney,' I said. 'Daniel and I are throwing a party to celebrate our ARIA, and we were wondering if you would DJ? I'd pay, of course.'

To my surprise, he was down. He agreed on the spot, saying he'd drive down in a few days to meet us. And that was that – DJ Kool Herc himself, the Godfather of hip hop, would be playing a show in our living room. In the bloody 2620. *Am I fkn dreaming?*

***

26 October, 2004.

To my One and Only Son,

I have a feeling that you are disappointed with our response to your most wonderful and prestigious Aria award achievement.

Son, I hope that after 28 yrs with your Dad and I, you'd know us well enough to understand how much we love you. As for your achievement, or not only you have made us proud, the proudest parents in the world, but you have given us Happiness in its fullest, the ultimate since your sister's and your birth. Your father and I cannot explain to you the way we feel. You have given us so much happiness in the last 28+ years, mostly with the way you have managed to live your life, determination and so much hard work and effort and always on your own, with little input from us. That way, you have taken a big load off our shoulders knowing that you are a very capable and responsible young man and a very clear head, always focused on whatever your goal and direction you have chosen to guide your life. We can never thank you enough Son

I could always rely on my parents' honesty to keep me grounded. When I got back to Queanbeyan and told them about Herc coming, they replied with, 'Oh, that's nice.' *Haha!* They had a cultural icon coming to visit and they were none the wiser. But when it came to rap stuff, they never needed to understand anything more than how much it meant to me. That part, they got.

The day of the party, Mum and Dad helped me get the house set up. It was all the usual stuff: barbecue in the backyard, decks and dance floor in the extension. All the boys were there – they weren't about to miss the opportunity to meet Herc – as well as all my extended family, who were as unphased by Herc as my parents, but happy to be there.

Herc was in top form. Each time I went into the living room and saw his imposing frame behind the turntable, I had to pinch myself. During a break in his set, I found him in the backyard, talking to my dad and uncles. Herc was mid-story, taking them through a graphic account of life in the Bronx in the '80s, detailing how he was stabbed and shot at back in the day. For my uncles, this was a lot to take in. All of them born and raised on plantations in Tonga, Queanbeyan had taken a bit of getting used to. Crack-era Bronx was another level altogether. They just smiled and nodded.

All evening I felt like I was in a dream-like state, floating from one room to another, soaking in the experience, willing time to stand still for just a few moments longer so I could preserve the memory. Thankfully, it sits in my mind today just as strong and vivid as it was then. Not even Tunks' antics on the night could change that.

TUNKS

Oh God, do we have to tell this? I want to be able to go back to the Bronx!

Look, I was out of order. At the party, I hooked Herc and his boys up; I didn't really smoke but they wanted weed so I got it for them. We went out to the car, and it was me and Herc plus a couple of his boys from the States. We got talking about the origins of hip hop, as you do. A few things I said annoyed Herc, because I was saying the Latinos played a big role, and he was adamant that they didn't come 'til much later and their role was fuck all. So I gave a few examples, which probably pissed him off even more – here was this kid from Canberra trying to tell him about hip hop.

I started talking about Rock Steady Crew, and some other acts like Prince Whipper Whip, and these were people he actually knew. He was just like, fuck this guy. This was around the time of the whole 'Hip Hop owes me money' campaign to try and get Herc paid for his contributions. He felt aggrieved, and rightly so. But in my state and being a natural smart-arse, I didn't appreciate that or care – I just wanted to argue my point.

Let's be honest, I shouldn't have been arguing with Kool Herc about hip hop! But he started getting a bit heated, and I responded in the only way I knew how. He was telling me, 'This is how it is, and I'm Kool Herc, and my word is law.'

I said, 'Alright, mate, you're not in the South Bronx now.' I didn't care who he was, and that I might have been wrong, I was just like, 'Nah, this ain't about to happen.' I didn't threaten him or anything; I just let him know that I didn't give a fuck that he was Kool Herc. I didn't tell him I was grateful for him creating this thing that I owe a large portion of my life to – I just switched straight into smart-arse mode. And the other boys in the car weren't happy, either. I was lucky they didn't turn around and start pounding me!

So Herc got mad offended and went back into the party pissed off. It affected the vibe a bit, so I apologised. I didn't pull my head in, but I went over to him and tried to make it sweet.

'You were supposed to be cool,' he said. 'They told me you were the cool one.'

Daniel or someone must have mentioned beforehand that I was going to be there and this and that. I wasn't trying to argue. I apologised, we shook hands, and it was all cool. But it would've pissed Hau off a lot, and Daniel too. This was their day, and it was incredible to have Kool Herc there. That was their way of paying him back for what he gave them, for kickstarting their careers. And Hau put a big chunk of cash in his hand to show his appreciation, which he didn't have to do.

Look, I didn't have to do what I did either, but that's me. I couldn't help myself. When Hau and Daniel heard, they were just like, 'Ahhhh, fuck, not again!' Everywhere we went together, I would cause trouble. Backstage at shows, I'd steal booze from the riders, start paying out the other artists. It was funny shit but it was annoying. Hau was always super respectful, so he allowed me to get away with it, but I know for a fact I caused a lot of dramas.

When Herc left I made sure we were all good. I did it for Hau, and also because I had just disgraced myself. I think I was just overexcited. I'd been up the front, dancing all night, spilling shit everywhere. Because Herc was playing all the classics, ya know. It was a complete spin-out, a mind-blowing moment. You have to remember, I started getting into hip hop around '81, and years and years later all these things had happened that had led to this moment. I just couldn't believe it.

It was a big moment for Hau and Daniel but also for all of us. Everything they did, every victory they had, every accolade they earned, was for the team. It was always a big family effort. And Hau was big on that; everything he's ever done has been for his family and his boys. Daniel, too. Because Daniel didn't really grow up with a proper family and always wanted one, we were his family. And we were a real family. It was years of mega-intense relationships, in and out of each other's lives. We lived together, we worked together, we travelled together, we made music together. It was a tight family, and all their victories were our victories, too.

But when I look back, that night is one of my biggest regrets. It's funny, I guess, but I would have found it a lot funnier if it had happened to someone else!

SYD–NYC

When the dust had settled on the ARIA win and Kool Herc's visit, I was able to reflect on what we'd achieved. The best part for me was what the award meant for my parents. Partly because they had grown up in Tonga and their cultural reference points were so different, and partly because they were that much older, but the very idea of hip hop – and making it your career – was a foreign concept to them. Literally. So, when I came home with such a prestigious award it confirmed the belief they had placed in me. It was something tangible for them, something that let them see how far I'd come but also to show their friends and feel proud. When a reporter for *The Queanbeyan Age* visited our house to interview me, my mum kept the article and proudly hung it on the wall. It's still there today. Growing up, I was usually found in the back pages of the sports section, but here I was, front page. Tunks got it framed and gifted it to me while jokingly saying, 'YOU'VE FINALLY MADE IT!'

I realised the timing was perfect to move out and join Shani in Sydney. It was the beginning of 2005, and I'd just turned twenty-nine. I still loved being around my parents every day but it was time to go my own way. I wanted to be with Shani and a change to my routine couldn't hurt. Now an ARIA winner, I was ready for new challenges in the big smoke.

I quickly learned a few lessons about big-city life. Number one, it pays to have someone acquainted with the area to help you choose a place to live. While Shani was at work I went to visit a few flats before I found one I liked on New South Head Road in Darling Point. It had a view and a beautiful park just opposite. *What's not to like?* We put the deposit down before we realised the Eastern Suburbs has a stigma of being its own little privileged enclave. To be honest, I didn't really care. The spot worked just fine for us.

With living expenses in Sydney a lot higher than in Queanbeyan, I knew I was going to have to get a job. Besides, cashflow in music is too inconsistent to rely on at the best of times. So a mate of mine hooked me up with a casual job at a clothing shop called SP. It was a really cool store, stocking brands outside your everyday Aussie fare. A few of the guys working there recognised me, and there was a good vibe among the crew. They got me hip to a bunch of Japanese denim brands and labels like EDWIN and G-Star, before they were everywhere. It was also my first introduction to proper sneaker culture. They'd have drops of rare new sneakers, like the Nike x De La Soul collaboration, and kids would queue up for hours to get their hands on them. I now own over a hundred pairs myself, so safe to say it had an impact on me.

For some people, getting a casual job so soon after winning a national music award might seem like a let-down, a fall from grace maybe. For me, it was straightforward: *until music is paying* all *my bills, I need another source of income.* Being a cool, broke rapper is not the vibe I was going for. Plus it kept me hungry. Trust me, you work a full shift selling clothes and you'll come home itching to work on your craft. I spent all day thinking up rhymes in my head, or sneaking them onto my pad when there were no customers around.

When I got home, I couldn't wait to put them into song. Daniel would email me beats to write to, and I'd hit up my cousin Hounga's home studio set-up to record demos. It wasn't Watson but it worked.

The life Shani and I started building in Sydney was blissful. I had moved from one house full of love and laughter straight into another. Now in our late twenties, we had done the whole clubbing thing, so we were more content to chill and take in the city at a slower pace. Shani was working a job in marketing on William Street in the city, so we'd often meet up afterwards at the gym before walking home together. This was back when Sydney still had a real vibe to it. It felt *alive*. The constant traffic, the hustle, the sounds and smells – some good, some bad – all of it was new to me and combined to give me a fresh drive to create.

Growing up, I'd always wanted to visit New York – the Holy Land of hip hop – but I never got a chance. Tunks had done it and came back with shitloads of records to play and stories to share. Now, it was finally my turn. When we found out a friend of Shani's was getting married in Brooklyn, I practically booked tickets on the spot. When I say 'I', I mean Shani. She was and still is the most organised of us two.

It was the end of 2005 when we went; Damian Marley's 'Welcome to Jamrock' had just been released and became the unofficial soundtrack of our trip. We had four weeks planned out, staying in Manhattan before flying home the day after the wedding. I was partly joking but partly serious when I told Shani not to expect a proposal during the trip. I suspected she thought it might be on the cards, considering the significance of the occasion, but I needed to let her know this trip wasn't about that. I loved Shani but that stuff could wait – I was making my pilgrimage to Mecca.

The timing of the trip felt ordained. After meeting Herc, it was like he had given us his blessing. We ended up discussing what Daniel had said on stage about not imitating US artists, and Herc agreed.

'You've gotta be yourself and be proud of where you're from,' he told us. Hearing that was like the protégé being told by the master he's on the right path. It gave me a sense of confidence visiting New York, like I wasn't so much an outsider but part of an international scene. A brotherhood, almost.

Being that it was such an iconic trip, there was always a danger it might not live up to expectations. But thankfully, the US – and in particular New York – has a way of smacking you around the face with its American-ness, making you feel like you're in a movie. Sure, that movie can turn from a comedy to a horror in a matter of seconds, but it's one hell of a watch nonetheless. The first thing we did was hail a cab – yellow, of course – and head for our hotel in Manhattan. One of my favourite movies at the time (and even now) was Eddie Murphy's *Coming to America*, so you know I was picturing the scene when Prince Akeem and Semmi arrived in the Big Apple and the taxi driver yells out, 'You dumb fuck!' *Haha*.

New Yorkers found me to be a curious commodity. They could never figure out where I was from. Each interaction would go along similar lines. When they heard my accent, they assumed I was British.

'Nope, I'm Australian,' I'd tell them.

'What? You don't look Australian.'

'Well, my heritage is Tongan.'

'What's *that*?'

'A small Island in the South Pacific.' *Blank face.* 'Near Fiji.' *Blanker, still.* 'And Hawaii.' 'Ohhhhhhh!'

At this point we did our best impressions of a geography teacher to better illustrate the dot in the ocean we were from. We got there in the end.

On day two, Shani told me about a hip hop sightseeing tour where they take you to all the cultural landmarks around the city. It was a cool concept but I knew it'd be corny so I wasn't into it. Then she told me who the guide was: none other than Kurtis Blow, the first rapper ever to sign a major label deal. *What the fuck!* I haaaad to go. When we rocked up, we were handed a Kangol and a fake gold chain to wear. For me, that was a step too far.

'Yeah, nah . . . I'm good, thanks,' I told them as we took our seats.

With a rap legend as our tour guide and a bunch of European families as our companions, we cruised around New York, learning about the history of hip hop from one of the very first to do it. We started the day visiting the famous Apollo Theatre on 125th Street in Harlem and eating soul food. In the afternoon, they took us to the famous graffiti wall run by the Tats Cru, affiliated to the rapper Fat Joe, where they had huge murals dedicated to the late Big Pun. It was all a bit surreal. Here was this legend and *this* is what he'd been reduced to? Performing for busloads of tourists? It wasn't 'til years later that my perspective changed. Here was this legend who *still* gets to share his story, *still* gets to do what he loves and *still* gets paid for it. That I could get behind, but the fake gold chains? Them, you can keep.

The sightseeing stuff was amazing, but the best thing about New York was all the chance meetings that occurred. One night we booked tickets to see a show by Cormega, a New York artist who came up with Nas, at the famous SOB's theatre in SoHo. It was cool enough in itself to see a gig in the same place Jay-Z and others had caught their big break, but the real trip was who was in the crowd. Casually watching the show by himself was the legendary producer Pete Rock. When I caught a glimpse of him between songs I thought I must have got it wrong, then I realised: *This is New York*. That sort of thing was normal. After all, this was the birthplace of the culture. But what was standard for the locals was unforgettable for me and Shani. We danced until the lights came on.

Another hip hop icon was also in attendance: Ghostface Killah of Wu-Tang. I'd known for some time that it was a dangerous game meeting your idols. They have a habit of disappointing you, tarnishing the memory you have of them. When we opened for De La Soul back in 2003, I knew not to try and kick it with them. I bumped into Trugoy backstage, dapped him up, told him I loved De La Soul's music and I kept it moving. With Ghostface, it was different. Maybe it was the fact it was in New York and I was so excited in general, but I made the mistake of talking to him.

'Ghost! Respect, bro,' I told him. 'When you going to come to Australia?'

He looked at me with his face all screwed up like I'd just dissed his mother. 'Man, I'll get there when I get there!'

Crikey. Alright, bro, you have a good one. Interactions like this one are half the reason why I'm always polite and engaged when fans come up to me at shows. Tunks used to tell me to hold back, create a little mystique so the fans keep wanting more. But that wasn't me. I was genuinely grateful for their support, so why not show it? The other reason was simple: regardless of who you are, paying someone some courtesy if they've gone out of their way to show you love is the least you can do. I don't care how big and important you are, manners cost nothing.

A few days later we had the evening free so I checked out a street press mag to see if anything was happening. Sure enough, Mark Ronson was playing a DJ set with none other than Q-Tip. I couldn't have planned it better if I'd tried! By this point, I'd figured out the go with the drinks. Tipping wasn't common in Australia but in New York it was mandatory. As soon as I realised you had to tip big on every drink, not only did we get quicker service but the servers got liberal with their pours. By the end of the evening we were slightly tipsy, to say the least. Which probably explains what I did next. On the walk home from the bar to the hotel, I took out my sharpie and tagged a cop car with 'KOA'. You can tell Shani was a few drinks deep too because, rather than tell me not to do it, she provided cover – then took a photo of it.

When we got back to the hotel, I got a bit paranoid. *What if someone saw? Ah shit, what about CCTV cameras?* Luckily, the conveyor belt of anxious thoughts was soon brought to a halt as the booze took over and I was dead to the world, waking up the next morning with a bloody great hangover and some awesome memories.

I was a man on a mission in New York, energised to do, see and hear everything I possibly could. After watching *The Warriors* as a kid, I always wanted to see all five boroughs – Queens, Brooklyn, Manhattan, Staten Island and the Bronx. One day we were hanging out with our friends Sash and Richie, whose wedding it was, and I asked them if they minded taking me to Brooklyn to visit a famous record store in Bed-Stuy. When I said this, they looked like I'd asked them to take me into a warzone.

'Erm ... You sure you wanna go there?' they asked. 'It's pretty dangerous.'

Yes, I was sure. I knew where they were coming from – I'd heard the stories, too – but Bed-Stuy was home to more hip hop stars than anywhere on the planet. Talib Kweli, Big Daddy Kane, Mos Def, Biggie, Jay-Z – they'd all grown up in and around the area so I needed to see the place for myself, walk the same pavements (sorry, 'sidewalks') they had and visit the same record stores they visited. Besides, I've always thought averting danger was about the way you carry yourself. This wasn't my home so I was always on alert to my surroundings; I showed respect to everyone I met and knew to leave if and when shit got dicey.

My friends relented and took me to Bed-Stuy Do or Die. When we arrived they decided to stay in the car. *Fair enough.* Leaving them behind, I flicked through record after record. This was the mixtape era when DJs were producing compilations of all the biggest new tracks. In Australia, we had to wait for anything new and hot to reach us. In New York, it was like getting it straight from the faucet. Realising I couldn't keep my friends waiting all day, I bought some dancehall and hip hop mixtapes then headed back to the car.

'You won't believe what we just saw,' they said as I got in. 'Six police officers on patrol together. Six! Told you it was rough here.'

After that, and seeing their reaction when I mentioned taking the ferry to Staten Island, I decided to drop my five boroughs quest. Several years later those same friends had permanently relocated to New York and bought a house in Brooklyn, close to where they had dropped me off in Bed-Stuy. I think that's called gentrification.

A couple days before we left, we went to a dancehall festival out in Queens. And I mean *proper* Queens, way out in the hood. Man, that was an amazing experience. Beenie Man, Elephant Man, Bounty Killer . . . the line-up was like the who's who of dancehall. That was my first time seeing that sort of show live. They'd perform a couple bars then the DJ would pull the beat up and everyone would go crazy, all whistling and waving flags from their home countries. It was cool being in that environment with other people of colour. I'd never had that in Australia. Come to think of it, Shani was about the whitest person there! Like everything in New York, it had this awesome energy about it, like you're right in the heart of the culture.

Then it began to get dark and you could feel the energy shift a little. It was time to go. Being so far from home, we knew not to push our luck.

The wedding was on the final day of the trip. The ceremony was out on Long Island, and Shani and I did our part by kicking off the dance floor. They started playing some MJ (remember, this was '05 guys, pre all the . . . well, let's not get into that) so we got up and others soon followed suit. It was a beautiful day and the perfect way to close out the trip.

The flight home quickly brought me back to reality. When we took our seats, the in-flight entertainment was playing some mundane Australian domestic news. Something about livestock. It bummed me out, reminding me that I was leaving this magical place behind. Shani was the same – she enjoyed New York so much that she wanted to move there.

'Let's do it, Hau!' she said excitedly as the plane took off. 'We both love New York. Imagine, we could do a year out here and barely miss anything at home.'

I was tempted, but I knew I couldn't do it. What about my family? If anything happened to Mum or Dad and I couldn't get home in time, I would never forgive myself. Then there was Koolism. Yeah, Daniel and I were having some issues, but our journey was far from over.

NEW OLD GROUND

Daniel and I were getting booked for more shows after the ARIA win helped raise our profile. We even got a call from a few major labels, including Sony, but nothing ever materialised. We'd been doing our own thing for so long, it seemed kinda pointless to sign with a major now. With our follow up to *Random Thoughts*, we knew there were a lot of people expecting us to go pop, to try and capitalise on the award and make a play for some more mainstream commercial success. Faaark that, we did the opposite.

It was never even a consideration. Sticking to our creative guns is what made us popular in the first place – why would we switch that up now? So we doubled down, creating an album that was our toughest and grimiest yet. While *Random Thoughts* had its fun moments, giving our fans something to dance to, *New Old Ground* was way on the other end of the spectrum. From the tone of the music to the attitude of my delivery, everything about it was tough and unapologetic. It was the anti-pop album.

We were in a really good place by the time I got back from New York. A lot of the songs were already written before we went, so it was a case of tightening a few things up and recording. Though, with Daniel, that was easier said than done.

I was still recording demos at Hounga's place, and I'm not gonna lie, I was enjoying the hell out of the stress-free environment. There was none of the tense atmosphere that was increasingly defining my time with Daniel. With Hounga, we were just two brothers having fun and making music. It was effortless. In many ways, I'd forgotten how that felt.

From the jump, I knew exactly how I wanted to open the album. Daniel sent me a raw, thumping beat and I finally felt ready to address the incident of our stolen gear. Inspired by Public Enemy's 'Who Stole the Soul?', the song's called 'Talent', and it's basically me ripping whoever the thief was, saying you can have all the gear in the world but without talent it won't mean shit. 'This is a special dedication to all those dirty snakes,' I say on the intro, 'who broke into my girl's car and stole our gear while we were on tour, you suckers!'

It was controlled aggression, setting the tone for the album and allowing me to take out my anger in the best way I knew how – on wax. Conceptually, the album paid homage to Run-DMC's *Tougher Than Leather*. You can see that in the cover art, which we shot in Canberra before Daniel moved to Melbourne. With the name *New Old Ground*, we wanted to offer our own fresh take on a classic: paying respect to the traditions that came before us while also looking forward.

More than ten years deep in the game by this point, Daniel and I had a lot to reflect on, both in music and in life. With one song, 'Tapes', I rap about that tape I handed over to Dr Phibes that ended up getting copied and doing the rounds, giving us our first bit of buzz around Australia. It was a way to document our legacy and chart the progress we'd made since those early days just trying to get noticed. Another highlight is 'All of the Above'. My parents' house has a tin roof, so whenever it rained you could really hear it. That was one of my favourite memories growing up; I loved either going to sleep to that sound or waking up to it. It was very calming and I did a lot of thinking in those moments. A lot of the time was spent thinking about Bain.

> Under the tin roof with headphones on
> all I need to do is be myself and stay strong
> The rain trickled down, pain settled down
> now we live life like Bain's still around . . .

RIP, bro.

I was at Daniel's new spot in Melbourne, putting the finishing touches on the album when we got the news from Tonga that Uncle Sele had died. I was devastated. Since Sione passed away, he was the head of the family; he held the Lātūkefu title and would lead us in prayer and at formal celebrations. He was a fearless rugby player who played for his tiny nation, but to me he was a loving uncle who'd pick me up with one hand and throw me on the back of his horse to go join him as he worked in the fields. The man was all heart, so it was cruel that he died of a heart condition, particularly one that I'm sure could have been treated. In Tonga, it's not like they have regular check-ups for things like that, so it went undetected. Sele was in his sixties when he passed, another one taken way too soon.

Getting the news at Daniel's place was disconcerting. Usually, my spirit would feel so punctured I'd end up going to sleep. I couldn't do that at Daniel's, so I decided to go for a walk, plugging in the sounds of Mos Def to keep my mind from wandering. It was cruel timing; just a few months earlier Shani and I were toying with the idea of moving to New York. This felt like the world was reminding me that I can never venture too far without death finding me.

THE BOOM BOOM ROOM

It took me a while to acknowledge it but, really, I always knew I wanted to marry Shani. At the same time, I was in no rush. With music and adjusting to our new life in Sydney, it seemed like it could wait. Then something happened that changed my perspective. I came to work one day and found out that one of my co-workers had died. He couldn't have been older than twenty-one and had gone to visit his family in Singapore. That was the last we saw of him. As I was digesting the news, I realised life is too short – who knows what might happen tomorrow? I needed to take control of my life, starting with asking Shani to marry me.

I wanted the moment to be just right: something low-key but special, reflecting who we were as a couple. One of our favourite restaurants was Mezzaluna in Potts Point, so I booked a reservation and made up a plan with the maître d'. After dinner, they would lead Shani upstairs to a private bar where I would be waiting on one knee, with the champagne ready.

I rarely get nervous – at shows, there's a few butterflies before going on stage but nothing that serious – but with the proposal, I felt like a kid again. When the night arrived, my hands were sweaty and I kept double-checking that I had the ring and everything else ready. I knew this moment would be a key one in our story together, so everything had to be perfect. After we ate, I snuck off, pretending I needed the bathroom. One of the waiters then brought Shani upstairs, telling her we had drinks waiting at the bar. As she walked in, I had our song playing – a cover of Luther Vandross's 'So Amazing', sung by Stevie Wonder and Beyoncé.

As soon as Shani saw me, the tears started falling. The good kind, of course. With the song playing in the background, I spoke from the heart about our relationship and how much she meant to me, how I couldn't imagine my life without her. As Beyoncé sang her final note, I was finished. Holding her hand, I looked her in the eye.

'Shani, will you be my wife?'

A few months later, *New Old Ground* came out. It didn't do as well as we'd hoped. The critics liked it, but that didn't translate to more people at our shows or more records sold. I knew this was the deal we'd made when we decided not to change our sound, but it was still painful putting so much work into something and then feeling like it underperformed. Balancing creative and commercial goals was the albatross around our neck that never really went away.

But I had other things to think about, like planning a wedding. Okay, I'll admit, Shani did most of the heavy lifting, but I had one job to handle: the music. And if I do say so myself, I nailed it. Hounga and his wife Juanita's band Suite Az were a no brainer. A mix of funk, hip hop and R&B, Shani and I would always see their shows whenever they played in Sydney, so it only seemed right to have them perform at our wedding. Sorted.

Then there was the important issue of the bucks party. Knowing where this was likely to go, I made it clear from the outset: no strippers. And I wanted some sort of activity before it inevitably descended into drunken chaos, so I booked us in for some paint-balling at a spot in Canberra. It was an interesting mix of people. Obviously Tunks, Daniel and all the boys were there, as well as Shani's brother and a few guys from her side. Metro came along and, judging by his behaviour, he was a few days' deep into a bender. As the instructor was taking us through the safety precautions, he kept pretending to shoot the poor guy. Everyone at the bucks not familiar with Metro's antics didn't know what to make of him.

'Who *is* that guy?' I heard Shani's brother whisper as Metro took aim at the instructor. Tunks had to pull him aside and tell him to calm it down.

'You know there are normal people here, right?'

But that was Metro. He was a handful and you either loved him or hated him. After we spent a few hours shooting the shit out of each other, it was back to the aptly named Boom Boom Room. Situated in the back of my cousin Mai's place, this was the location for a lot of debaucherous nights over the years. Man, if those walls could talk.

Both Shani's dad and mine joined us at Mai's and helped get the barbecue going. It was exactly as I'd hoped: all my boys in one place, talking shit, listening to music and sharing a few drinks. Towards the end of the night, I felt someone nudge me in the back. I turned round to see Mai with a cheeky grin across his face.

'It's time,' he said before leading me inside. *Ah, man!* I knew exactly where this was going.

Despite *New Old Ground* not doing what we'd hoped, it still did well enough for us to tour the country. I was grateful for that. This was late 2006 and 'Aussie rap' was in full flow, so we were okay with swimming against the tide. Most of the scene was either still trying to sound

American or were making shameless rip-offs of the Hoods. With Aussie rap on one end of the scale, and Daniel's esoteric genius on the other, I always saw my role as balancing the two. We didn't want to be like everyone else, but at the same time, we couldn't afford to get *too* bold with it. Who knows, maybe with *New Old Ground* I didn't get the balance right, veering too far from what the mainstream was doing.

By the end of the year, with the tour wrapped up, Daniel and I started thinking about our next move. I was still working retail in Sydney, so I'd visit Daniel in Melbourne every month or so to record demos and think up ideas for our next project. Before long it was time to get married. The ceremony was in Hickson Road Reserve in Sydney, under the Harbour Bridge, with the Opera House in the background. It was an idyllic location, but in the week leading up to the big day, it rained non-stop before the clouds finally cleared on the morning of the wedding. I'm not a superstitious guy, but I saw that as a good sign.

The night before, we stayed in separate places: Shani and her bridesmaids at a hotel near the Opera House and me at home with my groomsmen – my cousins Mai, 'Uli and Supi. I had the boys looking slick in these brown suits while I stepped out in a full Kenzo two-piece. (Sorry, boys, the purse strings didn't quite allow for Kenzo suits all round.) I had my hair long but decided to freshen it up on the morning of the wedding. One of Tunks' many talents was cutting hair, so I got him to shave my head, asking him to cut a line into my hairline like a crescent moon. (Look, I'm not trying to say I initiated the trend, but I will say this was a few years before everyone started doing it. You do the math.)

The day started when I saw Shani walking down the aisle. *Man.* She looked stunning. The wedding dress was off-white and shoulderless, flowing over her curves like syrup on pancakes. With her father by her side, Shani slowly made her way to meet me. She was in tears when the celebrant – a Tongan minister Mum had recommended – kicked things off. I saw this coming and had an icebreaker up my sleeve.

'Here, take this,' I said, offering Shani a hanky. As she pulled it, another came out, then another. She kept pulling as a long line of brightly coloured handkerchiefs emerged from my sleeve while the guests watched on in hysterics.

'Let us begin,' said the minister, quietening the laughter.

After the ceremony, the bridal party went to Balmoral Beach for photos before everyone met back up at the Wharf for the reception. We asked that kids be left behind so everyone could let loose and enjoy themselves. My cousin 'Alopi MC'ed and made sure I had Grey Goose on deck and the evening flowed smoothly. Shani decided to do the bridal waltz right at the beginning of the night so Suite Az kicked things off with a lover's rock version of Whitney Houston's 'My Love Is Your Love.' After that, the dance floor was on and poppin'.

At one point, Shani and I snuck off to enjoy a private moment together. It was a piece of advice I was given before the wedding and one I always share with other people now: weddings can often seem like they are for everyone but you. Like you're just hosting a party for other people. Make sure you take time away from the action to contemplate and savour the moment. With the reception at the Wharf, a big warehouse on Circular Quay, there was a long walkway leading up so we took a Vintage Dom Perignon from the bar and sipped it from the bottle as we strolled along the waterfront. It wasn't long, but it helped distil the memory, as if setting it in amber to preserve it for the future.

We had the honeymoon in Greece a few days after the wedding. Neither of us had ever been to Athens, so we spent a few days there doing all the touristy stuff before heading to Santorini. We stayed in a cute little hotel, and even though it was too cold for a dip in the infinity pool, Shani and I made good use of the spa. The town was a bit quieter than we'd anticipated – there was literally nothing to do at night – but we were okay with that. All we needed was each other. My favourite moments were breakfast on the balcony each morning. Just me, Shani, some coffee and that view. Perfect.

On one of the final days we were off on a long coastal walk when a few feral dogs started following us. As we kept walking, more and more joined until we had a whole pack behind us. Something about it felt significant, as if they were protecting us. We saw them as our guardians; as we set off on this new journey together, our ancestors were reminding us that they had our back. And they've had it ever since.

At that moment something occurred to me. Maybe it was as I said my vows, maybe it was when I proposed to her – or maybe I was wrong all along – but Shani was no longer second to music.

SHANI

Hau and I grew up as family friends but there's a four-year gap, so it's not like we were in each other's pockets. The earliest memory I have of him was when I started high school. I was in Year 7 and he was in Year 11. Knowing someone in the senior school when you're a kid is really cool, and the fact it was Hau, and he was actually cool already, every opportunity I got I was like, 'Oh, hey Hau!'

He was kind of the same guy he is now, just more shy. Always wired for sound, he'd have his headphones running through his school uniform with his Walkman in his pocket. We became good friends and actually wrote letters to each other. Did he tell you that? For Year 7 or 8 kids at our school, it was cool to write a letter to someone a bit older. So Hau was my pen pal, and when we passed each other in the playground we'd give each other a letter. There was nothing romantic at all. It was just like, 'Hey, today I went to the oval. Someone was kicking the footy. Did you see this thing on TV?' You know, stuff like that.

It must have gone on for a year or so. Then one day – it had been ages since Hau had written me a letter – I saw him at the front of my house, because we lived on the same block. He walked up the steps and I was like, 'Hey, what are you up to?' And he's like, 'Oh, I'm giving you a letter.' He had wrapped a cassette tape in a piece of paper; it was a letter, but he'd also written me a song. Oh my Lord, it was so cool! I still know all the words.

I know this girl
And she's swell and she's Tongan
She's strong in the mind and she's fine
So I thought I'd write a rap just for her
Cos I forgot to write a letter cos my memory's a blur . . .

So on a rainy day, Shani hey,
Keep your head up
Do well at school, be cool,
Don't get fed up
Cos for now you might hate it
But in the end with the intellect you create
You'll be glad you made it.

Then he left school and, you know, life goes on. So I guess we saw each other very sporadically for the next four years. I started hanging out with his sister, Sabne; we worked near each other and became really good friends. I then moved to Sydney after I finished university. I didn't know anybody and had gone from a really active social life to living in this city on my own, not knowing anyone. Hau messaged me one day and said, 'Hey, I'm coming up to Sydney. If you want to come out with us, let me know.' So I took them up on that. And, yeah, lo and behold, the chemistry kicked in. Because, I got to say, there was something between Hau and me even before that.

It just happened. Then it was six months of him coming up to Sydney probably every weekend or second weekend, and we'd hang out together. It was a bit weird, too, because in the time that we were kind of secretly seeing each other, I didn't want to tell anyone, just in case it wasn't a thing. Our families were very close, so if we did get together and then it didn't work we'd make it difficult for everyone. It was six months of that before I was like, 'Okay, are we doing this?' And he was like, 'No, no, we're never gonna do this. I've got music. Music's my priority.'

And then, and I'm sure he's told you, he called me and was like, let's do this. But music's always going to be number one. I was like, okay, that's fine. I can be number two! I was really accepting of it. I was just like, I hear what you're saying, but at some stage that's going to change. Or it won't and it'll be over. I guess I just had faith that it would work out.

When I'd just started my new job, in my first week, we were having team drinks and everyone's asking questions, 'Where are you from?' and 'Do you have a boyfriend?' Things like that. I remember because it was the first time I'd actually really said to anybody that we were together. And then they asked, 'What does he do?' I was like, 'Ah, he's in Canberra, he's a musician. His name's Hau and he's from a group called Koolism.' And there were about five mouths around the table that just dropped. It was a creative agency, and it just happened that they all loved Koolism and would play their songs in the office all the time. And I thought, Man, my cool factor seriously went through the roof.

And then the incident with the records happened. That was a moment. I think Daniel and Hau's relationship was getting a little bit tense by then, anyway. So I was thinking, How are we going to tell Daniel? *I didn't actually realise how bad it was at the time. I just thought it was his records that were gone. I didn't know it was a whole album.*

I had a friend who worked at Sydney Confidential. *I called them and asked if we could put a story in the paper, explaining how Hau from Koolism had had all his records stolen. They ran the story, saying if anyone has seen anything to call, blah, blah. But nothing came of it, obviously.*

If I could turn anything around, I would go back and bring back that bag.

HAU'S HIP HOP HISTORY

A few months after the honeymoon, triple j made an announce-
ment: the host of *The Hip Hop Show*, Maya Jupiter, was leaving. She'd
been doing the gig for a few years but had decided to move to LA to
live with her partner, the singer Aloe Blacc. Me and a few others got
a call and were asked to submit a demo.

To be honest, I was a little bemused. This wasn't the first time I'd
been called by triple j about *The Hip Hop Show*. I'd been asked to fill
in for Maya a few times when she was ill or on holiday, so I figured
I'd already done the hard part. I remember thinking, *Why don't they
just give me the job?*

But I'm a big believer that if and when opportunity comes knocking
you give it a chance – appreciate it, pursue it, at the very least consider
it. It may not be for you, or the timing might not be right, but that
attitude will serve you well for embracing the things that *are* right for
you. So, I swallowed my pride and submitted the demo.

I still wasn't convinced. I knew I wouldn't be able to play any
Koolism tracks myself and was okay with that. To be honest,

I wouldn't really want to, anyway. But would Koolism get *any* airtime across triple j if I was on the station? I spoke about it with them, and they assured me that wouldn't be the case. 'If we like it, we'll play it,' they said, letting me know that they were prepared to face any criticism they got if it ever came up. I spoke to Daniel about it, and the more I contemplated it the more I realised what an opportunity it was – not just for me but Australian hip hop as a whole.

Having a mainstream radio show dedicated solely to hip hop was an indication of how much the genre had developed compared to when Daniel and I started out. It actually came about as a result of a petition. A producer named Thomas Rock, who worked with Def Wish Cast and some other acts, began gathering signatures at shows, and before long triple j were paying attention. But there were a few growing pains. The first person to helm the show was Nicole Foote, who was a great host but not embedded within the culture. She approached it like any other hosting gig and did all the right things to make the show a success. The thing is, this wasn't any old show. It was the long-overdue representation of a culture that had never before been represented on a national stage. *The Hip Hop Show* was the crown jewel in the landscape of mainstream Australian hip hop. Done right, it could have a huge impact on the trajectory of the scene.

Maya was definitely an improvement. She was a rapper and dancer herself, so no one could say she wasn't part of the culture. It felt like we had one of our own running things, but she got a lot of pushback. Some of it I understood. There were moments when she mispronounced artist names, like *Most* Def and *Dee* La Soul, which would drive me crazy. The rest of it was unjustified and said a lot more about the misogynistic views of those dishing out the criticism.

Nonetheless, I started to feel like the scene would benefit from having someone in the role who, like me, had a deep cultural understanding of the music itself, as well as the respect of the artists and listeners. I'd been in New York a few years before, witnessing first-hand how hip hop had grown into this juggernaut of an industry – a cultural force that initiated social trends as well as a source of opportunities for artists old and new. Australia could follow suit. We just needed the right people with their hands on the steering wheel.

I had made my mind up by the time I got the call from the program director, Chris Scadden. I called Shani immediately.

'Guess who's going to be the new host of the triple j *Hip Hop Show*?'

It was a few months before I officially took the role. I joined Maya for her final show, so there was a handover period before I did my first solo episode on 21 April 2008. I remember the date because it was Shani's and my one-year anniversary. Not the best timing, I'll admit, but she understood.

I put a lot of thought into that first show. When I'd filled in before, it was with Daniel and Tunks, and we were there as Koolism. All we did – all we were expected to do – was play the tunes we liked. We spent most of the time playing hard shit from New York, guys like Mob Style and Tim Dog. But, as I learned, being the official host of the show involves a lot more work.

I was grateful to Chris, who really went out of his way to tell me the show was mine to make my own. I embraced that, first asking Hounga to help me put together the theme music, which I used until recently, more than a decade later. With the playlisting, I wanted to continue to only play the hip hop I liked, but I knew I had to broaden it so it wasn't just the likes of Tunks and Daniel who would tune in. I ensured my playlist was diverse with a decent mix of local and international artists, and I started a thing called 'Hau's Hip Hop History', where I would take one of the OG local or global acts and explain who they were and why they were important. It featured groups like AKA Brothers as well as Rize and Tarkee (later known as Mama's Funkstikools), one of the first groups I ever heard who rapped in an Australian accent *and* sounded wavy. It was groups like these who had laid the foundation, allowing the scene to get to where it is now, but never got the recognition they deserved. It was my version of edutainment – educating our listeners on the culture while playing some banging tunes. It became so popular I was soon presenting the segment for a triple j TV show on the ABC, my first TV gig.

When it came to my debut show, I turned up at the triple j studios a full hour before my set, nervous like a kid on his first day at school. I sat down and just stared at the dials as I watched the time count down. It occurred to me then that this was my first 'proper' job. Everything up until this point was casual work that served the purpose of fuelling my rap career. This felt different; it felt important. I was thirty-two years old and had been gifted an opportunity to make a lasting impact on the culture that I knew and loved. What a privilege.

That's not to say everyone was into it. There was this platform where listeners could leave comments about the show and, unaware at the time of how toxic those places can be, I wanted to check out what people were saying about me. Those from within the hip hop community were into the new direction, but there were a few anonymous voices who talked shit about my accent.

'Why's he trying to sound American?' one asked.

What?! Comments like that pissed me off, but more often than not they were proof of one thing: the idiot had clearly never met an Islander. Their loss. It also said something about the typical triple j listener and what their expectations were of the station. Most listeners were accustomed to hearing hosts with thick Aussie accents, and I just didn't fit that mould. I quickly learned from other DJs that those comment sections were best left alone.

Soon after my first show I started having a recurring nightmare: dead air. Anyone who's done radio work will understand. A song would end and in my dream I'd be scrambling around for the next one, that awkward silence feeling like an eternity. Thankfully, it's a dream that, so far, has never come true. Touch wood.

LOSING MY RELIGION

It's difficult to imagine a Tongan without religion. They're pretty much one in the same thing. Growing up, at any family event or community function, faith played a role in some shape or form. It's not like Mum and Dad sat us down and quizzed us on scripture or anything – they didn't have to. It was everywhere. Every Sunday there was church, every meal there was grace, and after every major achievement there was Mum telling us to thank God. I never questioned it. As I got older I stopped attending church as regularly as when I was a kid, but I still wore my crucifix around my neck and considered myself a religious person. It was an identity more than an action. I was proud to be Tongan, therefore I was proud to be a Christian.

Until I went to South America.

Shani and I had always wanted to go. My visit with Torch when we were in Germany was fun, but I'm not quite sure that counts. Then Shani's cousin Mele died and we decided we needed to get away. Plus, with things still tense between me and Daniel, I definitely needed a break. So we booked ourselves on a plane to South America in April 2009 to explore Argentina, Brazil and Peru.

Machu Picchu was a highlight. It had been on my bucket list

for years, but nothing can truly prepare you for seeing it in person. No wonder the place has such a history. Built in the fifteenth century, its construction was way ahead of its time, and it's a great example of Indigenous people's ingenuity. The Incas were no joke.

But it was the visit to a small colonial town that really left its mark. The tour guide clearly knew his stuff, and while he was doing a routine he had probably done a thousand times, there were moments throughout the tour where he was clearly going off script and speaking from a place of personal experience. It happened when we visited a church. He spoke passionately of the way the Spanish colonists destroyed the Indigenous culture, about how Catholicism was brought over as a means of brainwashing the local community and used to justify the slaughter of innocent people.

It was shocking stuff. And for me and Shani, it was soul-destroying. We'd both been having doubts for a while – we decided against getting married in a church – but for someone to lay out its evils in such unapologetic terms was mind-blowing. More to the point, it made complete sense.

This was the sort of stuff my uncle Sione had written about in his book *Church and State in Tonga*. He wrote about the impact of the missionaries there and, man, he paints a bleak picture:

> They saw as their mission, the conversion of the heathen at all cost if necessary, even if it entailed martyrdom on the one hand and a complete destruction of the traditional culture on the other . . .

> They identified Christianity with the moral standards of their own middle-class background at home, and anything which deviated from these standards, they regarded as sinful and deplorable and to be eradicated.

And that's what they did. *Eradicated.* A similar thing happened at Machu Picchu. This civilisation-defining creation was abandoned just a hundred years after it was built because of the Spanish invasion. More than that, in order to justify their invasion, the Spanish had to pretend the Incas were savages – and not a creative group of people capable of engineering an entire citadel nearly three kilometres up a mountain! – so no one bothered to find out how they had built Machu Picchu in the first place. All that knowledge and cultural history lost. *Eradicated.*

As Shani and I sat there listening to the tour guide I thought of Tonga, where Christianity still has a huge influence. *Is it a force for good or evil?* I asked myself. The answer, overwhelmingly, was the latter. There is so little money in Tonga, and yet the majority of families give money to the Church, depriving themselves of opportunities. This creates generational cycles of poverty.

Looking back, the boys had been trying to steer me away from the Church for some time. Daniel would make the occasional comment, and Travis would often ask me if it was hypocritical of me to believe in God and wear a crucifix every day, while regularly racking clothes.

'Isn't that one of the Ten Commandments?' he'd ask. 'Thou shalt not steal?'

Each time, I'd brush it off. I wasn't ready to hear it then. Just as I wasn't ready to hear it when King Kapisi was rapping about it a decade earlier. But now things were different. Now I was all ears.

The trip was a life-altering moment for both me and Shani. Having lost her cousin a few months before, Shani was already questioning her faith. She didn't understand what justification God could have in taking Mele from us. Hearing the tour guide only confirmed how she felt. Afterwards, we bought a bunch of books and began educating

ourselves on the impact of modern-day religion, specifically its relationship with Indigenous peoples. We both had the realisation that
this institution no longer held the same significance it did when
we were growing up. The role it played in our parents' lives didn't
resonate for us anymore. In a way, that was upsetting. Part of it is
normal generational growth; the things important to one generation
aren't necessarily the same for the next. But for Tongans, and other
countries where much, if not most, of the population live overseas,
it holds a deeper significance. It means the traditions and way of life
of our parents and their ancestors slowly but surely disappear. And
then there's no going back. Just as I didn't share my parents' affinity
for the Church anymore, my kids would likely feel it even less and
therefore have even less in common with their grandparents. My
mind was made up, but that doesn't mean it was easy.

And while Shani and I knew the Church would no longer be a
part of our everyday life, that didn't mean spirituality would disappear from our lives altogether. For us, it became about gratitude and
embracing the seasonality of life. Our ancestors – before Christianity
came along and left its mark – would worship the seasons and give
thanks for the ways in which the weather and the natural world
created life. That stuff made sense to me. And so we started replacing
things like grace with a message of gratitude. We could still appreciate
our place in the world without having to defer all our thanks to God.

Despite this, I was still unsure if I wanted to discuss it with my
family. I didn't really know how. Then one afternoon I was at Daniel's
and he played a new beat he'd been working on. It had this dark,
sinister tone to it, with this gritty, driving bassline pulsing through
it like the trains through the New York subway. As soon as I heard
that, I knew what I was going to do. I wrote the song 'Turning Back'
right then and there, approaching it with a real sense of aggression
to mirror the internal conflict I felt.

My parents were far from strict, didn't force the church card,
But my heart was with the Heavenly Father's kid,
Jesus Christ Lord, me na wan turn back
    but I'm a little concerned that we've been brainwashed,
Our generosity served as the main course
    and for the dessert, honey, our hard-earned money.

The writing and recording process was easy – therapeutic, even. But I knew when the record would eventually come out, it could well be a different story. I had witnessed Islanders take issue with Kapisi when he discussed his distrust of religion. *Am I prepared for the same treatment?* I wasn't sure, but I also knew this was something I had to do. I thought back to a piece of advice my mum would often give me: forget the 'right' decision, make the decision that's right *for you.*

Whatever the reaction – from my family, my community, my fans – ultimately it didn't matter. This was the right thing to do. For me.

The following year we were in Tonga. All the family was there and, as always, we were about to go to church. Shani and I had spoken about it before and told each other we would stay behind. We weren't going to make a big deal about it, but Sabne asked why.

'Oh, we don't believe in God anymore,' Shani said casually.

Sabne stopped dead in her tracks. 'What did you just say?'

Shani told her about South America, about the things we'd learned and the fact we were doing things differently these days. Sabne couldn't believe what she was hearing.

'I don't know what you saw over there,' she said, 'but it's wrong.' She walked off and that was the end of it.

I think Sabne didn't want to turn it into a big thing and risk having an argument, particularly not in Tonga with all the family around. But it showed how serious it was. After all, Sabne had her own history with religion. She'd converted to Islam when she met her husband, and it caused a few issues in our family. She would have other Tongans coming up to her asking, 'How could you leave our culture behind?'

But Sabne never fell out of faith, she just found a new one. When Mum and Dad heard, they were okay about it – it's almost expected in Tongan culture for the wife to follow the husband – but when she started wearing the hijab, covering her face, that was a different story. That's when my parents felt like they had lost a daughter. When Mum found out she called me straightaway in tears. Dad, meanwhile, went to the pub.

But Sabne and I talked about it, and I managed to calm Mum and Dad down. They saw it as a failing on their part, but I convinced them that's not how these things work. It had nothing to do with them; just as it was for me and Shani, this was about Sabne and her journey, no one else.

I never had the same conversation. To this day, Mum still reminds me to thank God after something big in life happens. I just shrug and say, 'Sure.' Maybe, when she reads this, we'll find the time to talk about it. I know she'll understand. At the end of the day, we're still family. That's all that matters.

THE 'UMU

The triple j gig made things difficult when it came to recording with Daniel. With him in Melbourne and me having to be in Sydney every week for the show, there weren't many opportunities to get together. The situation became an issue for Daniel, who was desperate to recreate the studio vibes of our past albums. I tried to convince him that while I also loved recording with all the boys coming and going, that part of our life was over. We'd end up having the same conversation again and again.

'Man, it's not the same anymore,' he'd complain.

'Yeah, exactly – because it's *not the same anymore.*'

Our lives had evolved, we had changed as people, and our living situation was completely different. We needed to adapt, but Daniel is such a vibes-oriented person he found that really hard. He wanted us to be back in Watson: Tunks talking shit in the background, a half-eaten Cherry Ripe by his side and cat litter on the floor. It made me think of Outkast, who were famous for recording all their early stuff in a basement studio known as The Dungeon. After they were able to afford their own places, do you think they continued to record there? In a fucking *dungeon*?!

289

With Daniel in Melbourne and me in Sydney, I would take off the occasional Thursday, prerecording my show or taking holiday, so I could spend some time recording with him. Those sessions were tough. We were making some progress musically, but the energy was way off. Daniel could go a whole eight-hour session in the studio without talking. Slouched over the keyboard, he'd barely show any interest in what we were doing. In turn, I just got pissed off. Hardly the best environment for creativity.

It was clear he wasn't in a good place. I tried to be there for him, but on the occasions he did open up, I realised I wasn't equipped to help. I tried to get him to see a professional and told him this album was not worth destroying his mental health over. I'd rather he was in a better place emotionally than see us make music. He agreed and ended up going to a few sessions, but it didn't last long. Then it was back to just the two of us, alone in a makeshift home studio, barely talking.

I stayed with Alvin most of the time I visited Melbourne. He copped an earful of my frustrations with Daniel on many occasions. I'd come back after several hours of torture and just had to vent. There were days when I decided I'd had enough. *Man, fuck the album and fuck him. I'm done.* But I'd always come back the next day. We'd worked too hard together to give up now and leave it like this. Sure, I could have cut my losses, but that would have meant accepting the fact I had given years of my life to something that didn't even get released. And I wasn't about to do that.

Things came to a head when our manager, a lady called Sam Cameron, who had taken over from Blake, called us in for a meeting. She knew we were in a rough patch and wanted us to come in and air any grievances we had so that we could move past it and finish the project. We met at a cafe in Melbourne, with the three of us sitting around a small table, trading awkward small talk before getting to it.

As I was trying to tell my side of things, Daniel kept talking over me. I asked him to stop and he did it again, refusing to let me finish. Then he did it a third time, at which point I'd had enough. Getting up off my seat, I slammed my hand on the table.

'You talk over me again,' I warned him, 'and I'm gonna punch you in the face.'

He quickly shut up, but at that point the meeting was over. After we left and I'd calmed down, I tried to tell Daniel I didn't mean it and would never *really* hit him. He was cool, brushing it off like it wasn't a big deal. But I knew it was; the damage had been done. I had spent my entire life being someone who preferred to defuse conflict. I think that comes from my dad and uncles. They were strong, tough men, but their disposition was always peaceful. Even when Hasim and I were running the streets, yeah I got into some fights, but I was never the instigator. Now, here I was threatening to punch my best friend and bandmate.

It was 2010 and the world was changing again, and with it so was hip hop. Just as Australian hip hop went through a transitional period in 2003, a similar thing happened at the end of the decade, only this time the changes were global. The internet was connecting us in ways we'd never imagined. And the consequences were huge.

First off, rap become less regionalised. Before the internet, each region had their own distinct sound that reflected the culture of its birthplace. In the same way hip hop in Canberra was different to what was happening in Western Sydney, artists from the West Coast in the US sounded a world away from those on the East Coast, and the South was something else altogether. As the internet grew, these distinctions began to have less meaning, as every artist and producer had access to the sounds and flavours of things outside their hometown. They didn't have to visit a place to experience it; they just had to go online.

It also meant a shift in the types of artists we were used to seeing. Hip hop was traditionally born in the streets, and MCs came up via the local scene. Like me, they performed in all the bars and clubs and would freestyle wherever, whenever. You first had to get the support of your city before the rest of the country or world would pay attention. In the internet age, an artist could blow up online, even if they'd never played a sold-out show. This is when the likes of Kid Cudi, Wale and Asher Roth were getting their major break. Children of the internet, they understood how to use this emerging medium to grow their profiles.

Internet blogs became the breeding ground for MCs, replacing traditional forms of hip hop media like *The Source* magazine. There was NahRight and, my favourite, 2DopeBoyz. What started out as small online blogs became the place you visited to get up to date on the hottest artists at the time. As a result, hip hop started a process of democratisation: there was less need for the financial support of a major label to get everyone's attention; you just needed to be smart about how you marketed yourself, and your music, online.

This meant there was less emphasis placed on the music itself, and more on the overall package. It was less about being an MC and more about being a rapper and an artist. You needed to think about your brand image, and the different ways fans could interact with you outside your music. Artists like Joe Budden had YouTube channels where they would video blog their everyday lives, recording themselves doing things like playing Monopoly and chatting with friends.

Everything was different. Baggy jeans were replaced by skinny ones, and artists began to embrace emotional vulnerability over the 'tough guy' image that defined a lot of earlier hip hop. Cudi's debut album *Man on the Moon: The End of Day* really paved the way. He was open about his struggles with mental health, positioning himself as more of the relatable guy-next-door, rather than an enigmatic MC of past generations.

Meanwhile, I was paying attention to all of this. At thirty-four, I wasn't part of the generation who grew up with the internet at their fingertips, but I knew enough to understand its value. The tectonic plates of hip hop were shifting again, and you either jumped on board the new direction or risked getting left behind.

With these changes going on in the background, Daniel and I finally released the album we had been working on since the end of 2006. It was nearly four years of at-times excruciating work but we got there. We called it *The 'Umu*, referencing the Pasifika cooking practice; just like the underground oven, making the album was a laborious process, but the end result was worth it. Daniel and I were close to giving up at points, but we stayed the course and created a project we were both proud of.

A review from *The Brag* summed up the album and the direction we had been trying to take for the past decade:

> Aussie rap genius, sure; but the best thing about Koolism is that they don't sound, and never have sounded, like any of the other Aussie hip hop acts . . . I like the way this record doesn't sound overthought, or overproduced; it's just fat in an effortless, confident way.

The album was dope, but there was no denying things were different between me and Daniel. It took four long years to make that project, and by the time it was finished my love of music was at an all-time low. Daniel would overwork songs to the point that I almost didn't care anymore. And while I was getting fed up with Daniel, I think he was just fed up with life. After several attempts to try and get him to seek help, it got to a point where I had to move on. I needed a fresh start.

But our journey wasn't over. Not yet. In February 2011, just after *The 'Umu* dropped, we got booked for our biggest show to date, on the Good Vibrations tour, featuring Nas, Damian Marley, Ludacris and, among others, Erykah Badu. This was a huge moment for us. We were used to playing festivals, but we would usually get booked for just the Sydney show – this time we were on the full bill, hitting stages in Sydney, Melbourne, Gold Coast and Perth. Besides, we were performing alongside Nas, Damian Marley, Ludacris and, among others, Erykah Badu! (I know, I already mentioned their names, but I thought I'd repeat them for the ones at the back.) No matter how bad things were between me and Daniel, this was an opportunity we weren't going to miss.

It was almost like going on a holiday with your partner when you know you're about to break up. The tickets have already been bought, so you're like, *Fuck it, let's go anyway*. And considering the other names on the line-up, it wasn't hard to enjoy ourselves.

I'll never forget laying eyes on Erykah Badu for the first time. When she walked on the tour bus, everyone stopped what they were doing. I've heard people talk about what it was like to meet Prince. He didn't walk, they said, he *floated*, like you were meeting an aura rather than a person. That's what it was like with Erykah Badu. You didn't just notice her presence, you *felt* it. The different artists on the bus looked at each other, acknowledging the cosmic event that had just visited us. It was as if making noise would somehow puncture the moment and she would realise she was on the wrong bus before disappearing forever.

On the final date, I got to interview Nas – the God MC himself – along with Damian Marley. As soon as Nas opened his mouth, I had to pinch myself. *There's* that *voice*, I told myself. That voice that had been with me through everything since he dropped *Illmatic* in '94. And next to *him* was Damian Marley, a legend in his own right and son of the most iconic performer of all time.

If things were different, it could have been a stepping stone to something new and exciting – our final, triumphant chapter as Koolism. But, instead, it was one of the last things we ever did. We hit the stage together, giving the Koolism faithful one last blow-out, and there was a huge afterparty following the Perth show, where we drank and hung out with some of the biggest names in hip hop. Daniel and I had fought for twenty years to get to this place, but having it happen like this felt bittersweet.

We played one final gig a few months later. It was in honour of MC Hunter, our mate from Perth who had devoted so much of his adult life to promoting local hip hop before dying of cancer at the age of thirty-six. Following his death, the big names in Australian hip hop came together for a footy game and concert in his memory. After all his selfless work putting on for other artists, it was the least we could do. At the show, Daniel and I performed 'Blue Notes', the one and only time we ever played that song live. It touches on the death of family members – uncles, cousins and grandparents, as well the sibling I never got to meet. It was like a funeral not only for Hunter but for Koolism. Both Daniel and I knew our time was up.

Afterwards, we went our separate ways, then we just . . . stopped talking. And it would be another ten years 'til I heard his voice again.

PART 4
RETURN
2011 . . .

The phoenix can only fly if its feathers are grown
An insight to what the veterans know
So I rose from the ashes like Cassius, straight off the canvas
Fresh and I'm clothed better than most
Devilish grin, heavenly flow, but down to earth
Lost a few bucks but I found my worth (what else?)
I wore a new tux and renewed my vows
'Cause when you married to the game there's no moving out

– 'The No End Theory', Hau, 2015

DEATH AND LIFE

It was the morning after Shani's birthday, 12 January 2011, and we were both still in bed when my cousin Mai called. As soon as the phone started ringing, I knew something was up. Those early-morning calls are never about anything good. When I answered, Mai was already crying uncontrollably. I braced myself.

'Travis is . . . dead,' he cried down the phone. 'He's dead.'

Mai was really close with Travis' younger brother, Trent, so he got the news first. He could hardly get the words out, as if each time he said the word 'dead' he was learning of the news for the first time. For both me and Mai, coming from such a big family, we expect a degree of loss every now and again. It's just part of having more family members – we all have our time to go. But when it comes to friends, those are the ones you never see coming.

Tunks, on the other hand, *had* seen it coming. The thing about Travis is, he was a man of extremes. When he was into something, he'd go all in; it's in part why he was so likeable. He had that type of contagious energy people want to be around. Even the guys we used to beef with liked Travis. You couldn't *not* like the guy. I've seen him knock a dude unconscious on more than one occasion, but that was never really him. At heart, Travis was a joker.

The lengths he went to for a laugh were extreme. Let me run you through a few of his greatest hits. You often hear talk of someone as the 'life and soul of the party'. Even that didn't do Travis justice – the party *didn't start* until Travis got there. One time, we were having a drink-up for Tunks' birthday and we noticed that Travis had gone missing. Half an hour or so passed, and we figured he must have gone home. As it turned out, he was in the garage, planning an elaborate joke. Finally, he strolls in wheeling a lawnmower.

'Alright, guys,' he said cheerfully, 'meet my mate Victor.' Named after the lawnmower brand Victa, Travis put a cricket cap on top of the lawnmower and proceeded to spend the party hanging with his new pal.

Then there was the time Axe introduced the crew to his girlfriend. He was rightfully a bit anxious, hoping we'd all make a decent first impression. We were chilling in the living room, chatting, and after half an hour Travis wanders in wearing a long blonde wig, midway through an animated phone call, looking and sounding like a mad real-estate agent wanker.

'Oh, yeah, *totally*. I mean, that's *exactly* what I said!'

Travis continued his 'call' until he finally, and dramatically, noticed us.

'Oh, so sorry, didn't see you there!'

Man, Axe was mortified! Then there's my favourite. Though, I'm not sure I appreciated it fully at the time. I would often stay with Travis when I visited Melbourne, and on one occasion he was kind enough to pick me up from the airport. I'm waiting in the pick-up zone when I see Travis beeping his horn and waving out the window.

'Hau!' he shouted. 'Hau, over here – *cooee!*'

Sitting next to Travis in the front seat was a big inflatable sex doll that he'd purchased specifically for the purpose of embarrassing me. I tried to pretend I didn't see him, but he pulled up right next to me and started theatrically manoeuvring the sex doll to make room, all the while ensuring as many people noticed as possible. My face was redder than The Game's wardrobe, which, with my complexion, is no easy task, believe me.

He was the sort of person who reminded you that life was supposed to be fun. His gags brought us all closer together, and when you were with him, you felt a giddy energy as if anything could happen. The term FOMO was invented for people like Travis: miss a party and you risk missing some classic Travis moments. But where there's that much light, there's often a degree of darkness.

He'd been starting to live recklessly. Working as a fly-in fly-out scaffolder in Western Australia, he was cashed up, doing shift-work a few weeks in a row followed by seven days off. His days off would turn into sessions, which would turn into benders. Noticing a pattern emerging, he asked Tunks to help control his spending by managing his finances. At the end of 2010, he wanted to go to Thailand and then India, and also train to become a yoga instructor, his new passion at the time.

Tunks tried to warn him against it: 'You go to India and I'll never see you again. You'll wind up dead.' As with a lot of things, Tunks was right.

Recovering from Travis' death wasn't easy. When Bain died, we were all in Canberra, so we could meet up that same night and be together. With Travis, we were all dotted around Australia, in different phases of life. Plus, with his body in India, we had to wait a long time for it to be returned before we could give him a proper burial.

In truth, I've never fully recovered. And I think that's okay. As with all my close friends, Travis changed my life. His presence was always joyful; in darker moments, he was a reminder of what is actually important. That's the same in his passing. I may have moved away from God, but my spirituality means I can still feel Travis – and Bain, my uncles and everyone else – by my side constantly. I can remember the ridiculous skits he'd devise, and rather than feel a sense of pain at his loss, it brings a smile to my face. Even in death, he can still make me laugh.

And besides, life goes on. What I learned was, even though you feel like time has stood still, the world actually continues to fucking move – sooner rather than later, you've got to move along with it. If you can persevere through the pain, more often than not, there's joy waiting at the other end. That's what happened to me. After experiencing the loss of Travis not even two weeks into the year, 2011 still turned out to be one of the most momentous years of my life. And Travis was with me every step of the way.

Shani and I always knew we wanted to have a family, but we weren't in a huge rush. But after losing Travis, we decided not to wait any longer. And even though things with Teniela had ended the way they did, it hadn't dimmed any of my enthusiasm to have a child. So when Shani told me she was pregnant, I was overjoyed. People often say you're never ready to be a parent; it's just something you get used to. I *was*. And finally, it was about to happen.

Since it was both of our first time, we did everything we could to prepare ourselves. We read the books, got ourselves an expensive obstetrician and put headphones on Shani's belly so the baby could listen to music. I played all the classics: from Roots Manuva and Jay-Z to Bill Withers and Bob Marley. I even played some classical music to really get the balance right. My kid could be whoever they wanted to be, but having bad taste in music was not something I was about to let happen.

During one of the meetings with the obstetrician, Shani explained that she wanted a natural birth. It's the way she'd always envisaged it. The doc, on the other hand, had other ideas.

'Your pelvis is *this* big,' he explained, 'and the baby's skull is *this* big. You can have a natural birth but you may be there for two days.'

Shani and I looked at each other. *Well, when you put it like that . . .* He went on to explain that a lot of mothers will insist on a natural birth, have an excruciating labour that lasts twenty-four hours, then still have to have a C-section anyway. It took some time for Shani to readjust her expectations but we took his advice.

Because Shani had decided to go with the C-section, we could pick the date we wanted to have the baby, as if we were planning a trip up the coast. The due date was Christmas Day, and because the obstetrician only did scheduled C-sections on a Monday, we could either pick one week before or two. We looked at the diary and settled on 12 December, two days after Sade was coming to Sydney. We had already bought tickets so it'd have been a shame to waste them, right?

We arrived at the hospital at 6.30 am. After getting Shani into her gown, the doc came to meet us.

'Okay, you'll have a baby in five minutes,' he said.

Sorry, what? That fast?

Apparently so. They gave Shani an epidural, sliced her open and brought out our first child, a beautiful boy named Aki with a big, beautiful head. It literally took all of five minutes. Just enough time to get through the first song on our birthing playlist, 'Lovely Day' by Bill Withers.

My head was spinning. In the operating room, I thought of my dad and my uncles: the family barbecues where I felt untouchable perched on their shoulders; the footy matches with Dad watching from the sidelines; the trips to Tonga when I would ride the fields on horseback with Uncle Sele. I always wanted to be just like them, to one day have a child of my own so I could make them feel as safe and as loved as I did. Now, finally, my dream had come true.

As they stitched Shani back up and checked her vitals, they told me it was important for Aki to have 'skin-to-skin time'. It helps them adjust to the outside world by feeling the touch of their mother, but with Shani occupied by the doctors, the privilege was all mine. They handed Aki to me and left us alone. With the door closed and the frantic energy of the operating room silenced, we had our first talk, father to son. I took off my shirt and held him close to my heart.

'Aki, welcome to the world,' I whispered. 'Your mum and dad are overjoyed to have you with us, and you have an even bigger family at home who can't wait to meet you.' I told him about Tonga and about his Uncle Travis. 'He passed away this year, but he's watching over you,' I said. 'We all are.'

ALL HEART, NO SOUL

Ever since Sione and I first hit the stage at Firehouse, I've considered myself an artist. It's an identity that is as much about your state of mind as it is your creative output. I carry a notepad and pen with me everywhere I go so I'm ready to jot down some ideas or pen a few rhymes whenever I feel the urge. Going through that process helps me make sense of the world and my experiences within it. When I lost Bain, when I lost faith in God, when Daniel and I got all our gear stolen – I couldn't fully process these events until I put them into song. Even if no one ever bought a Koolism album, I would have still made music in some shape or form. Without it, I start to feel lost.

During the final stages of making *The 'Umu* I could feel something changing. I no longer felt excited to open my notepad. Usually, a blank page staring back at me is a sight of opportunity. The stream of ideas starts flowing and I snatch at one, put it into words and start running with it. If it doesn't go anywhere, no big deal, I turn over the page and start again until something sticks. But for the first time, that excitement was starting to fade. Daniel and I had hit such a rut; I'd become stagnant. For an artist, that feeling is terrifying.

It's like when Samson's hair was cut; without the very thing that gave him his power – that made him who he was – he no longer understood his place in the world.

Rather than labouring away, trying to rekindle my love of writing rhymes, I looked elsewhere for my creative outlet. The joy of making rap music, for me, was about being the first to do something. Pushing boundaries has always excited me. Money, accolades, adoration – all of that comes and goes, but no one can ever take away from you the fact that you were the first to go somewhere no one else has. So, if I couldn't do that with my music, I needed a different avenue.

I had started to notice different music platforms pop up around the world. In the UK, there was SBTV run by Jamal Edwards (RIP) as well as Grime Daily, now rebranded as GRM Daily, and in the States there was VladTV. These were self-funded projects that had the sole purpose of showcasing hip hop culture in all its forms. Rap had begun to go mainstream but mainstream media was slow to catch on, so in true hip hop fashion, innovators like Jamal Edwards said, *Fuck it, I'll do it myself.* They aired freestyles, interviewed artists and covered news within the scene with the respect and integrity it deserved. It was a way to drive the culture forward when no one else was willing to do it, and more importantly it was created from people *within* the culture.

Australia didn't have an SBTV, a Grime Daily or a VladTV. (Though, let me shout out Gunsta and Hustle HARD TV. That platform did great things for the culture and even helped launch a few careers, but I wanted to do something different.) I was interviewing artists on *The Hip Hop Show*, but the format only allowed me to do so much. So I came up with the idea to launch Hauie TV, a video series aired on a relatively new platform called YouTube, wherein I would showcase Australian hip hop culture in a visual form.

***

My first interview had to be big, and because of my history in the scene, I had the contacts and respect to go right to the top: Hilltop Hoods. Since *The Calling*, they'd only gotten bigger, selling out arenas, touring abroad and knocking out number-one album after number-one album. They had raised the bar, and if I was to cover Australian rap, the Hoods was the only place to start.

I travelled to Adelaide to interview them at DJ Debris' house a few weeks after Aki was born. I know, what an understanding wife, right? What can I say, when the inspiration hits, you gotta run with it. Aki was actually part of the reason I was so desperate to get cracking. Before his birth, I thought fatherhood might sap my energy and enthusiasm, slowing my pace down to a nice, comfortable family life. It did the opposite, inspiring me to step my game up. So, I set off for the Adelaide Hills, joined by my guy Rush, who I tapped as my videographer and editor (and who shot the cover picture for this book).

I knew the Hoods were a big deal, but seeing Debris' house put their success in a different stratosphere. The man was living in a mini-mansion, complete with a split staircase in the foyers, an in-home studio and floating floors. All he needed was a handful of bikini-clad babes and a robe and you could call him DJ Hefner. I was amazed. It reminded me of visiting Kapisi in New Zealand. This was money from hip hop – *Australian* hip hop.

For me and Daniel it was never about the money. We were driven by creating a sound that was fresh, new and exciting. Like I said, we wanted to push boundaries. Our journey coincided with the Hoods', and while we always got critical acclaim, they also got the album sales – and with it the money and the mansions. I wouldn't trade our legacy for anything, but damn, I wouldn't say no to a crib like that!

One afternoon, I got an email from an artist named Syreney, who wanted to work with me. She had a beautiful voice, and after we talked I found out she also had Tongan heritage, which only made the offer more appealing. I told her to send me some of the music she was working on.

A few weeks later I received a bunch of MP3 files with a few instrumentals and some rough demos. It sounded promising, but there was one song in particular that had me hitting rewind. It was a posse cut featuring a collective of artists, and right at the end was a young rapper whose verse knocked me for six. I emailed Syreney back right away, asking who it was.

'That kid has got it!' I told her.

'Yeah, that's Remi,' she said. 'He's our secret weapon!'

Turned out he was an up-and-coming rapper from Melbourne who was acting as hype man for former 1200 Techniques frontman N'Fa Jones, who'd started going solo. Remi, N'Fa and Syreney were part of a collective called Run For Your Life, and in February 2012 they'd just released a mixtape.

It may have just been their warm-up mixtape, but the whole project, front to back, was the breath of fresh air Australian hip hop so desperately needed. There was a lyric from Souls of Mischief that I always felt summarised rap in this country. It's from the song 'Do You Want It?', and in the first verse Tajai calls out rappers who are 'all heart, no soul'. That was Aussie rap in a nutshell. In 2012, the country was still rooted in the boom bap era of the '90s, all about hard bars and gritty beats. It was cool, but it just wasn't funky. I could appreciate the lyricism and all that, but it didn't move me. Run For Your Life, on the other hand, had heart *and* soul.

And it wasn't just Remi and N'Fa. The group was led by two producers, Sensible J and Dutch, who were clearly listening to the same music I was at the time – artists like The Roots, J Dilla and Little Brother. It all had that lazy funk to it with a touch of electronica. I hit them up straightaway and asked them to come on *The Hip Hop Show*.

The crew clearly had hunger to go with their talent, because they dropped everything and drove in two car loads from Melbourne straight to the triple j studio. That's when I knew they were serious.

'We weren't gonna miss this opportunity,' J told me when they arrived.

That night, the studio was popping. We chopped it up for a bit, speaking about the different roles in the group and the various projects they had planned, before getting into some freestyles. Their energy was new school but they still had that old-school ability to rap anytime, anywhere.

You know that feeling you get when you hear a new artist for the first time and the hairs on your arm stand up? It grabs you by the scruff of the neck and reminds you why you fucking *love* music in the first place. That was the feeling I got hearing Remi rap.

He was only twenty-one, but damn he had steez for days. In fact, he had everything: charisma, cadence, charm, plus his lyrics were tough but they also had a sense of humour to them. He was having fun with it, which in turn was fun to listen to. He was a shot of youthful energy, but more importantly it was Black energy, something Australian rap was sorely missing.

After the show, I encouraged him to hook up with two other young Black artists I had just discovered.

'Sampa the Great and Baro – they're both based in Melbourne,' I told him. 'You guys gotta link.'

I was excited at the thought of what they could create together, how they could push the scene forward and help the country find its soul. But more than that, I realised how much I enjoyed playing that role – the facilitator, the voice of experience who could guide the next generation. Remi would have only just been born when my and Daniel's first project came out, but here he was inspiring me to get back in the booth.

For the first time in a while, I was feeling that itch again.

STYLE
KRS told me... YOU GOTTA HAVE
    STYYYLE!
learn to be original - keep it versatile
so you can't be pigeon-holed
can't be boxed
can't be compared to the rest
of the flak, I mean...
I gotta team, who's not concerned
with what's popular nor what's
poppin' off in the scene
I mean..@ the expense of not
getting any radio play
I do... what I do and what
I do is ok!
I am... comfortable with myself
and my music
Do you understand where I'm
 coming from?!
I push it along like Phife
  & QTip
that's been my tip through every
summer gone
And when winter approaches
buena as noches!
theme for the hopeful, theme for the
hopless! stick to your guns, it'll
come stay focussed!

BROWN MESSIAH

Like a lot of people, I've lived my life by a motto. Some go for things like, 'Be nice to the people on the way up, because you may need them on the way down.' For me, it's been, 'Never run for the bus.' Not heard of that one? I'll explain. There's the literal interpretation: I don't like the thought of running for a bus, only for it to leave as I arrive all hot and sweaty, looking like a goose. But it's deeper than that. I don't like putting effort into something unless I can be certain I'm going to be good at it.

I've lived a blessed life and achieved some incredible things, but opportunities have tended to present themselves. When they arrive, just like the proverbial bus, I jump right on board. Some could call this lacking ambition. So what. It had never held me back so I was content doing me. Then one day, as I was minding my own business, Shani gave me a reality check. She was visiting a therapist and encouraged me to book a session, too.

'You're not reaching your full potential,' she told me. 'You have your music and the radio show, but I know you, Hau – you could be doing so much more.'

Damn. I'm not gonna lie: I was shocked and more than a bit hurt. But Shani doesn't say things for no reason. Our relationship is built on honesty, so I figured I should at least think about it. I agreed to do one session with her therapist, a lady named Sonja.

Sonja was no ordinary therapist. I've heard her labelled a healer and a clairvoyant, while her title on the invoice just reads 'business consultant'. She's said to have 'the gift' to see into the future, but that's not what she trades in. Sonja is there to help you gather the tools you need to become the best version of yourself.

Shani has been seeing therapists like Sonja for as long as I've known her. She sets high goals for herself and likes to seek guidance and validation that she's on the right path. I'm not against the idea in principle and went along with her on a bunch of occasions in the past. Sometimes I'd get something out of it; other times they seemed like complete frauds who just dished out generic advice. *I'm sensing there's a difficult decision looming . . .* Yeah, no shit, Sherlock. There was even one who told me I was about to achieve something so momentous it would attract the attention of Barack Obama. Barack and I were, I was told, going to meet in New York City and ride a taxi together dressed in dark suits. Still waiting for that one to materialise but, nonetheless, I've always tried to keep an open mind. If that's your disposition, opportunities and inspiration can come from the unlikeliest of places.

Her office was in North Sydney. From the jump, it was unique compared to the other ones I'd visited. No generic mystical crap on the wall, no mood lighting or the therapist sitting mysteriously behind a veil of shadows. This was more like a corporate office; there was a couch if you wanted to lie down – I didn't – but other than that it felt serious, professional. Sonja was one of those no-nonsense white women. Medium height with curly hair and a slim build, she was warm without being friendly. She was all business, and I liked that about her.

'So, why are you here, Hau?' she asked me. 'What is your intent?'

'*Err*, my wife says I could be doing more,' I replied.

'Well, what do *you* think?'

Should have seen that one coming. 'I mean, I guess she has a point. I haven't really thought about it before.'

'Okay, we're going to start by looking at your priorities in life,' Sonja said. 'I want you to make a list of the most important things in your life and the order in which they come.'

I did as I was told: Shani and Aki at the top, followed by my family, my work and then music.

'*Hmm*. My understanding is that music is the driving force in your life,' she said. 'So why is it so far down the list?'

'It just is.' I shrugged. 'I have a family now and other priorities. It's the way life goes.'

Sonja nodded. 'We're going to do an exercise,' she continued. 'It might seem weird, but trust me. I want you to look at the chair next to you and pretend music is sitting in it. I want you to talk to music and tell it how you're feeling.'

Hesitating, I looked at the chair. *Keep an open mind*, I told myself. *This only works if you keep an open mind.*

I uttered the words 'I'm sorry' before an overwhelming feeling of embarrassment and shame took over. It was like bumping into an old friend on the street who you've been avoiding. You just have to cop it and level with them. But I was making excuses.

'I've got a family now, bro,' I explained, getting emotional. 'Things are different.'

Sonja paused for a moment, forcing me to sit with the shame I was feeling.

'Okay. Now I want you to swap seats and pretend that you're music,' she continued. 'Take a look at yourself next to you. What would you say?'

It was my friend's turn to talk, and he wasn't holding back. At this point I started crying. I couldn't hold it any longer.

'It feels like you don't make time for me anymore,' I said. 'We went on this journey together all those years ago, and now we don't even hang out. It's like you've forgotten about me.'

Tears streaming down my face, I was overwhelmed, but at the same time I felt a release. Like a weight had been lifted off my shoulders that I didn't even know was there. The session would have been productive if we'd just left it at that, but the thing I like most about Sonja is that she has one foot in the spiritual world, one in the practical. We'd covered the spiritual side of things, now it was time to get practical.

'I want you to make a schedule,' she explained. 'Break down for me what your week looks like.'

I told her when family time was, when I went to the gym, what hours I worked, what time I went to bed and so on. Being a musician and stay-at-home dad, I've always kept odd hours, so it's not unusual to be up at 2 am.

'So, from now on, you work on music from 10 pm to 1 am,' she told me. 'It's up to you to find the time and make it a priority.'

Sonja fixed something in me I didn't even know was broken. I knew I hadn't been doing much music for the past few years, but I didn't appreciate how deep-rooted the issue was. I figured I'd get back to it when I was ready. And it was more than just my issues with Daniel; I had my own issues to deal with.

Leaving her office, I felt energised. I was ready to run for the bus.

I stuck to the schedule like glue. Every night, from ten to one, with Shani and Aki in bed, I devoted myself to music. It was like rekindling a love affair. Rather than jumping straight into making music,

I focussed on listening – and I mean, *really* listening. Of course, I still had *The Hip Hop Show*, so I was never out of touch, but there's a difference between the way you consume the culture as a radio host versus as an artist. I immersed myself in the new trends that were emerging, how tastes had changed and which artists were able to capitalise.

Trap music was on the come-up, and while I could see the appeal, it didn't move me. Then there was a young artist named Kendrick Lamar, who was being hailed as the new king of the West Coast. When Kendrick dropped *Section.80*, there were some really dope moments throughout the project, but I wasn't quite seeing what others claimed to see. On his next album, 'Swimming Pools (Drank)' demonstrated some impressive musicianship but, again, it wasn't blowing me away. Then I heard 'm.A.A.d. City', featuring MC Eiht, and I was hooked. MC Eiht was part of Compton's Most Wanted, a rap group from the '90s who came up in the wake of NWA. I grew up on CMW, and while Eiht may not be a household name like Snoop or Dre, the man is a legend nonetheless. When I heard him on a track with Kendrick, I realised this was a young artist who under-stood his history and his place in the legacy of West Coast rap. That was an artist I could get behind.

I always wanted to make a solo record, and I knew this was my time. Like an athlete rediscovering his form, I needed to warm up first, so I decided to open with a mixtape. For this I took it right back to basics. I was back to writing rhymes whenever I had a spare moment, filling not just my notepads but napkins, the back of receipts – anything I could get my hands on. I downloaded GarageBand, a free piece of software that enables you to make beats from your laptop without a full studio, and I chose a photo of my dad, uncles and cousin in Tonga for the cover art. Featuring solely Australian instrumentals, it was called *Football, Feasts and Funerals*, tapping into that feeling I had when I was a kid, surrounded by family, discovering my love of hip hop for the first time.

The whole project was written and recorded in the space of a few months. I asked Dutch from Run For Your Life to mix and master the mixtape, and working with him reminded me how fun the whole process of making music can be. Don't get me wrong, Daniel and I had a super-collaborative relationship for the most part, but during the making of *The 'Umu* I knew what his reaction would be if I tried to broach an idea. I couldn't be bothered with the dramas so I tended to just leave him to it. With Dutch, I was in the driver's seat. When I went to him with suggestions, he was *always* receptive. I'd forgotten how that felt.

Football, Feasts and Funerals was released in August 2014 via Bandcamp, an online platform that enabled you to upload projects and sell directly to your listeners without an intermediary like a record label. I made a bundle to go with it, with signed CDs, as well as a cassette and a pencil, the sort we used to rewind our cassettes back in the day. This was a project for the hip hop heads, but more importantly, it was a project for me.

In December, Shani and I had another baby on the way so we were back looking at the calendar again. Maila – a name we'd made up that was part my mum's maiden name, Ma'ilei, and part my Uncle Maile – was due, just like Aki before her, on Christmas Day. This meant we needed to find the right time for the C-section. We settled on 15 December 2014, a date you may remember from the news. The date of the Lindt Cafe siege in Sydney.

Shani and I watched the events unfold from the waiting room. The Lindt Cafe in Martin Place was a few doors down from our obstetrician, so their chocolate cheesecake became our post-appointment treat. It was always full of tourists and couples on dates, but on 15 December it was the setting to something else entirely. A crazed gunman held ten customers and eight employees hostage while he made a series of nonsensical demands, like talking to then-PM Tony Abbott live on radio. The scumbag even used hostages as human shields. The situation hadn't been resolved when we went into theatre for Shani to deliver Maila, distracting me with depressing thoughts about the sort of world we were bringing our daughter into. But as soon as the doors closed behind us, any fears I had vanished.

Having a baby will do that. From before her birth to now, Maila has a habit of making me forget anything else that's happening on the planet. Her light shines so brightly it doesn't matter how dark the world is. Then again, on that day she did have just *a little* bit of help – in the form of R&B legend D'Angelo. While the day of Maila's birth coincided with one of the bleaker moments in Australian history, it was also the same day D'Angelo dropped *Black Messiah*, his first release in fourteen years. After the birth, we had that album on repeat, a fitting soundtrack to the arrival of our very own messiah.

THE NO END THEORY

By the start of 2015 I was in full album mode. As a solo artist I was going simply by Hau – I know, a long cry from the days of Cruel-T, X-Kwizit and Fatty Boomstix – and I'd hooked up with a manager named Sam Dutch. My man. A champion of a guy who has done a lot for the local scene, he was working hard to get me a record deal.

Sony were interested again. I'd never been into the major label idea when I was with Daniel; everything we did was off our own back, and we preferred it that way. To us, that was the essence of hip hop. But in 2015, my life was in a different place. I had two kids now, so if a major wanted to throw some cash my way I wasn't gonna complain.

But after several conversations they never came with any paper-work. Instead, I signed with a New Zealand label. They were an indie set-up who understood the culture so I trusted them with the project. They handed over a $10K advance and I got to work. One of the first things I did was come up with the title. I think people can forget the significance that comes in a name. Before I even began writing this book I knew it was going to be called *King*. It embodied the story I wanted to tell and the message I wanted to get across.

As soon as you have a name, you give life to the story, creating the vessel that allows it to take shape.

Months before its completion, I called the album *The No End Theory*. It was a tip of the hat to my favourite Tribe Called Quest album, *The Low End Theory*, and it captured my place in history – the history of my Tongan heritage as well as of Australian music. In music and in life, I've tried to honour the legacy of my ancestors, and now that I have kids myself I hope they do the same. My art, as well as the Lātūkefu legacy, has 'no end'.

As a solo artist operating in the new age of hip hop, I was doing things a little differently this time. Rather than simply coming up with album merch to sell to fans, I approached a local fashion label called Sydney Romantics to create a collaboration T-shirt for the launch. They were a new label making dope clothes, but more importantly they aligned with my values. Rather than ripping off international designs, they were rooted in Australian culture and had a vision to celebrate and promote *our* identity in fashion, just as I wanted to do in music. Plus, one of the main creative minds behind the label was a guy named Ricky Simandjuntak, who was a real hip hop head. As soon as we hooked up, we clicked instantly.

Everything was going smoothly until Sam got a call from the label in New Zealand, telling us they'd gone bankrupt and folded. You see – this is why you do things yourself! My first response was, 'Do we have to pay back the advance?' Thankfully the answer was no. So we were $10K in the black but without a distribution partner. It was back to the essence.

We never expected my dad to inherit the title of *Tauhifonua*. As the youngest of nine, it had a lot of hands to pass through before it fell to him. But in April 2015, that's exactly what happened.

Tongan society is very hierarchical. There's the King, then the nobles, then the people. In each village there's a noble who then picks someone to act as *Tauhifonua*, becoming their ceremonial stand-in when they're not there. In Dad's village, that responsibility has been with our family for generations. Following the death of my grandfather, which happened before I was born, the title should have gone to Sione, as the eldest son. However, as he and the majority of the siblings were overseas, Sione decided to give the title to Uncle Sele, who was still in Tonga. Sele stayed behind to take care of my grandparents, so instead of a proper education he got the privilege of the title. When Sele died, the responsibility fell to his son, Siosiua. But Siosiua died when he was in his 40s, and because his son, Elikena, was only in his early teens at the time, my dad, as the only living son left, took on the role of *Tauhifonua*.

It was a huge honour for Dad. And while I was thrilled, I also knew the burden that came with it. Each time there was a ceremony or a fundraising event in his village in Tonga, Dad's presence would be expected. Dad loved it; he received a special reverence from the community and was able to give back in a way that made him feel immensely proud. He saw it as a privilege. But that privilege comes at a cost. A big one. It's one thing if you hold the title as Sele did, and you live in Tonga, but each time Dad got the call-up it meant a return flight from Australia plus money for family while he was there, then of course a sizeable donation to whatever cause they were raising funds for. Mum had got several degrees and worked non-stop since she'd arrived in Australia, and when she retired, she imagined a future of leisure and travel. Now she was watching her pot of hard-earned money slowly but surely disappear. All because of my dad's title. His *privilege*.

And there was little recognition for the sacrifices that went into Dad doing what he did. In Tonga it's expected. You just have to find the money by whatever means necessary. No one asks questions. If, for example, the church needs money, the community – however hard up people might be – is expected to pay for it. Growing up in a Western country, this dynamic is hard to conceive. But in Tonga, the Church, cultural traditions, even the Royal family, all take precedent over the individual.

What people outside the Islands don't understand is how readily these sacrifices are made. They're not done out of resentment but joy. They give Tongans like my dad a purpose in life. Without it, their life doesn't have the same meaning and their attachment to home becomes unmoored. My uncle Sione wrote about this in his book. One of the ancient Kings, Toogoo Ahoo, who was known to be particularly cruel and vindictive, wanted a way to distinguish his twelve cooks from the rest of his attendants. So he asked them all to chop off their left arms. Without complaint, all twelve immediately did as they were asked. Elsewhere, the book mentions sacrifices the Tu'i Tonga (sacred King) expected of his subjects:

> You will see fathers tie the rope round the necks of their children, whose death is demanded to prolong the life of this divinity; more than once you will see the child smile as it is being killed.

Now, to be clear, Dad wasn't about to chop off his own arm or sacrifice me for the sake of Tonga, but he was always ready and willing to do what was asked of him for the sake of his community. I admired the strength of his convictions, but I felt bad for Mum. A strong-willed, independent woman, she'd achieved so much in her life but was always being asked to play second fiddle to Dad, just because she's a woman. Once, when they were at one of these events in Tonga, she and Dad were bickering, like they often do. Nothing serious, a minor couple's disagreement. A woman a few rows back piped up and told my mum she shouldn't speak to her husband like that. Mum had had enough. She turned round and told the women exactly what she thought of her 'advice'.

You're probably wondering, what will I do if the title falls to me? My answer is simple: I'd decline. I'm conflicted about this. It's traditions like these that define my cultural heritage. And I'm immensely proud of the role my dad, Sione, Sele and all those who came before them have been able to do for our community. But whether it's because of my own internal make-up or, more likely, the fact I didn't grow up in Tonga, my priorities are different. Like I told Sonja, it goes: Shani, Aki and now Maila, then my immediate family before all else. No title, privilege or tradition will get in the way of me providing for them. For Dad, it was slightly different as Sabne and I had already moved out and could support ourselves, but it still came at a cost – a cost I am unwilling to pay.

In 2015, the tide was starting to turn in Australian hip hop again, this time for the better. Remi and Sensible J formed a duo, transforming from exciting up-and-comers to one of the best acts in the country. They dropped their debut album in 2014, called *Raw x Infinity*, which won the Australian Music Prize and launched their record label, House of Beige. The label would bring some much-needed funk to the scene, or as Remi puts it in the opening song of the album: 'We're here to change the Australian rap game / We add colour like blood on white walls.'

Then came Bad Apples Music. Set up by Indigenous rapper – and future PM – Adam Briggs, it aimed to nurture First Nations artists, helping to break the likes of Nooky and Kobie Dee. Finally, with new, diverse voices holding the steering wheel for the first time, Australian hip hop was finding its soul.

Dutch and J were the main producers behind *The No End Theory*, so when the NZ label folded I took the opportunity to House of

Beige. It was a perfect match: they respected the work I'd already put in for the scene, and I loved what they were doing in pushing it forward. We dropped on 25 September 2015 and took the album on tour in December.

It was like my victory lap after putting in over two decades of work. As an elder in the game now, I made a conscious effort to include a wide range of voices and textures. I had legends on there like New Zealand's Che Fu, as well as new-school artists like Oddisee. And I was sure to include a bunch of female vocalists throughout the album, like Ngaiire, who went on to receive three ARIA nominations in 2021. Not only were they all dope singers, but they helped offset the macho energy that can define a lot of hip hop.

The tour ended in Canberra. It was more like a celebration than a gig; Tunks and all the boys came through, Axe got on stage, and I ended with a remix of a Resin Dogs song called 'Re-Fizzla' that I renamed 'ReFizzLātūkefu', featuring only Canberra MCs. It was a homage to the local scene that gave me my start in rap. Back in the '90s we were outcasts. Adults like my high school principal Mr Marks told us hip hop wouldn't take us anywhere, sound engineers looked down their noses at us, and radio wouldn't play us.

Twenty years later, I was deciding who gets played on radio, my friends were running labels, and our music was winning the most prestigious awards in Australian music. So, for all the haters and naysayers out there: how you like *them* apples?

THE COULD LIFE
ft. CHE FU
We work like a slave til
the pay packet is gone /
Went from plantations
→ a factory job /
tryin' to save up
e-nough for a better day/
end up sending the
money back hooome
anyway !

FOREVER EVER

The music industry can be cut-throat. A lot of people won't lift a finger until they know they'll get something in return. Even something as simple as an introduction will get held up because Person A wants to ensure they will get a kickback for introducing you to Person B. It's tiring having to tiptoe around the egos and the hidden agendas, but occasionally you'll meet someone who's an exception to the rule. Someone who will think about the bigger picture and happily do something to push the scene forward regardless of their own personal gain. In my life and career, I've been fortunate enough to meet a few such people, and one of them is Petrina Convey.

Petrina owned and ran a marketing firm specialising in hip hop and R&B, so we'd known each other for years. She'd bring her artists to *The Hip Hop Show* to be interviewed and would always ensure I had tickets to their gigs and all the access I needed. In 2016, when she took her talents to Sony, one of the first things she did was call me. Straightaway, I could tell from her tone that this wasn't our normal conversation.

We met in the cafe at the ABC offices on a day I was prepping for the show. Home turf. I trusted Petrina but I still wanted to figure out what it was she was after. I got myself a cappuccino and for Petrina a soy flat white. In typical fashion, she got right down to business, explaining that she was now the Director of Cultural Marketing at Sony, with a focus on hip hop and R&B, and she wanted me involved in some way. 'I told them if this is the direction Sony wants to go in,' she said, 'they are going to need people like you who are actually connected to the culture.'

I was intrigued. Sony and I'd had our own history, but our conversations hadn't led to a recording deal. Now, with a whole section of the business dedicated to the culture, they were taking things more seriously. This was a good sign for the local scene and an even better sign that they were talking to people like me.

We arranged a follow-up meeting at Sony's offices a few weeks later. This was an away game with unfamiliar opposition, so I knew not to overcommit myself. Sitting opposite me was Tim Pithouse, Sony's General Manager of International Marketing and Artist Development. I'd never met Tim before so my approach was the same for all meetings where I don't know the person's intentions: just sit back and listen. They will either earn your trust or they'll talk themselves in circles until they expose themselves. Either way, it's win–win.

Tim seemed the real deal. We discussed hip hop and the things he was listening to at the moment – Kendrick, J. Cole and Joey Bada$$ – as well as some of the classics. He dropped references to A Tribe Called Quest, at which point I became more receptive. Of course, I didn't show any sign of this. I was straight poker face.

What I appreciated most was Tim's honesty. He acknowledged head-on the fact that if they want to connect with artists of different backgrounds, it's not easy coming from him – a white Brit from a corporate world – whereas I was an artist with credibility in the scene, and an Islander at that. After he'd said his spiel, he turned the tables on me.

'So, what do *you* want from all of this, Hau?'

What's that sound? It's a bus, about to pull away. But, man, you're gonna have to run . . .

'I want my own record label,' I told him. It was a spur of the moment thing, but why not ask, I thought.

'Okay,' he said, nodding. 'Well, let's talk about it.'

The first order of business was, of course, the name. Negotiations were still a mile away, but a name would give life to the idea in my head, and I needed it to be real before I could agree to any of the fine print. I knew from the jump that any label I was involved in would be two things, first and foremost: it would be run *for* and *by* artists, and it would be here for the long haul. I had rejected the idea of major labels for most of my career because they have a habit of cashing in on artists' hard work then dipping when the going gets tough. I was going to do things differently.

I think it was Shani who came up with the name Forever Ever. If this was trivia night at the local, I'd be expecting my readers to know this one off by heart. It's from Outkast's 'Ms. Jackson': *I hope we feel like this forever / Forever, forever, ever, forever, ever?* Yeah exactly, you knew that.

The reference was perfect. Not only was Andre 3000 one of my favourite MCs, the line spoke to my idea of permanence. My label wouldn't be a short-term thing; I was playing for keeps. For *forever ever.*

Next, I reached out to a few artist mates for advice, including Sydney rapper Urthboy. He entered the game around the same time as me and went on to found the indie label Elefant Traks, so I was keen to hear what he thought of the idea. As an underground head at heart, just like me, he was sceptical about the major label connection but told me, 'If anyone can make it work, it's you.'

The last thing I did before everything got signed and sealed was talk to Petrina again. I'd come clean to Sony about what I wanted, but I needed more assurances about what they wanted from the label. While artists like Remi were doing their thing and doing it big, the major looks were still reserved for white dudes who played sing-along festival rap, guys like Illy, Allday and 360. Did Sony want more of the same?

'Trust your instinct, Hau,' Petrina told me. 'You're here to take risks.'

That was all I needed to hear.

THE NEW AUSTRALIA

I've always had a rule that if I'm going to work with someone I need to like them first. Talent, work ethic and all the rest are important, but I need to want to spend time with them if we're to have any hope of succeeding together. This was especially the case with Forever Ever. I wanted to work with people I respected as artists and liked as individuals. You have to tick both boxes or it's a no deal.

My vision from the start was Top Dawg Entertainment (TDE), the label out of Los Angeles, California. For a small operation they had platinum-selling rappers like Kendrick Lamar, Isaiah Rashad and ScHoolboy Q, as well as the R&B star SZA. But most importantly, these artists were with TDE *before* they blew up. The label and the artists grew alongside each other, making their success all the more meaningful.

Like Kendrick before he dropped *good kid, m.A.A.d City*, I wanted a diamond in the rough – an artist I could nurture and develop, guiding them towards their dream. Not a fully-fledged product who I could just throw the weight of Sony behind. I *could* do that, but that would be boring. I also knew I wanted to sign a female artist first. I wanted to set an example. Rap has always been a male-dominated scene, and all that testosterone isn't healthy. It can create a toxic space and means that a lot of super-talented women get overlooked. Not at Forever Ever.

When I finally signed the paperwork with Sony I was in discussion with two artists: Genesis Owusu, a charismatic rapper/singer from Canberra, and Ziggy Ramo, an Indigenous artist born in Bellingen, NSW. After several months of conversation, both discussions led to nothing. I think Genesis and Ziggy were already in talks with other labels but went on a journey with me mainly out of respect.

Both have gone on to become stars. When Genesis Owusu released his debut album in 2021, *Smiling with No Teeth*, it reminded me of a conversation we had where he told me he wanted to make an album like Childish Gambino's *Awaken, My Love!*, the one with 'Redbone' on it. Psychedelic and funky, it's an R&B record in hip hop clothing, and it's an epic piece of work. Listening to *Smiling with No Teeth*, you can hear the traces of Childish Gambino in there. It's a big, impressive debut and exactly what Genesis envisioned for himself. I was proud of him. Ziggy, meanwhile, has gone on to release tracks with the folk icon Paul Kelly, and while his 2020 album *Black Thoughts* is awesome and powerful, he's more known for his activism these days than his music.

If they had signed with me, would I have been the right person to steer their ship? Would I have encouraged Genesis to stick to his rap roots, causing him to veer away from the feel of *Smiling with No Teeth* that gave him his major breakthrough? And with Ziggy, would I have been sitting in the studio wondering when he was going to pause on the activism and get back to music?

I honestly don't know. But I do know I was happy to wait, for the right artist at the right time. Like I said, Forever was in it for the long haul.

✳✳✳

I hadn't been checking for Islander rap in a minute. They were still rooted in the American West Coast gangster rap scene, and while a few acts like Pistol Pete & Enzo out of south-west Sydney's Campbelltown were impressive rappers, everyone was still imitating Americans, so I wasn't paying it much attention.

The first artist I heard who broke the mould was Hooligan Hefs. A Samoan-Australian with Chinese heritage, Hefs released a song called 'Dem Boyz', and it wasn't like anything I'd heard in Australia. He was rapping in his own accent and was clearly inspired by the grime scene coming out of the UK, offering his own version of it. Grime, which is all about the fast-paced tempo and energetic lyrics, is what catapulted UK rap to the world stage. As soon as artists like Skepta and Dizzee Rascal started embracing their own culture and identity, people got behind it. It was like I'd been saying all along: be yourself, and people will mess with it.

I reached out to Hefs over social media. Like all artists I hit up, I don't mention the label or anything like that at first; I just offer a hand if they need it and see where the conversation goes. It's like meeting a girl – you don't ask her to marry you on the first date; you gotta get to know her first. Turned out, Hefs already knew who I was, telling me he'd listened to *The Hip Hop Show* while serving time in prison. It made me realise the impact the show was having. It's one of the main sources of rap releases in this country, so I know it's a big deal in general, but for those of us living behind four walls it offers something more. For young men like Hefs, it's a symbol of hope. We exchanged a few messages back and forth, but before I knew it Hefs was back inside.

Then I heard ONEFOUR, a rap group out of Western Sydney's Mount Druitt, consisting of members Celly, Lekks, Spenny, J Emz and YP. It was Ricky Simandjuntak, my guy from Sydney Romantics, who put me onto them. Like Hefs, their sound was also inspired by the UK, but instead of grime it was drill, the new subgenre of rap that had taken over Chicago in the early 2010s before spreading to London. While grime is based on rave culture, drill is rooted in portrayals of crime and violence. Darker than all other hip hop subgenres to come before it, drill holds a mirror up to tough neighbourhoods, like Mount Druitt, and forces the listener to pay attention. It's relentless and for a lot of people it's tough to stomach, both in the lyrics and the aesthetic, with a lot of drill rappers covering their faces with balaclavas while they perform. It's a sign they either have legal troubles and don't want to reveal their identity given the theme of their raps, or it's just some savvy marketing – like it or not, rapping about drugs and crime from behind a mask is one powerful image.

Hefs had the energy but ONEFOUR were serious rappers. Particularly Lekks and Celly. On one of their very first releases, 'Ready for War', Celly raps:

> I've got ten steppin' with ten weapons
> You disappearin' in ten seconds
> If you get away in a better place
> You must really have ten blessings.

Fkn oaf! The rhyme scheme was advanced and for a rapper with only a couple releases under his belt? That was impressive stuff. I had to meet these boys.

I reached out to Celly, the group's founder, first, through another rapper/producer, Lux, and we started messaging back and forth on Instagram. I kept it simple, letting him know I was there if he or the group wanted advice. They were talented but they were also raw. As you can hear in the lyrics, their music – just like their neighbourhoods – was full of violence, and had the potential to attract a lot of negative press. This didn't bother me. Hip hop was born in the streets; the whole point is that it can offer kids like ONEFOUR a pathway *out* of them. They just need to be given a chance.

By November 2018, I got wind that Celly was in prison. He'd broken his bail conditions for a previous crime and wasn't about to be released anytime soon. Sensing their position dangling on a knife's edge, I reached out to ONEFOUR and suggested we meet in person.

We met at a steakhouse in Mount Druitt. As I waited, the restaurant filled up with Islanders wearing *tupenus*, coming for their post-church feed. The image warmed my heart. I hadn't been to Mount Druitt before and didn't realise the extent of the Pasifika population. When I was ONEFOUR's age, you could fit the Islander population of Canberra into a few restaurants like this one. In Mount Druitt in 2018, they were barely even a minority.

With Celly in jail and Spenny busy, it was J Emz, Lekks, YP, their producer HollaBack Beats (RIP), as well as their mate T, and L, the older brother of J Emz and YP. They sat down, offered a round of polite hellos and immediately hit the buffet, returning with plates piled high with steak, potatoes, curry and chop suey – a standard Islander feast. I was fine with my cappuccino.

J Emz did most of the talking. I couldn't tell if he had done his research on me or was genuinely aware of my history, but he asked if I was still rapping.

'Not really,' I told him. 'The label and the radio show are my priorities now.' (This time, it really *was* different, Sonja.)

They were sweet lads. Staunch, but sweet. They reminded me of some of my cousins and KOA boys like Metro and Mahem. There was a tight bond that reflected where, and how, they had grown up.

While they were all polite and respectful, you could tell this was a group of lads you didn't want to fuck with.

We spoke about music first. I wanted to know who they were listening to that had inspired them to rap in the way they did. Rather than street dudes who had a passing fancy in rap music, they were clearly well schooled, identifying with artists in the UK like Harlem Spartans and Brixton's 67. Then the conversation turned to their bail conditions. Both YP and Lekks were on bail for their involvement in the same alleged crime that put Celly inside. They explained they had strict curfews and couldn't enter licensed premises – which made me turn over the drinks menu in front of us.

They answered my questions but, aside from J Emz, they were clearly wary of saying too much. I respected the attitude – I would have done the exact same if I was in their shoes. But despite their quiet demeanour, I could see they meant business. Their first few songs were recorded in a studio that was part of a youth centre called Street Uni. They were given one-hour access each week, and returned week after week until they were finished. That's the sort of dedication you just can't teach.

'Aside from the police stuff,' I asked them, 'what's the one thing that's holding you back?'

'Studio access,' replied J Emz, the others nodding their approval.

'If I was to book you a studio, would you come?'

J Emz responded without hesitation. 'Name a time and a place and we'll be there.'

A week later, I was back at an ARIA event with Zane Lowe. It was November 2018 and Lowe was hosting a masterclass on 'The New Australia' – a celebration of the fact hip hop in this country was at its most stylistically and culturally diverse. I was on the panel alongside Briggs of Bad Apples, hip hop journalist Chris Kevin Au, and the young dons Sampa the Great and Kwame. It was a milestone for me personally but even more so for the scene in general. There was an exciting energy in the room. We could all feel the shift that was occurring, with the big corporations finally paying attention to the wide range of voices in Australia. What we didn't know at the time was that the most exciting thing to *ever* happen to rap in Australia was bubbling away thirty miles west in Mount Druitt, about to explode.

After the masterclass I had the opportunity to sit down with Lowe. We'd never met but, as he'd grown up in New Zealand with a few of the KOA boys, we had a bunch of mutual friends. He was tripped out when I brought up names he hadn't heard in years. After we caught up, I played him a few recordings of ONEFOUR. At that time there was nothing official to show other than some rough demos I had in my email. With both of us hunched over my phone, I played him recordings of 'Want the Money' and 'Ready for War'. The sound was tinny but the energy was there, living proof of the 'New Australia'.

SHANKS AND WHAT?

There're a few times in life when you know you're witnessing history. As if life is about to take a divergent course and you're right there in the moment that a new path is being trodden. When it came to Australian hip hop, I'd had a front-row seat to a few of these mile-stones, like winning the first urban ARIA in 2004 or watching Remi enter the game in 2012. Witnessing ONEFOUR in the studio for the first time was another.

Manu, AKA HollaBack Beats, was the first to arrive – and for some reason he turned up lugging a massive suitcase.

'What are you doing, bro?' I laughed. 'Moving in?'

'Nah, this is my computer,' he replied. 'It's got all our beats.'

It reminded me of meeting Daniel at the youth centre in Woden Valley all those years ago. Technology had improved a lot since then, so Manu wasn't dragging around a small car like Daniel, but the sight was still humbling. It was a reminder that these boys were doing whatever they could to make it work. They didn't have laptops with Logic preloaded, ready to make beats; what they had was one desktop computer between them. Plus, it showed their dedication. They had been given an opportunity to record in a proper studio, and they weren't about to miss their shot.

Each member of the group has a hugely different rap style to the next, so whenever they appear on a track together, you get a lyrical assault on all fronts. Lekks is the rapper's rapper; like Celly, his verses are full of complex rhyme schemes that reflect the types of artists he listens to, like East Coast legend Big L. Spenny is cut from the grime cloth, so his flow is more up-tempo, and he always comes with funny, offbeat cultural references to things like wrestling, Captain Cook and even *Wreck-It Ralph*. Then there's J Emz and his younger brother YP. Less technical than the other two, they're all about presence and confidence on the mic. You hear J Emz on a song and it's as if you can feel him in the room next to you, while YP, as the youngest of the lot, has a habit for coming up with the most memorable – and shocking – one-liners.

When they arrived in the studio, it was unfiltered potential straight from the faucet. As they were getting used to the surroundings, Manu played a few of their songs that they'd roughly recorded themselves. There was one track that resembled Bone Thugs-N-Harmony, with them singing rather than rapping. The contrast to their drill stuff was crazy, but it still had the same captivating energy. I encouraged them to re-record it, but they said that one was just for them. Instead, they had a song called 'Shanks and Shivs' that they wanted help with.

YP was the first to enter the booth. He hadn't been a part of their previous releases, so this was literally his first time recording anything. And it showed. He had the conviction in his voice but the skill level wasn't there. After a few failed attempts, he and the others went outside to listen to music in their headphones and get in the zone. When they returned, they were ready. The diamonds in the rough, ready to be polished.

***

When I read the reports about Sony Australia Chief Executive Denis Handlin, I was hardly surprised. Everyone in the building walked on eggshells around him, and I'd heard rumours of how much of a hardarse he could be. Whenever I'd met him, he seemed nice enough. Looking back, I think I was far enough removed from the Sony structure that I wasn't really a part of his world and therefore not a target. Forever Ever was close enough to Sony that they could take credit for its success, and far enough apart that they could wash their hands of it if it was a failure. And so to Denis I wasn't a threat. He always offered me a smile around the office whenever we bumped into each other and reminded me he was available for anything I needed.

A few weeks after we recorded 'Shanks and Shivs' I met him in a boardroom at the top of the Sony building. It was one of those special boardrooms, where you needed a different access key to the other plebs in the building. This is where Denis spent his days, separated from his staff and cocooned in his plush executive office with his view of the city. If 'Ivory Tower' had a steel and glass version, it would look a lot like this.

Petrina and Tim thought it was best coming from me. With Denis' reputation for being difficult to please, they thought having me speak directly to him about why I was so passionate about ONEFOUR would help our case and get approval to make a formal offer. Fine by me. These boys were the real deal and the exact reason I started Forever Ever in the first place. Ideally, I wanted to open the label with a female artist, but I knew a group like this doesn't come around often.

In the room was Denis; his son Pat, who headed up artist rela-
tions; Tim; Petrina and some execs from the legal team. I gave them
all a run-through on ONEFOUR and why they were the perfect act
to open the label. Hip hop in this country is changing, I told them,
and these boys were the face of the new generation. If we're going to
sign anyone, it should be them.

Denis sounded keen. 'If you're into it, I'm into it,' he said. 'Let's
do it.'

Wow. That was easy! Hearing that, I was ready to escape the Ivory
Tower while the chips were still in my favour. But Denis had other
ideas.

'Do you have anything to show me?' he asked.

Damn! I'm about to undo all my good work, I thought.

'Yeah,' I told him. 'They just dropped a song called ... *erm* ...
"Shanks and Shivs".'

'Well, let's hear it,' he said.

They pulled the video up on a big screen while Denis instructed
someone to dim the lights. The darkness was convenient for me
because it was precisely at this moment that I started sweating
bullets. With the room silent, I took a deep breath and pressed *play*.

Shanks and Shivs, (shanks and what?)
I swear that's all we need when we go there to take that trip . . .

YP's voice filled the room while the video opened with a
disclaimer that 'all the characters in this music video are entirely
fictional'. Having listened to all types of hip hop over the past thirty-
odd years, I'm so desensitised to certain lyrics that they barely even
register as controversial. But, trust me, in a boardroom surrounded
by a bunch of suits, I was aware. *Very* aware. And it wasn't just the
lyrics. Because of their impending cases, YP and Lekks kept their

identities hidden with balaclavas and scarves wrapped around their faces. Here I was trying to get Denis Handlin to front up some cash to sign a group of faceless artists.

It was like a comedy sketch. *Is it me or did this room just get hotter?* I was worried that if I pulled open my collar steam would rise out of my shirt like I was boiling a kettle. It was the longest three minutes and thirty-seven seconds of my life. When the lights finally came back on, I'd lost several kilos in perspiration but, to my surprise, Denis was a fan.

'Great, I love it,' he said. 'Let's do it!'

This is why I can't talk down on the guy. After the way he is said to have behaved for the best part of three decades, I'd love to pile on and rip him a new one. After all, that *is* what he deserves. But I can't – to me, he was always a gentleman and a supportive ally. I mean, how many execs would have given the green light to work with ONEFOUR at that time, when one member was already in jail, two others were also facing time and the Sydney papers were labelling them a gang of heartless thugs? Yeah, not many.

'Is there anything else I can help you with, Hau?' Denis asked, signalling an end to the meeting.

'Yeah,' I said, standing up. 'You don't mind lending me the keys to your Benz this weekend, do you?'

TUNKS

I understand what ONEFOUR are doing. If I was a kid today, I'm not sure if I'd be super into them. Only because I was always resistant to being into what everyone else was into. In fact, when I hung around Sydney as a kid, our crew never really got on with Mount Druitt, so I probably would've found a way to be saying, 'Fuck ONEFOUR.'

But as an adult, there's a lot in their music that I like. I'm feeling it that there's these Polynesian kids from out west who have latched onto this culture and then made their own version of it. And they're going hard with it. Even if I was a kid, I'd be able to recognise how much they've put into it and how good they are at it. They're definitely the best in this country at that form of music. They're polished. They go hard. And they're really dedicated to their craft, so, objectively, I rate them. Let's put it this way, when I was a kid, I was listening to NWA. So for kids who grew up here, ONEFOUR is their NWA, and it's in a local accent.

But I called Hau one day and I had to ask him, 'Do you let your kids listen to this?' Because I saw he's got Aki in a film clip; he's wearing a balaclava and he knows all the words. I know it's harmless, because to him it's just music. But I wanted to see what Hau's thoughts were on that because, let's be straight about it, almost every single one of those songs is about killing opps, selling drugs and territorial violence.

And like, I'm cool with that. But I wouldn't necessarily want my kids rapping along to a lot of that. Then again, Hau's an artist and he sees the artistry and the pure musical side of it. And I don't think Aki listens to it on that level. Aki hears the songs and he hears the catchy raps, and he likes the posturing and the fact they're Islander boys and, you know, he feels cool. And I know Hau has open conversations with his kids about this sort of stuff.

I also wanted to know what Hau's position was on being involved with ONEFOUR. Because the impression I get is some of those boys have had one foot in the streets – and some of them maybe more than one foot. And that's dangerous territory. 'Cause some of those kids, even if they're not really doing that anymore, their boys might be, and so they're always on the edge of that world. Hau's not really about that. He's been around it his whole life but that's not really him, so I was just checking in to see how he was handling it, how he's carrying himself through it, and what role he has with the group. And the thing about Hau is, he's really trying to be a positive role model, to help them get up and outta that lifestyle.

Still, I wouldn't encourage my kids to listen to that shit!

SANTA CLAUS

I don't believe in him. Never have. I'm not saying I don't believe he's actually a person; I think we can both take that as a given. What I mean is, I don't believe in the *idea* of Santa Claus. Every year, parents around the world work their arses off to afford gifts for their kids only to give all the credit to some fictional white bloke with a beard and a bunch of reindeer as his chauffeurs. Not in my family. Any present I give my kids, they *know* Shani and I are the ones who paid for it.

It's like religion. Whether it's saying grace, praying in general or just giving thanks, we defer all our success and joy to God rather than ourselves. Not in my family. It's going to hurt my mum to read this, but everything I've done and achieved in my life has been because of my hard work and the support of my friends, family and community. *Not* divine intervention.

I've tried to communicate this to Aki and Maila since they were born. Don't worry, it's not like I sat them down on Christmas Eve and explained that Santa Claus was a fraud. I didn't have to. All I did was be completely honest with them and ensure we have open conversations about these things. When, as a five-year-old, Aki asked me if Santa was real, I put the question back on him.

'What do *you* think?' I asked. 'Do you think it sounds possible?'

I didn't force it but I encouraged him to come to his own conclusions. And I've done the same with rap music. He and Maila can listen to ONEFOUR, Ice-T and Jay-Z, and they can listen to the *Frozen* soundtrack on repeat if they want to. (I'd prefer if they didn't, but they can.) When Aki got into ONEFOUR, we talked about it. Just because he knows what a shank is doesn't mean he's going to use one. I also explained to Aki that some of the group were in prison. I told him they had done some bad things, things they shouldn't have done, and now they're paying the price. That's what happens in life, I explained; there are always consequences for your actions.

I started bringing him along with me when I visited the boys out West. Aki has been in music videos and promotional artwork for their songs, and he's loved every minute of the experience. From before they were born, I wanted my kids to mix with people of all different backgrounds – rappers, artists, teachers, business people – because diversity is *always* a good thing.

On one of our visits to Mount Druitt, he made the same observation I did when I used to visit New Zealand as a kid: there are *way* more Brown people there than back home.

'Why's that?' he asked.

I explained about immigrant populations and how they often live together in suburbs out of the city because it's cheaper to live there than, say, where we do in Woollahra. Did he fully understand? Maybe not. But that information will be stored in his brain for when he's ready to process it.

He likes visiting Mounty and being around the Brown faces there, but I suspect he also likes returning home. I used to laugh at the thought of Eastern Suburbs kids and their privileged lives by the beach – now I have two of my own. But Aki and Maila are Eastern Suburbs babies with some flavour: raised on honesty and hip hop, *not* Santa Claus.

AIN'T NO MAYBES, IFS OR BUTS

When an artist blows up, it's a lot like a chemical reaction: there's nothing you can do to stop it. If you combine pure, unfiltered potential with the right circumstances, all you need is a spark then – *BOOM!* – you'll light the whole place on fire. That's what happened in 2003 when Hilltop Hoods dropped *The Calling*. Their rap skills and natural ability to write a catchy pop song, combined with white Australia's yearning for hip hop that they could identify with, meant that the Hoods were sent into another stratosphere. Sixteen years later and Australian hip hop was prepping itself for another seismic shift. All I needed to do was create the spark.

We were back in the studio soon after 'Shanks and Shivs' dropped. It was just me and Papertoy, an Australian music producer/engineer who happened to be living in Brixton when the London drill wave was kicking off. He knew the vibe and aesthetic of what ONEFOUR were going for, so I brought him in to add another opinion. He's talented and, for context, he's white.

The first to arrive, J Emz offered his polite hellos before whispering to me, asking why the cleaner was in the studio with us.

344

'Bro, that's Papertoy,' I told him, bursting out laughing. 'He's the engineer.'

It was a funny misunderstanding, but it was also an encouraging sign that the face of local hip hop was changing. The days of 'Aussie hip hop' – the Bliss n Eso era of Australian flags draped on white shoulders – were shifting, and whiteness was becoming the minority. With this, the 'circumstances' for the ONEFOUR explosion were set in place.

After we went through the intros and clarified everyone's roles, we got to work on a song called 'The Message'. With Celly still locked up, I wanted to find a way to keep him in the mix, so I'd asked the boys to record a phone call with him when they next spoke. I cut his vocals so they were in time with the intro, and with that, we had the foundation for our next release.

As Daniel knew well, good energy in the studio is key to making good music – especially hip hop. ONEFOUR always arrived with a crew of mates who would be the litmus test for each song we recorded. If they got hyped when one of the boys laid down a verse, we knew it was a keeper; if not it was back to the drawing board. The studio became our colosseum; the boys would emerge from the booth like gladiators before the crowd would offer either the thumbs up or the thumbs down.

When YP dropped the first line of his verse, there was no need to survey the room for opinions: 'Retaliation is a must, ain't no maybes, ifs or buts . . .'

The line is iconic. The sort of line that comes round every once in a while. It's catchy and easily repeatable, but more importantly it captures a truth. Growing up in a place like Mount Druitt, all ONEFOUR had was each other. And when you feel like you're on your own in the world, you'll do anything to protect yourself because you're all you've got. When you're at war, retaliation isn't a choice – it's about survival.

***

When it came to street-based rap, Kerser, Nter and Sky'high were the first ones to make waves in Australia. But no one could have foreseen the way ONEFOUR exploded with 'The Message'. After dropping on 30 March 2019, it had millions of views within weeks, with teenagers from Western Sydney to Bondi and all the way up to Queensland entranced by ONEFOUR's raw energy. The video had the group and literally hundreds of friends walking around Mount Druitt, lighting flares in front of the courthouse and other local landmarks. It put the neighbourhood – and other similar forgotten pockets of Australia – on the map for the first time. Even overseas, established artists like the UK's Mercury Prize-winning rapper Dave offered his endorsement. Soon profiles in *GQ* and *Rolling Stone* appeared, before a cover for *NME* magazine. At that point in time, ONEFOUR weren't the biggest thing in Australian hip hop; they *were* Australian hip hop.

But the thing about viral success is that it can often bring the wrong kind of attention. ONEFOUR had extensive legal troubles, with YP and Lekks still fighting court cases that threatened to put them inside along with Celly. Both had strict bail conditions, and with the extra eyes on them, any slip-up was going to prove costly.

They were shooting the video for their next single, 'Spot the Difference', when YP was seen on Instagram Live out and about on the streets of Mount Druitt after dark, rather than at home where his bail conditions specified he should be. The police, savvy to social media, saw this and visited his home. When YP wasn't there, a warrant was issued for his arrest.

The lawyers called me and I was able to explain that YP was there for work reasons. In a written statement, I told them that as an employee of Sony Australia I was trying to sign the group, and the video shoot was part of our ongoing working relationship. YP was released a few hours later but, as we were about to find out, the problems had only just begun.

***

Celly was the one with the vision. He started rapping first before the others followed his lead. But ever since he appeared on ONEFOUR's first few tracks, 'Ready for War' and 'Want the Money', he'd been watching the group's success from inside a prison cell. I'm sure he was as happy as everyone else to see them flourish, but still, that can't have been easy.

I'd already seen first-hand the impact of visiting people in jail. When I went to see Mahem in Parramatta, he never let me forget it. Nearly every time I've seen him since, he'll bring it up, telling me how much he appreciated it, that it let him know he wasn't forgotten. It gave him hope, he told me, and if there was anyone in need of hope at that point in time, it was Celly.

When I went to see him with the other boys, we mainly chopped it up about life on the outside, but with a formal offer on the table now, there was more to discuss. It was actually his mum who suggested I visit him again. Fiercely protective of her son, she wanted to make sure he wasn't being forgotten about. If I was in his shoes, my mum would have done the exact same thing. Immigrant mums aren't to be messed with.

After what felt like a lifetime waiting, I was brought inside the visitor's room to face Celly. Opposite me in his prison-issue greens, he seemed in good spirits, full of questions about how the deal was structured and what it meant for him, in jail. I was keen to put his fears at rest about being forgotten, explaining that the boys talk about him all the time and, from what I could see, have his best interests at heart. He seemed excited and at one point even asked how it would work signing the contract from inside. At that point, I had to explain that from his position there was little he could do.

I wanted to give him the reassurance he needed, but at the same time I was powerless. Whether the boys signed or didn't was out of my hands, and the fact of the matter was Celly was in jail while the others were outside doing the actual work. All I could offer him were some empty words and a vague message of hope.

'You're just going to have to trust the boys to make the right decision,' I explained.

There was nothing else I could do.

There's a reason rap videos often feature an artist standing in front of dozens, if not more, of their friends. When a folk singer makes it big, you don't see all his mates coming along for the ride. But when you come from the same environment as some of these artists, your friends are more than just companions – they're your protectors. The same went for ONEFOUR. Everywhere they went, a group of loyal friends was there too. They contributed to the vision, and just because they didn't rap any verses didn't mean they weren't part of the movement.

Since I'd brought them into Sony studios, I had been acting as a de facto manager for ONEFOUR, connecting them with different people and putting them in a position to grow. But as time went on, I became less and less confident they would sign the deal. I understood their dilemma. Their streaming numbers were so huge that they were making decent money already, so why would they want to give a good portion of that over to a label? Plus, their legal fees were mounting so they needed all the cash they could get.

And so, the group started taking advice from friends within their circle who had ambitions to manage them. They were taking meetings elsewhere and encouraging ONEFOUR to move in a different direction. That was fine by me but it got to a point where they needed to choose. The friends had their best intentions at heart but they had no experience in management, so things were falling through the cracks. All these cooks in the kitchen were spoiling the broth.

It all came to a head the night YP broke his bail conditions for a second time. He'd entered a licensed premises, and this time there was nothing I could do. After that, J Emz called me and asked to meet.

When he turned up at the steakhouse, he was in a bad way. Celly, Lekks and his younger brother YP were all inside facing lengthy prison sentences, and with the police pressure increasing, it looked like things were about to come crashing down for ONEFOUR before they even really started. The chatty confidence he'd displayed the first time we met was replaced by a look of dejection. There were tears in his eyes when he spoke.

'What would *you* do, Hau?' he asked me. 'If it was you, would you sign the deal?'

I explained that I would. I knew what I could do with ONEFOUR with the support of a major behind them. But I also knew I was only one person. They had five people to think of, five mouths to feed and five families to support. That was a very different situation. I also acknowledged that me giving them advice on whether to sign or not sign was bordering on a conflict of interest. I couldn't be their manager *and* their label head.

I suggested to J Emz that they speak to Ricky. We'd stayed in touch since the clothing collab and he was getting more and more involved with hip hop, working with artists like Sampa the Great and the young rap phenom The Kid LAROI. Ricky had come through the studio a few times when we were working, and while the boys didn't trust many people, they trusted him.

J Emz agreed and we left it at that; I was going to send the offer to Ricky so he could talk it through with the boys. As we left the steakhouse, the same place where we'd had our first meeting, I realised in a strange way we had come full circle. In the space of a few months, they had gone from just a group of lads from Mounty with a chequered past, to the biggest hip hop act in the country. Now they were at risk of being right back where they started.

YO! I'M ON TV

When I was a kid, *YO! MTV Raps* wasn't shown in Australia. There just wasn't the market for it. Then I met Daniel. He had a mate with a relative in Germany who would record episodes on VCR tapes and send them to Australia for us to watch. Daniel would get them first before passing them to me, then I'd hand them on to Alvin. We never dreamed of one day being featured on the show – that was too lofty a goal. All we wanted was for it to be aired in Australia so we could watch it just like all the other hip hop heads around the world.

There was this one episode where they showed videos from artists starting with each letter of the alphabet. It opened with A Tribe Called Quest, then Big Daddy Kane, Cypress Hill and so on. I must have watched that video five or six times front to back, hoarding it for a good week before passing it to Alvin. None of the videos featured had been released in Australia; to be honest, I reckon half the artists wouldn't have been able to point to Australia on a map.

In 2019, twenty-six years after I'd got my hands on my very first episode, MTV announced they were arriving Down Under. The show was relaunching in America, and they were doing one-off episodes in territories around the world with emerging hip hop markets.

The best thing about it: they wanted me to host. Along with presenter and internet personality Flex Mami, I was given the task of curating a line-up of artists to showcase Australian rap.

It was like assembling the Avengers of Australian hip hop. With ONEFOUR's legal troubles they weren't in a position to perform, so I started with Remi – he was a no-brainer – and then tapped one of the best female artists in the game, Okenyo, to join him as co-headliner. Then there was Tasman Keith, a proud Gumbaynggirr man whose dad, a rapper called Wire MC, I had come up with; as well as Sophiegrophy, a Nigerian-born artist making a mad mix of hip hop and club anthems. Rounding off the list was Shadow, from Perth; Sydney's That Kid Kearve; and Carmouflage Rose, out of BrisVegas. It was a line-up I was proud to show the world: diverse, talented and full of both heart *and* soul.

Like a small plucky nation getting its first appearance at the Olympics, it was Australia's arrival on the hip hop world stage. I imagined a young Hau and Daniel watching the episode from home, dreaming of one day rocking the very same stage. For the first time, that dream wasn't such a long shot.

Even though Daniel wasn't with me when I hosted *Yo! MTV Raps*, I soon realised that in a way he was. Because, really, he's never truly left my side. Every studio session with my artists, he's there, offering words of advice. He used to tell me to reflect the emotion of the song in the way I recorded. If it's a happy song, make sure you're smiling when you record, he would say. It always sounded weird to me, but he was right. Small details like that fill songs with real emotion that the listener can feel. His attention to detail and obsession with perfection is another. Yes, Daniel took it too far at times, but it was because he cared.

When we'd set out on our journey together, there was no one to show us the way. So we did it ourselves. Yeah, we secretly had dreams of one day being as big as A Tribe Called Quest, but really, we were just two kids from Australia having a crack at something that seemed like fun. He made the beats, I wrote the rhymes, and we kept on driving 'til the wheels fell off. When that eventually happened, it happened in a big way. Following the loss of Daniel's gear in 2004, there was a wedge driven between us that only grew wider. There was just too much resentment and too much frustration for us to recover from.

In the process of writing this book, I'm pleased to say we started talking again. It's early days but we'll get there. After everything we went through together, we owe it to each other. Through the tours and the marathon studio sessions, the fights and the bickering, we became family – a dysfunctional one at times, but a family none-theless. Rather than blood, it was our mutual love of hip hop and a desire to make something new for Australia that brought us together. Thirty years later, I can confidently say, we did what we set out to do.

DANIEL

I don't get time to sit and listen to Hau's show as much as I'd like. Occasionally I'll catch an episode and remember life back in the day. But I'm just so disconnected to it all now, ya know. I wish I wasn't. I know there's this whole culture that exists now, but I was only ever close to it because I was along for the ride with Hau. I just enjoyed making music with Hau. Music is my only language. It's the only way I get along with people. I was just someone who was looking to make music with people. I mean, for all I know, if I hadn't met Hau and Sione, I might have ended up moving to Berlin to make techno music. I have no idea.

When Hau and I called it quits, I stopped making music altogether. I was sick of everyone asking me, 'When are you gonna do your solo album?' or, 'When's the next Koolism record coming?' And I was just struggling to feed myself. The frustration of everyone thinking that I should be doing music, but not being able to get the time to do it, was a level of frustration that I felt was cruelty. I was like, What kind of sick joke is this? So, sadly, I just buried it. I decided, I'm gonna stop caring because caring is too painful for me. And it worked. I stopped fighting 'cause I couldn't handle that frustration. When I let go of it, I could get up in the morning, look at my calendar, make some calls

353

and go and do what I had to do to make some money. Unfortunately, I've just burned ten years doing that.

But something changed recently. This whole process of talking to Hau again and digging through all these memories has been such a break from the journey I've been on over the past decade. I've been digging through the archives and I've been listening to everything. I found the original cassette demos of songs we recorded in 1999. Looking through these things has been a joy. Over the past couple of months, that's all I've wanted to do.

I had this one night recently, when I was working as a technician in a studio, and I had nine days to complete the job. They'd closed the studio for me to work through a whole list of issues, but going into the final night I'd done everything. So I brought in an 808 drum machine and my Moog synth. I plugged them into these incredible amplifiers, hit record and sat up all night making music. It was the first time I'd done that since Hau and I stopped, and I had this crazy outpouring of energy; all of this pent-up emotion from the past ten years just flooded out of me. I felt inspired for the first time in a long time. I stopped at six in the morning, switched everything off and went home. I was like, Wow, I've still got it!

That's given me hope, and I'm trying not to let go of that this time.

CHANGED THE GAME

I eventually got the call I had been expecting for a while: ONEFOUR had decided not to sign with Forever Ever. Was I disappointed? Definitely. After what we'd already done together in such little time, I knew there was no end to what we could achieve if I threw Sony's backing behind them. But, at the same time, I understood. They wanted to remain independent, enabling them to keep all of their streaming profits and do things their own way. Daniel and I stayed on the indie route our whole career, so that was something I could respect.

I think they also felt they didn't need a label anymore. In just a year, they had pioneered an entire scene. In Western Sydney, every man and his dog wanted to be a drill rapper after watching 'The Message' and 'Spot the Difference' go viral. They broke down doors for others to follow, proving it was cool – *finally!* – to rap in your own Australian accent. I'm not trying to detract from anyone's success, but if you make money off drill, or any other kind of street rap in Australia, you're here in part because of ONEFOUR. That's just a fact.

Remaining independent also helped when it came to the legal fees. YP and Lekks ended up being sentenced to a few years in prison, leaving it up to Spenny and J Emz to fly the flag in their absence. For most people, a knock like that could spell the end. But ONEFOUR aren't like most people.

Since we went our separate ways, I've stayed a part of the fold, mentoring the boys on the pitfalls of the industry and offering a helping hand in the studio when they need it. My relationship with them was never about the money – it was about seeing a group of Pacific Islander artists chase their dreams – so I could do that with or without a record deal binding us.

A big part of my role is connecting people. After all, an artist is only as good as the team around them. Daniel and I had Axe, Tunks, George and all the boys to help create the right environment for us to be creative. To help ONEFOUR, I brought in a producer named Solo Tohi, aka i.amsolo. He'd never made any drill music before but I thought his musicality could help the boys grow. He also had a proven track record in the industry. Before producing, he'd started off as part of Justice Crew, a breakdancing group that won Season 4 of *Australia's Got Talent* before becoming recording artists and touring with everyone from Janet Jackson to One Direction. In a display of typical Islander humility, they were huge and Solo never even mentioned it. I knew him for a good year before I noticed a plaque on his studio wall and made the connection.

A few months after the group made their decision, we were in the Sony studios again, finishing a song called 'Heartless'. It's the same ONEFOUR energy fans were used to – a defiant us-against-the-world attitude – but it also showed their growth as musicians.

It's the same with songs like 'Home and Away' and 'Welcome to Prison'. The musical arrangement is next level, adding real substance to their powerful lyrics. With these releases, ONEFOUR started to build their own unique sound and identity. Trailblazers in every sense of the word, they went from controversial outsiders to genuine stars.

After the 'Heartless' session, Solo and I went to grab some food at a nearby Japanese restaurant on Oxford Street. It was part of our routine: a quick break and debrief on the day's work over a feed. I was having my usual – a bowl of teriyaki salmon – and Solo the same. We'd been there dozens of times before, but on this night the food tasted particularly good. Between mouthfuls, we reflected on the work we had done with ONEFOUR.

'Can you believe we've actually changed the game?' I asked him. 'Not just for rap in Australia, but for *our people*, bro.'

There was no champagne, no big displays of emotion. Just a quiet smile and a nod. As if looking out on the horizon, our eyes wandered down Oxford Street and we saw a future as bright as the traffic lights that hugged every corner.

Then we got back to work.

A lot can happen in a year. In November 2018, I'd sat on an ARIA panel with Zane Lowe, heralding the sprouting of new seeds in Australian music, and exactly twelve months later those seeds were in full bloom. As the ARIAs came round again, ONEFOUR had three songs inside the year's top ten trending music videos on YouTube Australia, as well as a combined 73 million streams and counting. As Jay-Z once said, 'Men lie, women lie, numbers don't,' and Australia had never seen anything like those numbers. So, it would have been reasonable to expect to see ONEFOUR at the ARIAs, picking up an award or two to reflect the groundbreaking year they'd just had. Not quite.

Instead, the NSW police got in contact with Star Casino, who were hosting the awards, to offer 'advice' on ONEFOUR. Their presence, it seemed, was a threat to the upstanding citizens of the Australian music industry so they were banned from attending. And this was just the start. They had a headline tour planned, starting with a sold-out show in New Zealand, which in itself was huge for an Australian act. Since the Dawn Raid days, we were used to playing back-up to rap in Aotearoa, but with the undeniable success of ONEFOUR, the roles had finally been reversed.

But that was short lived. Again, the NSW police got in touch with the venues with more 'advice', and within days each one had pulled out, citing 'unforeseen circumstances'. So ONEFOUR ended 2019 as the most exciting, most talked about act in Australian music but without a show to their name and a ban preventing them from attending the one event designed to celebrate Australian music.

Now, some of this attention is justified. With their background, ONEFOUR are not like most bands you see every day. Their interactions with the law and experience growing up in one of the country's toughest postcodes are what makes them unique. But, the group were answering for their crimes in the courts. Being held accountable for your past is one thing, being prevented from building a different future is something else. For me, that's when the moral justification starts to lose its weight.

In rap music, this is hardly a new concept. In 1988, NWA were labelled a threat to society by the FBI after releasing 'Fuck tha Police'. But rather than stopping NWA's growth, the police attention made them even bigger, turning them into cultural icons. Twenty-seven years after the release of 'Fuck tha Police', the film *Straight Outta Compton* came out, documenting the group's career and run-ins with law enforcement. The film was a worldwide success, hitting number one at the box office.

What the FBI learned, and what the NSW police may well come to understand, is that in trying to put out the fire, they only fanned the flames.

J EMZ

Hau was the main guy that kicked it off for us. There was a lot going on in our lives at the time, but we just got straight to work. I saw him as an adult figure to look up to. He was like an uncle to us. It was nothing but good vibes as soon as we started locking in. We learned a lot from him, especially on how to work properly in the studio. We took a lot of traits from back then to what we use now.

The way we used to work before we met Hau, we wouldn't have a plan for anything. We were just going off our own knowledge of how music is meant to be made and what we liked to hear at the time. He introduced us to proper engineers and producers, and he got us comfortable in that professional environment.

And his knowledge of music definitely helped. He got us out of our comfort zone and showed us where we could go with music. While we were working, he'd be standing next to us in our ear the whole time with ideas: maybe pronounce this like that; maybe change this word to a word you actually use in your everyday life. He was also helping us with melodies. Stuff we weren't comfortable with at all back then.

In the end, we decided not to sign. With us being the people we are, we struggle to trust everything. And there were a lot of voices getting in our head at the time. So, as a group, we came together and made the decision to not listen to any outside noise and just take care of things ourselves.

We've distanced ourselves a bit since then, but Hau is someone I can always go to if I need advice. And if I want his opinion on something, he's always open – he's still that guy. And that's rare. It gets ugly out here, man. A lot of people say they're gonna be there for you through certain situations when really they're not. They switch up real quick when things don't go the way they want.

But Hau's never switched on us. Whenever I see him, it's always good vibes. I appreciate the man he is. He definitely played a big role in where we are today.

THE NEXT EPISODE

There's a lot of smoke and mirrors in today's game. With social media at the forefront, real artistry can take a backseat while rappers search for a shot of viral fame to catapult them to stardom. Sometimes it can work. There're artists like Lil Nas X and Bobby Shmurda who have gone on to have real careers off the back of a viral clip. But for every one of those, there's a dozen whose careers shot up then disappeared overnight. Remember Stitches? Yeah, exactly. Since ONEFOUR took off, this was becoming even more common. Wannabes thought they just had to slip on a balaclava and repeat some violent lyrics to get the same attention. But the whole point about ONEFOUR is they had the talent to back it up. Sooner or later, it's always talent that will determine whether you stay or go.

At triple j, we had the idea to launch a new initiative called Bars of Steel. It was designed as a freestyle platform where we invited established or emerging artists to hop in the studio and show us what they've got. It's a celebration of pure hip hop: just a rapper and a beat, with nowhere to hide. To launch the platform, I enlisted a young artist by the name of Hoodzy. While I was trying to sign ONEFOUR, I had been quietly working with Hoodzy, building a relationship with her in and out of the studio. There wasn't much music to show for it yet, but the potential was there. She reminded me of a young Remi: playful and cheeky one minute, then staunch the next. She is also Brown and queer, representing the new face of the next generation.

It was Hoodzy's first time in a recording studio, but she didn't show it. She rapped with a smile on her face, clearly enjoying the experience. As I watched from the production booth, I thought of my first time performing in front of others. I was either ripping off Ice-T's lyrics or impersonating an American. Hoodzy, on the other hand, was fearless. She was still rough around the edges, but she confirmed what I needed to know: she was ready.

They say hip hop's a young person's game. It's not like rock'n'roll where you'll see ageing stars like the Rolling Stones sell out arenas well into their seventies. Rap's more fickle. I always knew this was the case, but it took a conversation with Hoodzy's dad to have it truly hit home. Considering her age, I wanted to speak to a parent first before we discussed any paperwork. I expected a conversation with someone like my dad. That was what a parent meant to me – old, supportive and a little out of touch. But what I found was a man in his forties who seemed a lot like me.

'What's good, bro?' came the sprightly voice down the phone, forcing me to reach for a greeting other than 'Sir'.

We chopped it up like two mates, discussing music as well as his hopes for his kids' careers. He was supportive, just like my dad, but he had a modern mindset. Rather than wanting his kids to go to university for the sake of it, he encouraged them to find their passion and pursue it in the best route possible. Hoodzy's passion was music, so he was keen to see her sign a deal and go all in.

As I hung up the phone, I knew two things: Hoodzy was the right artist to officially launch Forever Ever; and my place in music was now to make way for the next generation. In this, a young person's game, it was time to really embrace my role on the sidelines – as a father, a mentor, a supporter of the next line of Kings and Queens.

So, it's time to retire the notepad. I spent decades pouring myself into those pages, but there comes a time when you need to pass the pen down the line so you can help bring a new generation of stories into the light. It's going to take some getting used to, but I think I'm ready. After all, it was never just about me.

Soon after Hoodzy signed, three more artists joined the Forever Ever family. That's the funny thing about running for the bus: you may miss a few, but sooner or later you'll be spoiled for choice. First, there was CG Fez, a lyrically minded rapper with Tongan-Turkish heritage, hailing from Sydney's west. Then Becca Hatch, a soulful R&B singer with an Aboriginal-Samoan background, also from Western Sydney. Finally, there was Kenzie From Welly, a NZ-born Māori-Samoan spitter who I'd known and admired for years. They're unique but share one thing in common: they're all storytellers. Just like me.

It's still early days for us as a label, but the foundations are solid. One of my favourite things from my short time working with them is their willingness to learn and help each other out. Whether it's appearing in each other's music videos, or promoting each other's songs, they know that if one of us succeeds we all succeed.

Like family, they bring me a lot of joy – and a lot of work. And so, after fourteen years as host of *The Hip Hop Show*, I'm leaving triple j at the end of this year. It's time for some new blood to take the show forward, and I have my family to focus on – both of them. But don't call it a retirement. Far from it. When I think about my career and the things I've done, from the tours and festivals to the albums and the ARIAs, it fills me with pride. But do you wanna know the really scary thing? I'm just getting started.

HAU'S OUTRO

I was approached by a big name in Australian TV recently. I can't say who, but let's just say you would have heard of them. They're making a show about an aspiring Pasifika rapper from Western Sydney who dreams of making it big. In his way are a series of obstacles from his former life that threaten to derail his future. Can he divert the danger to create a better life for himself and his family, or will he get sucked back into a cycle of poverty and prison? It's a story all about persever-ance, music and family. But, more than anything, it's an Australian story. And there's no prizes for guessing who it's based on.

They've brought me on board as a co-creator and consultant on the music side of things, to ensure it feels connected to the culture and not some corny rip-off. I didn't need much convincing – they had me at 'Australian hip hop story' – so I've been working closely with them to develop the narrative. COVID has stalled things, but when it does arrive, the show will be proof of the changing times in this country.

When I was a kid, I had my uncles and I had Ice-T. They were as close as I got to role models helping me to visualise the future I wanted. But it was deeper than that. I had to watch American films like Beat Street *just to see other Brown kids on screen. It fills me with hope to know the world Aki and Maila are living in is very different. Now, there's ONEFOUR, and soon there'll be a major Australian TV show that puts Brown kids' lives and experiences front and centre. Where they belong.*

When I was in my late teens I would drive Dad to work. It meant I could keep the car for the day, so I would get up early and drop him off at whatever house he was painting. I'd watch as he walked off in his work overalls, lunchbox in his hand, ready to start his shift. The sight made me feel conflicted, even a little ashamed. With my future a blank canvas at the time, house painting seemed a small ambition to me. Doesn't he want something more? *I'd ask myself.*

That feeling stayed with me until I had my own kids. I realised then how very wrong I was. Because my dad had won in life. He'd literally hit the jackpot, starting in poverty before coming to Australia with his brothers and improving his lot. I have no idea how difficult that transition must have been for him, but he did it. Then he had two kids of his own who had more opportunities than he'd ever imagined – all because of the sacrifices he and Mum had made. I hope it's the same with Aki and Maila. I hope they read this book and feel proud. But more importantly, I hope they want more. That, I've realised, is what real success looks like.

I recently asked them what they want to do when they grow up. Aki said he wants to be a professional Rubik's Cuber, and as funny as that sounds, he may be onto something. Within a few days of getting one, he managed to get his time down to one minute, nineteen seconds. Not bad, eh? Maila, on the other hand, hopes to either be a singer like her dad or run her own YouTube channel doing reaction videos. Good to know she's keeping her options open. Whatever they decide to do, I know they will carry the Lātūkefu legacy forward.

But they've got a good few years to figure that out. For now, I reckon it's time for a celebration. Throughout my career, I've been careful not to sing my own praises. After all, humility runs in my blood. Or as Mum would say, 'It's "the Tongan way."' But as I approach the end of this book, and I edge closer to fifty, I've been feeling a little reflective.

The day this book is due with the publishers is the same day as Tunks' fiftieth birthday, which seems the perfect opportunity for a party. We're all going to get together and have a proper drink-up for old time's sake. The barbecue will stay lit late into the evening; Daniel will be on the decks all night long, even though he'll promise not to; and Tunks will be the man of the moment, as always. We'll pour one out for Bain, for Travis, and for my uncles, aunts, cousins and grandparents, who are no longer with us. I may even grab the mic, not to rap any bars but to make a toast: to life, death and hip hop.

Burn my raincoat when it rains
Fed those ~~job~~ zombies all my brain 🙂
Whats for ~~breakFAST~~ fast nutri-grain 🙂
Gave my lion a new mane
Time to strike again ~~time to strike again~~
~~grah grah~~ X2 hoo hoo
verse
Pull ~~oua~~ a rabbit outta my magic hat
~~And~~ ethat was a savage rap
Next time ~~what~~ ohme when I have my backwards cap,
See me all around like a cd
dont come for a freebie
Cause those bars ~~aint~~ aint cheapy
~~Get~~ (Put your money up x2
Dis aint funny but this aint funny bat
O yeah!
~~makin flames~~ I'm on fire like a stoker
hold his neck like a choaker
were at war weres the ochre (Baking Bang Bang!)

Aki, aged 9

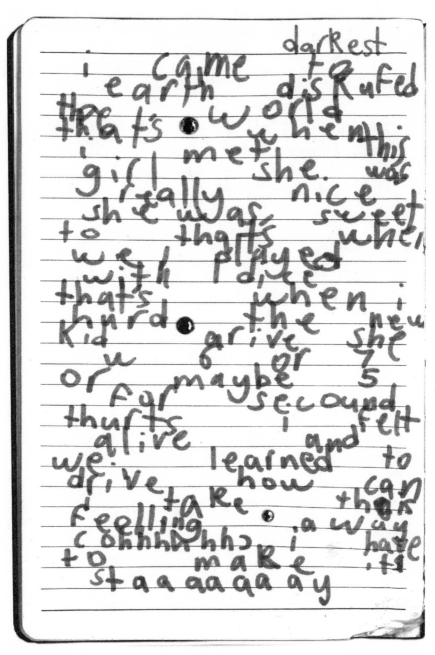

i came to darkest earth disRupted that's world when this girl met she was really nice she was sweet to that's when we with played that's diye when i hard the new kid arive she or maybe 5 or for maybe secound that's i felt alive and we learned to drive how can feelling taRe thats away i hate (ohhhhhh) i it to make staaaaaaay

Maila, aged 6

ACKNOWLEDGEMENTS

HAU

The journey of writing this book would not have started (or ended, for that matter) if it weren't for the encouragement and enthusiasm of my man, Christopher Riley. His patience, dedication, sensitivity and, of course, his way with words, have made this very surreal experience fun and exciting. Chris, I'm forever grateful, bro. You've not only immortalised my life, but also the lives around me.

Must big up our publisher and editor, Brandon VanOver, and the team at Penguin Random House. Thank you for joining us on this journey. Again, such a surreal experience not only to write a book, but to also have it published by the same people who have provided classics since I was a kid.

My incredible wife, Shani. Man. What a journey. You've been my constant inspiration, motivation, encouragement, support and unconditional love for the better part of twenty years. So much so, I know I wouldn't be where I am without you. Aki and Maila. My beautiful children. So proud of you two. Every time I look at you both I am filled with happiness, hope and optimism. I love you all.

Eternal love to my parents, my sister, my Lātūkefu, Maʻilei, Langi and Griffin families. My close friends. My acquaintances. Whether you were named in this book or not, you all played a role in my life that helped make me the man I am today. *'Ofa lahi atu.*

Since I was young, I knew I had both feet firmly planted on the broad shoulders of giants. And I knew that, one day, I would in turn be that giant whose shoulders would prop up the next ones standing. Young ones, be great, be kind. In the immortal words of the GOAT, Nas: 'The world is yours.'

CHRISTOPHER

I want to thank Hau first and foremost. Your contribution to hip hop is immense, but it's your integrity and character that I admire most. Being entrusted to tell your story has been a huge privilege. Thank you, bro – can't wait to see what the next chapter of your life holds.

I would also like to say a special thank you to Hau's family and friends, without whom this book wouldn't be possible: Lu'isa and Lesoni, Sabne, Shani, Aki, Maila, Daniel, Tunks, 'Uli, Hounga, Alvin, George, Axe, Talo, Sensible J, Ricky, J Emz, Petrina, N'Fa and Omar.

A huge shout-out to Brandon, who championed this book from day one, and whose careful edits and advice made everything we wrote immeasurably better. To my family and friends for their love, support and patience throughout the process. And finally, to my partner, best friend and the first set of eyes on anything I ever write, Gabby. I wouldn't have been able to do this without you.

ABOUT THE AUTHORS

Hau Lātūkefu is one of the pioneers of Australian hip hop. One half of the iconic ARIA-award-winning rap group Koolism, he went on to have success as a solo artist as well as becoming the longest-serving host of triple j's *The Hip Hop Show* – a role he's still in today. Now working with emerging artists through his imprint of Sony Music, Forever Ever Records, Hau has remained a central part of Australia's music scene for the best part of two decades.

Christopher Riley is a freelance journalist, specialising in music, sport and fashion. He has worked as deputy editor of *GQ* Australia, contributing editor for *Australian Men's Health* and as a columnist for *T Australia: The New York Times Style Magazine*.

Discover a
new favourite

Visit **penguin.com.au/readmore**